LIBERTY/LIBERTÉ
The American and French Experiences

Edited by

Joseph Klaits and Michael H. Haltzel

The Woodrow Wilson Center Press
Washington, D.C.

The Johns Hopkins University Press
Baltimore and London

Editorial Offices: The Woodrow Wilson Center Press
370 L'Enfant Promenade, S.W.
Suite 704
Washington, D.C. 20024 U.S.A.

Order from:
The Johns Hopkins University Press
701 West 40th Street, Suite 275
Baltimore, Maryland 21211-2190
Telephone: 1-800-537-JHUP

9 8 7 6 5 4 3 2 1

Library of Congress Cataloging-in-Publication Data

Liberty/liberté: The American and French experiences / edited by
    Joseph Klaits and Michael H. Haltzel
        p.   cm.
    "Based on a two-part international conference, held in Washington
(June 30–July 2, 1986) and Paris (October 22–23, 1986) on the
occasion of the one-hundredth anniversary of the gift from France to
the United States of the Statue of Liberty. The conference . . . was
co-sponsored by the West European Program of the Woodrow Wilson
International Center for Scholars and the Comité officiel franco-
américain pour la célébration du centenaire de la statue de la
liberté"—P.
    Includes bibliographical reference and index.
    ISBN 0-943875-18-8
    1. Liberty—Congresses. 2. Liberalism—Congresses. 3. Political
science—France—History—Congresses. 4. Political science—United
States—History—Congresses. I. Haltzel, Michael H. II. Klaits,
Joseph. III. West European Program (Woodrow Wilson International
Center for Scholars) IV. Comité officiel franco-américain pour la
célébration du centenaire de la statue de la liberté.
JC586.L425   1991
323.44—dc20   91-21328
                                                                          CIP

The Center is the "living memorial" of the United States of America to the nation's twenty-eighth president, Woodrow Wilson. The U.S. Congress established the Woodrow Wilson Center in 1968 as an international institute for advanced study, "symbolizing and strengthening the fruitful relationship between the world of learning and the world of public affairs." The Center opened in 1970 under its own presidentially appointed board of directors.

In all its activities the Woodrow Wilson Center is a nonprofit, nonpartisan organization, supported financially by annual appropriations from the U.S. Congress, and by the contributions of foundations, corporations, and individuals. Conclusions or opinions expressed in Center publications and programs are those of the authors and speakers and do not necessarily reflect the views of the Center staff, fellows, trustees, advisory groups, or any individuals or organizations that provide financial support to the Center.

Woodrow Wilson International Center for Scholars
Smithsonian Institution Building
1000 Jefferson Drive, S.W.
Washington, D.C. 20560
(202) 357-2429

CONTENTS

ACKNOWLEDGMENTS

Liberty/Liberté: The American and French Experiences is based on a two-part international conference held in Washington (June 30–July 2, 1986) and Paris (October 22–23, 1986) on the occasion of the one-hundredth anniversary of the gift from France to the United States of the Statue of Liberty. The conference, entitled "The Concept of Liberty: Its Development and Meaning in France and the United States," was cosponsored by the West European Program of the Woodrow Wilson International Center for Scholars and the Comité Officiel Franco-Américain pour la Célébration du Centenaire de la Statue de la Liberté.

Thanks are due to the Statue of Liberty–Ellis Island Foundation (New York), the sponsors of the Comité Officiel Franco-Américain pour la Célébration du Centenaire de la Statue de la Liberté, and the United States Congress Special Wilson Center Conference Fund, whose generous grants made this conference possible. The Woodrow Wilson Center is also grateful to the Embassy of France for the hospitality it extended to conference participants, and to Air France, which donated several transatlantic air tickets.

François de Laboulaye, Ambassadeur de France, deserves special thanks for his indefatigable efforts as head of the Comité Officiel Franco-Américain. The editors would like to recognize the late Jean-Claude Lamberti, Professor of Sociology, Université de Paris V, for having collaborated on creating the conference agenda and having made most of the conference arrangements on the east side of the Atlantic. We are also grateful for the translations of the Lamberti and Agulhon essays expertly done by Elborg Forster. Finally, we would like to thank Charlotte Thompson of the West European Program of the Woodrow Wilson Center and Roccie Hill of the Comité Officiel Franco-Américain for their superb work in the organization of the conference and assistance in the preparation of the final manuscript.

Joseph Klaits
Michael H. Haltzel

LIBERTY/LIBERTÉ

Introduction: The Theory, Practice, and Symbols of Liberty

Joseph Klaits and Michael Haltzel

Except perhaps for the Capitol in Washington, the Statue of Liberty is the structure that best evokes in Americans a sense of their national identity and common heritage. Miss Liberty's renovation and re-dedication in her centennial year tapped a deep well of popular senti-ment that would be difficult to stir for the restoration of any other monument. But the statue's power to inspire extends far beyond the borders of the United States, partly because immigrants from all over the world associate the statue with the promise of America. Also it is one of only a few national monuments whose symbolic power tran-scends political frontiers to represent a universal ideal. The *Statue of Freedom* erected in Tiananmen Square by Chinese prodemocracy dem-onstrators in the spring of 1989 captured this symbolism in the most powerful form imaginable.

Indeed this universal quality was part of the initial vision and hope of the Frenchmen who planned and designed the Statue of Liberty. Edouard Laboulaye, Frederick Bartholdi, and their associates envis-aged a symbol of the friendship of those French and Americans who had worked since 1776 and 1789 to achieve the victory of republican government. Moreover, because the battle was far from won in the France of the 1860s, the people who first conceived of a monumental representation of liberty not only were making a dramatic gesture to the United States but were pointing a course for their own country. A gift from the people of France to the United States in honor of the centennial of American independence seemed highly appropriate to those who profoundly believed in the possibility and the desirability of liberty's triumph everywhere. "Liberty Enlightening the World" was a watchword for the aspirations of the Western democracies in the late nineteenth century.

The hopes and fears that moved the statue's creators are if anything more deeply felt today. In both the country that created the statue and the one that embraced it as a national symbol, the definition of liberty has evolved against a threatening backdrop of war, social revolution, and economic crisis; and challenges to democracy from right and left continue to pose profoundly troubling questions about the endurance and applicability of the idea of liberty in the West and elsewhere throughout the world.

In the wake of the opening of the Berlin Wall, the crumbling of the Soviet bloc in Eastern Europe, and the apparent end of the cold war, there has been a worldwide revival of interest in democracy and the institutions that embody it. The Statue of Liberty's centennial, followed by these dramatic changes on the world scene, has provided an especially appropriate moment to encourage reflection on liberty's past and prospects for the future. The chapters that make up this volume of essays originated as papers delivered in 1986 at a two-part conference, in Washington and Paris, on "Liberty/*Liberté*: The American and French Experiences," cosponsored by the West European Program of the Woodrow Wilson International Center for Scholars and the Comité Officiel Franco-Américain pour la Célébration du Centenaire de la Statue de la Liberté. The papers and comments presented by distinguished French and American scholars at these meetings reflect the diverse messages suggested by the concept of liberty and by the statue's history.

The twin major themes of the conference, liberty and liberalism, are indicative of both the parallels and the divergences in the historical experience of France and the United States over two centuries. The essays in the first half of this volume primarily illuminate common patterns in the intellectual antecedents, political theory, and symbolic practices of the two countries. The essays in the second half of the book stress the varieties of liberty's formulations in the historical experience of France and America since the statue's construction. Here there are two main approaches: the comparative development of "liberalism" in both countries, and the conflict of liberalism with other political philosophies.

As many of the authors demonstrate in their essays, the concept of liberalism in Europe today continues to bear many similarities to what in the United States is often thought of as "classical liberalism," a set of ideas that is profoundly linked to contemporary American conservatism. Indeed, throughout the book, the contributions illustrate the multiple meanings of the concept of liberty in French and American history. One of the main goals of this volume is to indicate the rich variety of connotations attached to the concept of liberty. Although readers may find themselves baffled at times by the multiple senses in which our contributors employ *liberal* and *liberalism,* in a sense this apparent confusion is exactly to the point. French and Americans have been joined by their mutual attraction to these worlds, even though the meanings they have attached to them are various and shifting.

The modern world is heir to two related but not altogether compatible traditions, both of them legacies of the eighteenth-century Enlightenment. From Locke, Jefferson, and Rousseau we have received a deep faith in natural rights and popular sovereignty. But whereas Locke and Jefferson emphasized the need to develop political institutions to defend these rights, Rousseau spoke of a much more amorphous "general will," which it was the duty of government to identify and even create through some variety of representative institutions.

In the United States Constitution the principle of individual liberty is the cornerstone of government, embodied in the first ten amendments' statement of individual rights. The French Revolution's Declaration of the Rights of Man and the Citizen, like the American Declaration of Independence, proclaimed natural right as the foundation of society and government. But the various assemblies that met in France in 1789 and the following years found it difficult to reconcile the idea of individual liberties and the notion of a sovereign general will. In Chapter 2 of this collection, François Bourricaud shows that individual rights and the general will were the twin poles of revolutionary ideology, the former identified with the moderates who led the revolution until 1791, the latter with the Jacobins who presided over the subsequent radical phase. His essay also demonstrates that the tensions of faction and ideological stance were never resolved and that the legacy of the French Revolution was therefore a mixed message that would be interpreted in diverse ways over the next two hundred years of French political life.

Bourricaud's essay introduces the varied interpretations assigned to the idea of liberty in the modern world. Donald Kelley's contribution (Chapter 1) looks back to the complexities implicit in the notion of liberty in classical, medieval, and early modern times. Too often in the Western democracies, political reflection stretches no further back than to the age of democratic revolution. The long history of the idea of political liberty in ancient Greece and Rome, in feudal times, and in the Reformation era is an almost forgotten chapter in the development of the West's governmental arrangements. Kelley also shows that at the deeper level of private life the Western legal traditions cultivated a profound respect for liberty of person and action. This, he suggests, was the hidden source of the Enlightenment's "discovery" of the rights of man and representative government.

The opening essays' theme of looking both forward and back from the hinge of the late eighteenth century is continued and developed in the chapters on Alexis de Tocqueville and liberty. In Chapter 3, Jean-Claude Lamberti calls attention to three traditions that formed Tocqueville's idea of liberty: the feudal notion of individual independence, passed via Montesquieu's writings to the common consciousness of the age of revolution; political participation, a legacy of antiquity; and the Christian concept of equality before God. Similarly, in Chapter 4, James T. Schleifer calls our attention to Tocqueville's affinity for Puritan formulations of liberty built on a sense of Christian calling; and to his devotion to the classical idea of liberty in economic and private life that seemed to him a leading feature of the American scene. Tocqueville's prescriptions differed for France and the United States. In America he warned against the dangers of an excess of liberty; in Louis Philippe's France, where the liberal ideal rested on weak foundations, he encouraged the American model.

The contributors to this section build their analyses of Tocqueville's thought around the theme of his acute awareness of the strain, inherent in democracy, between liberty and equality. Tocqueville vividly described the contrary impulses of democratic states toward untrammeled freedom for the individual and toward restrictions of that liberty in the name of an egalitarian ethic. To him the tyranny of the majority, the tyranny of the despot acting in the name of a general will, and the abused individualism of laissez-faire capitalism all threatened the idea of liberty.

Edouard Laboulaye, the moving force behind the Statue of Liberty project, was, as Walter D. Gray demonstrates in Chapter 5, a liberal in the Tocqueville tradition. A man for whom support of the Union in the Civil War derived from his hatred of slavery, Laboulaye led a campaign for the statue that was to symbolize the friendship connecting liberals in France with an America they regarded as the homeland of liberty. In the context of French politics during the Second Empire, such a stance was also a protest against the illiberal regime of Napoleon III. In addition, as Maurice Agulhon reminds us in Chapter 6, the design of the statue created by Frédéric-Auguste Bartholdi set its sponsors apart from the Jacobin revolutionary spirit that had inspired the Paris Commune. If representations of women from 1789 on as leading and inspiring revolution had become symbols of combative radicalism, Miss Liberty was the revolutionary symbol of Marianne—

the French Republic—finally come to rest. Thus the statue can be viewed as a tangible embodiment of the reconciliation of liberal goals with the more moderate form of Jacobin aspirations. Whether one accepts the formulation of George Armstrong Kelly (Chapter 9) that the Third Republic was characterized by "liberal forms and Jacobin habits" or Jean Rivero's view (Chapter 8) that it represented the victory of liberalism over the Jacobin tradition, it is clear that, in the period of the centennial of the Revolution of 1789 and the dedication of the Statue of Liberty in New York harbor, the French government moved far closer to the liberal ideals of Tocqueville and his followers.

Although for Laboulaye, Bartholdi, and the other members of the Franco-American Union in the 1870s the American pattern remained the prototype of the liberal ideal, which the newly established Third Republic might emulate, in the United States during this period the practice of liberty remained limited in fundamental ways. In Chapter 7, Eric Foner argues that after the Civil War the classical republican liberalism modeled on the Jeffersonian vision of a society of independent citizen-farmers gave way under the pressures of industrialization to a democratic individualism that exalted capitalistic economic freedoms and majoritarian politics and made a mockery of the abolitionists' goal of true equality for blacks. William E. Leuchtenburg (Chapter 10) amplifies this theme as he describes the painfully slow implementation of constitutional guarantees of liberty of expression. Yet Leuchtenburg's account of the Supreme Court's extension of the Bill of Rights to all jurisdictions through a broadening interpretation of the Fourteenth Amendment suggests the underlying strength of liberal values in American society, values that have come to the fore in recent decades in the movements to attain equal rights for minorities and women.

In twentieth-century France the challenges to liberal values have been even more penetrating and destructive, as René Remond suggests in his essay on the decline of liberal models between 1900 and 1930 (Chapter 11). On both sides of the Atlantic, however, the postwar world has seen the rise of an updated liberalism—in some places emphasizing state controls and the social democratic model, elsewhere emphasizing free-market economics and deregulation. Compared with the illiberal fascist and Communist regimes that for most of the twentieth century challenged liberal-democratic ideals, however, the differences between Mitterrand's France and Bush's United States, for example, seem more matters of nuance than fundamental differences of political orientation.

These postwar trends are the starting point for the final contributions to this collection. In Chapters 12 and 13 Jean-Claude Casanova and Michael Novak consider the etiology and significance of contemporary liberalism. Novak, deeply influenced by the social theory of F. A. Hayek, summarizes the neoconservative rationale for free-market economic relationships. He further asserts the fundamental compatibility of such liberal values and human nature, drawing especially on Thomas Aquinas's views of man and the social condition. In this assertion Novak reaffirms, although from a much different point of view, the thesis of Donald Kelley that the roots of modern liberal values lie deeply embedded in the premodern history of the Western world.

In an essay that uses Novak's chapter as a point of origin for a rather different evaluation of the historical roots of modern liberal ideas, Pierre Manent (Chapter 14) observes that the Christian tradition historically has regarded liberal values with something less than wild enthusiasm, that such classical liberals as Tocqueville regarded themselves as Christians in little more than a formal sense, and that the moral absolutism implicit in Thomist and other theologies was precisely what the relativistic liberal theorists of the Enlightenment most vigorously opposed. Yet Manent agrees with Novak that liberal ideals rest on a moral vision of man and society and that a traditional religious stance need not necessarily conflict with a liberal political order, given mutual respect among those who make up the body politic.

The sweeping essay by Casanova (Chapter 12), connecting classical liberalism with the contemporary liberal vision, interprets the liberal surge of the past several decades in another light, one that also illuminates the essay by François Bourricaud that opens this book. Bourricaud's delineation of the deep tension between moderates and Jacobins in the French Revolution introduced the theme of liberalism versus democracy that runs like a leitmotiv through most of the contributions to this collection. Casanova's thesis is that the circumstances of late-twentieth-century economic and political life have created an extraordinary convergence of liberal and democratic values. Thus, the worldwide disillusionment with Marxist and other collectivist approaches to the organization of society and the demonstrable success of capitalism in producing economic improvement have combined with democratically inspired welfare state reforms to produce the amalgam Casanova calls contemporary liberalism.

Will this result provide a stable, lasting foundation for worldwide development in the future? Or will the apparent liberal-democratic consensus prove to be but a brief and passing phase in the history of the postwar world? These questions perhaps will be a starting point for scholarly commemoration of the Statue of Liberty's bicentennial a hundred years hence. As unknowable as the conditions and issues of that distant time are, the conviction shared by all the contributors to this volume is that, as Miss Liberty stands tall in her second century, the values of 1776 and 1789 will continue to shape the thoughts and actions of men and women everywhere.

I

The Development of the Idea of Liberty

1

The Private Life of Liberty

Donald R. Kelley

Over the centuries the concept and term "liberty" has had a colorful career. It has been symbolized by burning stamps, burning chateaux, and burning draft cards, by trees, poles, magical caps, and of course, by expensive statues. It has been the oldest of clichés and the most modern of demands, both a sign of privilege and a cry for liberation; it has been both a black flag and a red flag, or rather a tricolor, which could be brandished in defense of the most disparate of claims and protests. Finally, liberty, at least the term "liberty," has become an essential ingredient of social life and the legal order in Western society, and what Justice Holmes would call an inarticulate major premise of our political reasoning. As term and concept "liberty" has more layers and more uses than an onion, and it presents as serious a challenge to historians as it does to philosophers and, I suppose, to politicians.[1]

The idea of "liberty" assumed its modern form in the Enlightenment prelude to what has been called the "age of democratic revolution." In the late eighteenth century, talk about "liberty" was cheap and often loud, and it resounded across the whole social spectrum of the Atlantic community. Much of it, however, had to do with natural and what political theorists call "negative" liberty. This negative liberty contrasts, often sharply, with the kind of "positive" liberty, celebrated by the likes of Montesquieu and Edmund Burke and embodied in the great series of constitutions and codes of law, which forms the most enduring part of the revolutionary legacy. For present purposes let me pass over the revolutionary context, when talk was easy and illusions ran high, and focus instead on what preceded, what survived, and what went largely unexamined during eighteenth-century struggles for liberation. I prefer to look at the concept and term "liberty" not in its incendiary and public phases but rather in what I am calling its private life—which is to say, as it has shaped human language, perceptions, and social and political predicaments over the long haul of history.[2]

What were the factors of ideological *longue durée* that link us with ancient notions of "liberty"? Eighteenth-century revolutionaries (as well as conservatives) realized, though they usually failed to mention, that the idea of "liberty" did not originate with Locke, Rousseau, & Co., and that it had a classical as well a Christian background. Long before French citizens and American colonials demanded their liberties, feudal and municipal liberties also had been wrested from royal authority. Before Locke's "state of liberty" and Coke's liberties of the Englishman there had been the Protestant "liberty of the conscience," which had been the battle cry of French and Dutch Huguenots in the sixteenth-century civil wars. Before Luther's "Christian liberty" (which these Calvinist resisters often invoked) there had been the "liberty of the church," which eleventh-century Gregorian reformers had urged against the encroachment of secular power. And before Saint Paul's "liberty" (from which Protestants, Catholics, and agnostics alike took inspiration), there had been the human "liberty" of Roman jurists and Greek philosophers (on which all the foregoing drew).

The term *liberty* was thus haunted by centuries of cultural and conceptual ghosts. Yet from the standpoint of the Enlightenment the major vehicle and refuge of the idea of "liberty"—and indeed of most ideas concerning the human social condition—continued to be European legal tradition. In those days civil law was by no means the forbidding technical structure it seems today but instead was an integral part of secular, liberal education. The legal tradition was based on the progressively "modernized" civil law (*jus civile*) stemming from Justinian's great collections of the sixth century and on many subsequent layers of commentary and accumulations of European customs, barbarian and "feudal" in provenance but shaped by the methods, assumptions, and language of Roman jurisprudence. To some extent this also included English common law, which, despite its aversion to Romanism, evolved largely in terms of the Roman notion of custom (*consuetudo*).

In the seventeenth century the ghost of Roman jurisprudence continued to haunt European social thought, especially when champions of natural law (the *jus naturale*) like Jean Domat and Montesquieu tried to rationalize and systematize the old legal tradition. In many respects this "natural law" was little more than a sublimated version—the rational part and, one might almost say, the legal superego—of Roman law, which for centuries had been regarded by jurists as "written reason" ("raison écrite," "ratio scripta"). American lawyers, too, were familiar with this formula and with its philosophical implications, and we should not be surprised to see Thomas Jefferson, in a federal lawsuit of 1810, invoking the phrase *ratio scripta* and other allegations from civil law.[3]

Like John Adams, his old colleague and comrade in the businesses of revolution and state building, Jefferson always put law before politics, at least theoretically, and was a great admirer of the old tradition of civil law, which had fostered "natural rights." In general, as Jefferson recalled, writing in his youth, "The lawyer finds in the Latin tongue the system of civil law most conformable with the principles of justice of any of which have ever yet been incorporated into our own."[4] As a young law student, Adams had felt the same way, and at one point in the 1760s had even planned to translate Justinian's *Institutes*.[5]

Eighteenth-century lawyers, American as well as French, knew (as we too often tend to forget) that civil law has a liberal and even a revolutionary, as well as an authoritarian, side. The old legal tradition supplied abundant justification for new assertions of liberty and challenges to civil authority. It was only "natural" to support such claims by appealing, as civil lawyers themselves had often appealed, from the *jus civile* to its rational and moral aspect, the *jus naturale*—which was, in effect to say, from the existing state of civil society to the ideal state of nature. In other words, the loose talk of "liberty" in the anglophone world, as on the Continent, referred largely to the "natural liberty" derived ultimately from classical jurisprudence. "Natura omnes homines liberi sunt et aequales" ("All men are free and equal by nature")[6] was a rule of Roman law.

"Life, liberty, and property" was the famous expression of natural law, but this sacred social trinity had been enshrined in the Western legal tradition for centuries before the rational, or perhaps pseudo-rational, formulation of John Locke—it was embedded in culture and especially language, whether or not it can be imputed to nature. To unearth the foundations—to reveal the "deep structure"—of this concept, it is necessary to search what Paul Ricoeur calls our "Greek memory" underlying the legal tradition, but suffice it here to examine the derivative system of social thought which was, and is, civil law. At all written stages, civil law has been anthropocentric, voluntaristic, and vitally concerned with personal liberty and responsibility and their social consequences—and, of course, with property. The key text is given by the jurist Gaius in the second century A.D.: "All our law concerns either persons, or things, or actions."[7] From at least the time of the Twelve Tables assembled by the Roman decemvirs some six centuries earlier, Roman law possessed this fundamental tripartite structure, which down to the present has continued to dominate the European legal tradition through the countless "institutes" of civil law modeled on the work of Justinian, which had attracted John Adams. Let us turn briefly to this ancient trinity and some of its modern implications.

In the beginning was *personalitas*, the category of "person." In other words, the dynamic base of the Roman legal system and its later incarnations and offspring, including "natural law," was the force of human will. That Justinian's corpus was itself an expression of imperial will was a legal commonplace—recall the famous formula *Quod principi placuit* . . . "The emperor's will is law." But what is all too often forgotten is that the will of the emperor's "subjects" also was "law" in an equally fundamental way. The civic personality (first person of the sacred Gaian trinity) was defined precisely by the degree of human "liberty" he enjoyed—whether, technically, he was his own master or under the "law" of another, and whether he had the "absolute" power to use and to dispose of his belongings (according to another Roman—and French—formula).

What the *imperium* was to public law, in short, *libertas* was to the persons inhabiting the private sphere, and it is important not to forget that although the sovereign had "absolute" public authority, he had "absolutely" no power to act within this private sphere (except under extraordinary, "public" conditions). Not all of the emperor's armies could violate this domain. Private law could be altered only through consent, the "will" of the people, usually expressed by the three estates. In this sense "liberty" was indeed the other face of law.

Who was this "person," this "subject" of the law, this possessor of self-consciousness and "liberty," standing at the beginning of Greek thought and at the center of the Roman social world, looking out over the horizons defined by the *jus civile*?[8] Classically he was the Roman *civis*, the propertied male citizen, the masterful *paterfamilias* with power of life and death over his children and hardly less over his wife. The large majority of humanity—not only slaves, aliens, and barbarians, but also women, children, incompetents, and a wide range of dependents—fell short of full humanity. Slavery was civil death, and it was notorious that, as Papinian, the greatest of Roman jurists, admitted, "In many parts of our law the condition of women is worse than that of men."[9] In later stages of the legal tradition these requirements were relaxed, but the principle of male and paternal domination persisted in one form or another—as did of course the property requirement. The Code Napoleon, for example, followed the Roman model in virtually all these respects.

If the free person was the "subject" of law, what was his object? Here we come to the second category of Gaius's trinity, the "real" world, which was to say the world of "things" (*res*), including the "real estate" which was required for subsistence and which, in the Christian view, was created by God specifically for human use. Personality (*personalitas*) projecting itself onto reality (*realitas*): this social process defines the legal field and, more particularly, reveals the essential links between liberty and property, or rather shows how, conceptually, property can be seen as an extension of liberty and consciousness. In civil law this connection was reinforced by the requirement that private property in a "civil" sense (*dominium*) should include not only physical possession but a consciousness of—indeed the psychological intention and "good will" to maintain—possession (*animus possidendi*) and at least implicitly to use, as well as the capacity to "will" the property to others.[10]

In modern times this principle of civil law, inherited (along with so many other conventions) from the ancient legal tradition, was transformed by advocates of natural law into a formula of pure reason. These so-called jusnaturalists were fully aware of the historical dimension even if they did not attach much significance to it; and while searching for a "natural" form, they covertly or naively preserved much of the "civil" content of the old law, much as Descartes smuggled old scholastic formulas into his new "method." In particular they continued to endorse the famous Gaian trichotomy and, attendant on this, the consubstantial relationship between the first two members of that trinity—that is, the legal tendency to join and even identify liberty and property.

The third member of this trinity was designated classically as "action," although later jurists substituted the more spiritual category of "obligation."[11] Civilly (as distinguished from "naturally") *actio* is to be understood not as the mere physical or willful activity of a "person" but rather as an action at law by a free citizen pleading for justice in a particular "cause" (which more often than not, incidentally, involved "real" property). Historically (as distinguished from philosophically) law was the product of innumerable such *legis actiones*; and once again the analogy between the wills of sovereign and subject, between law and liberty, is evident. As the ruler made law through public "enactment," so did the "people," in their own way and by their own free will, through private "actions at law."

Historically, the more common name for what the people created through their collective will was "custom" (*consuetudo*), and this, too, is a major category of Roman law. According to Justinian's Digest, custom was a convention confirmed by time and the "will" or "tacit agreement of citizens" ("ex populi voluntate," or "tacito consensu populi"); and its continuing force was not less than written and officially "enacted" law.[12] In old regime France, this principle, which the late Walter Ullmann called "populism," was honored by the requirement that feudal customs could be written down or "reformed" only by the approval of the three estates, which again illustrates the assumption that the sovereign power of the crown did not reach into the sphere of private law. From the time of Bracton, English common law boasted that it was exclusively custom and so was its colonial offspring. In 1790 one of the few men to sign both the Declaration of Independence and the Constitution, James Wilson, argued that the American legal tradition, too, fulfilled the prescription of the Digest that law should be "a general convention of the citizens."[13]

So, in the eighteenth century, Roman law lived at least in the mentality of revolutionaries as well as royalists, and so did its original threefold form. How "deep" is the threefold structure of Western social thought? My allusions to the "trinity" are fanciful, but the sacred character—and divine origins—of law have been another immemorial premise of the legal tradition and the "priests of the law," as Justinian called them, who serve it. In his book *Trichotomy in Roman Law* Henry Goudy suggests several possibilities, including Roman pontifical conventions, Stoicism, and Pythagorean mysticism. A more obvious source, or at least homology, is Latin (and Greek and indeed Indo-Germanic) grammar, which is likewise based on relations between subject, object, and verb, but at this point, I suspect, we are all out of our depth.

In any case, as far as we can think, or read, back into our Greek (and Roman) memory, the free and conscious person, the "thinking subject" (as contemporary philosophers would say, perhaps with a grimace) has been a constant of law and language, if not literature and politics. So has the "liberty" that jurists took literally as well as legally to be the "cause" of the existence of this subject. A world of experience, pain, and tragedy (no doubt) lies behind the formulas of ancient jurisprudence that have come down to us as fragments and sound to us like the most tired of commonplaces.[14] "Liberty is a possession beyond price," asserts one of the ancient "rules of law" preserved by Justinian, and "Liberty is favored above all things." Eighteenth-century convention, of course, suppressed the original context—which had to do with the realities of slavery—and transformed such customs and rules into legal maxims and self-evident expressions of "natural law."

Political theorists and historians have emphasized the contributions of the legal tradition to questions of sovereignty, constitutionalism, resistance, and revolution, and to be sure these are major themes of political thought. Yet they make up only a very tiny fraction of Justinian's corpus; and in traveling the well-trodden paths of public law and political theory, scholars have overlooked the vast, mostly submerged continent of private law and social practice. Conceptually at least, the *jus privatum*, which forms most of the substance of the old legal tradition, has been the true refuge of "liberty," ancient and modern.

Perhaps the best illustration of this is title 5 of the first book of the Digest, devoted to one of the most repeated, glossed, interpreted, and inflated of all topics in the Western legal (and intellectual) tradition, namely, the "condition of men" (*De Statu hominum*), which was indeed the *locus classicus* of the idea of political liberty. Time had wrought many changes in the human condition, of course, and as Alberico de Rosate wrote in the fourteenth century, "In the modern times there are many human conditions not treated in this title" (referring to Jews and infidels in particular).[15] Two centuries later a French jurist, Barthélemy de Chasseneux, enhanced the ancient legal topic with reference to Pico della Mirandola's famous celebration of the "Dignity of Man," which argued that "liberty" was the defining feature of human nature, and, of course, this theme was carried over into natural law.[16]

By the eighteenth century this ancient topos, represented most conspicuously in the law, had spawned a massive literature devoted to the "dignity" and the "rights" of man. The harvest of this continuing discourse came in the various declarations of rights that accompanied the eighteenth-century revolutions and prefaced and adorned the postrevolutionary constitutions as the original title had prefaced and adorned the texts of civil law. Millennia and civilizations apart as they were, these manifestos had this in common, too, that they began with the premise that "by nature men are free"—though not necessarily denying that in fact, "everywhere they are in chains." This ideal premise has informed legal and political philosophy to the present. It furnished the basis for the new discipline of political economy, it occupied the center of German idealism, it was the lifelong obsession of Lord Acton, whose "madonna of the future" was his unfinished *History of Freedom*, and more recently it has furnished one of the foundations for Jack Hexter's Center for the History of Freedom.

In recent years the classical idea of liberty has come under attack from several quarters, and the main target seems to be that primary vehicle of liberty, the first hypostasis of the old civilian trinity, the "person"—the thinking, acting, perhaps writing, but, in any case, willful and responsible subject. Deconstruction and sociobiology are only the most recent of such postmodern assaults on subjectivity, but there are other more political spinoffs, such as Barthes's and Foucault's covert critiques of human autonomy. Classical liberalism, from Hegel to Hexter, is not well-equipped to handle such criticism. The main difficulty is that most parties in this debate are still caught up in what has been called the "Cartesian anxiety"—the demand for absolutes (coupled with the suspicion that they may not be present in the human condition).[17] For the Cartesian *Cogito* has no memory or respect for the deep structure and ambiguities of language, and neither does the natural-law view of human behavior in which this *Cogito* found its political definition and its conception of liberty. In fact the notion of "liberty" has roots deeper—and in that sense more "radical"—than imputations to "natural law," to the precultural and sociobiological or (as Thomas Hobbes would say) brutish aspect of humanity.

Invocations of nature and "natural liberty," by contrast, tend to obscure and even to obliterate the cultural inheritance I have talked about—and what is worse, to endorse habits of forgetfulness that are quite inconsistent with the sort of self-knowledge on which liberty has, conventionally if not naturally, depended. "In free countries," declared James Wilson, "—in free countries, especially, that boast the blessing of a common law, springing warm and spontaneous from the manners of the people—Law should be taught as a historical science."[18]

I do not intend this backward look into the old legal tradition to be a rehearsal of Burkean (or neo-Burkean) conservatism and complacency, only a reminder of the value of historical perspective. For the blessings of Western "liberty" are by no means unmixed, and the inheritance from antiquity, the images from our Greek memory, are not all reason for celebration. For most persons, perhaps, "liberty" is still a negative attribute—representing "freedom from," in the distinction made famous by Erich Fromm (and before him Nietzsche).[19]

In its positive form, on the other hand, it is a creature of human will. For Nietzsche, liberty is not a metaphysical or metahistorical attribute; it is "the complex state of delight of the person exercising volition, who commands and . . . enjoys triumphs over obstacles."

In general liberty is still an elitist preserve, associated with wealth, male prerogative, political power—and most primordially, with property. The idea of liberty has had a checkered, but also strikingly continuous career in connection with the Western practice of law, and it has reflected the evils as well as the benefits, the acquisitiveness as well as the tolerance, the small interests as well as the large ideals of society and its political arrangements. It is essential to remember that "liberty" was in fact a creation, or vision, of culture, not of nature except in revolutionary hyperbole and in movements that set out to under-mine, or to undo, the old regime—and so, in unexpected ways, it did. But ultimately history will not be undone by mere reason, true "en-lightenment" needs memory as well as reason, and "liberty" is serious and complicated enough to deserve critical historical examination as well as political commemoration.

NOTES

1. For views a generation ago, see *Nomos*, IV ("Liberty"), edited by Carl Friedrich (New York: Atherton Press, 1962).
2. For the basis of and bibliography for much of what follows see D. R. Kelley, *History, Law and the Human Sciences* (London: Variarum Editions, 1984).
3. "The Batture at New Orleans" (1810), in *Writings* (Memorial ed., 1904), XVIII, 1ff.
4. To Bernard Moore, August 30, 1814 (from a copy written fifty years earlier), in *The Writings*, edited by P. Ford (New York: G. P. Putnam's Sons, 1892-9), IX, 480-5; and see also Karl Lehmann, *Thomas Jefferson, American Humanist* (New York: Macmillan, 1947), 21ff.
5. Reported in Gilbert Chinard's biography *Honest John Adams* (Boston: Little, Brown, and Company, 1933), 29. See also *The Earliest Diary of John Adams*, edited by L. H. Butterfield (Cambridge: Belknap Press, 1966), 55; and H. T. Colbourn, *The Lamp of Experience* (Chapel Hill, N.C.: Published for the Institute of Early American History and Culture at Williamsburg, Virginia, by the University of North Carolina Press, 1965), chapter 6.
6. Endlessly repeated, but see, e.g., Eguinaire Baron's commentaries on Digest I, 5, in *Opera omnia* (Paris, 1562), 29, "Natura omnes homines liberi sunt et aequali"; see also G. Argou, *Institution au droit français* (Paris: Bailly, 1771); also royal ordinances as early as Louis X.
7. Heraclitus, fr. 45; and see Eric R. Dodds, *The Greeks and the Irrational* (Berkeley: University of California Press, 1951), 15; and Nietzsche's friend Erwin Rohde, *Psyche*, translated by W. B. Hillis (New York: Harper & Row, 1966); Digest I, 5, 1: "Omne ius quod utimur vel ad personas pertinet vel ad res vel ad actiones"; see also Henry Goudy, *Trichotomy in Roman Law* (Oxford: The Clarendon Press, 1910); and my "Gaius Noster," *American Historical Review* 84 (1979), 619-50, reprinted in *History, Law and the Human Sciences*.
8. A vast literature, including P. W. Duff, *Personality in Roman Law* (Cambridge: Cambridge University Press, 1938); H. Hübner, "Subjektivismus in der Entwicklung des Privatrechts," *Festschrift für Max Kaser*, edited by Dieter Medicus and Hans Hermann Seiler (Munich: Beck, 1976), 715-42; and now especially *Quaderni fiorentini per la storia del pensiero giuridico moderno*, XI-XII (1982-3), "Itinerari moderni della persona giuridica."
9. Digest, I, 5, 9.
10. D. R. Kelley and B. Smith, "What Was Property? Legal Dimensions of the Social Question in France (1789-1848)," *Proceedings of the American Philosophical Society* 128 (1984), 200-30.
11. A classic work, E. I. Bekker, *Die Aktionen des römischen Privatrechts* (Berlin: F. Vahlen, 1871-3).
12. Digest, I, 3, 35.
13. Again a large bibliography, but see Carlo Maiorca, *La Cosa in senso giuridico* (Turin: Instituto giuridico della R. Università, 1937), and C. Reinold Noyes, *The Institution of Property* (New York: Longmans, Green, and Company, 1936).

14. Three of these maxims are Digest L, 17, 106, "Libertas inestimabilis res est," 122; "Libertas omnibus rebus favorabilior est"; and 209, "Servitutem mortalitati fere comparamus." See also J. C. Dantoine, *Les Règles du droit canon* (Liège, 1775), "La liberté est un bien sans prix." And in general see Peter Stein, *Regulae Iuris* (Edinburgh: Edinburgh University Press, 1976).

15. *In primam partem ff. commentarii* (Venice, 1585), 44v.

16. *Catalogus gloriae mundi* (Paris, 1529), 17v.

17. Richard J. Bernstein, *Beyond Objectivism and Relativism: Science, Hermeneutics, and Praxis* (Philadelphia: University of Pennsylvania Press, 1983), 16.

18. *The Works*, I, 70; see also my *Historians and the Law in Postrevolutionary France* (Princeton: Princeton University Press, 1984).

19. Erich Fromm, *Escape from Freedom* (New York: Avon Discus Books, 1971), chapter 3; see also Friedrich Nietzsche, *The Birth of Tragedy and the Genealogy of Morals*, translated by Francis Golffing (New York: Doubleday, 1956), 19; and Quentin Skinner, "The Idea of Negative Liberty," in *Philosophy in History*, edited by Skinner et al. (Cambridge: Cambridge University Press, 1984), 193.

2

The Rights of the Individual and the General Will in Revolutionary Thought

François Bourricaud

Although the American Revolution and the French Revolution belong to the same *tradition*,[1] the revolutionary process took very different forms in the two countries. The stability of post-Revolutionary American institutions is generally lauded, while the fragility of the nineteenth-century French regimes is frequently deplored.

The French Revolution constitutes a process of an inexhaustible complexity. The historiography of this process is perhaps even more interesting than its history, assuming the two are separable. It is at least as instructive to ask what historians have said about the Revolution as to examine how it took place: *Wie es geschah*. Some, including Tocqueville and the moderates, are struck by the contrast between 1789 and 1794, between the "marvelous dawn" and the nightmare of the Terror. There is assumed to have been a break between the humanism of the Constituent Assembly members who, in the political sphere, are reputed to have fulfilled the hopes and demands of the philosophes, and the sadistic fanaticism of the Jacobins, marking a return to the spirit of the ancien régime and its brutal and compulsive conformity. The break is variously attributed to the tactlessness, blindness, or mediocrity of certain protagonists (the king, in particular); the premature demise of some of the most gifted men (Mirabeau, for instance); or to the interference of largely independent phenomena, whose conjunction brought about cumulatively destabilizing effects (the anti-religious policy of the Assembly, the emigration of the nobility, the bankruptcy of public finances, the food crisis in the towns, the breakdown of the army, the intrigues at the Court, and the proselytism and bellicosity of the Girondin left).

Other observers like Joseph de Maistre see no "break" but an implacable continuity that *necessarily* led from the follies of 1789 to the crimes of 1793–4. Moreover, the question of the "break" changes its meaning according to whether the series of events taken into account is more or less long. Between the Celebration of the Federation of 1790 and the September Massacres in 1792, there was perhaps a "break." But Napoleon repeatedly emphasized the continuity between Louis XIV and Robespierre, both defenders of a state that broke the power of the *grands* and the "factions" within France and protected the Nation against threats from outsiders.

Tocqueville, himself so sensitive to the "break" in the short period of the revolutionary episode between 1789 and 1793, defended the thesis of continuity when he empahisized that the centralization had started under the kings of France and accelerated even more because of the Revolution. But was not this centralization in the end fatal to individual liberty and the virtue of the citizen? By uncontrollably producing perverse effects, did the Revolution not only devour its own children but also deny the principles it had at first proclaimed?

In the wider perspective within which those who are called the "philosophers of history" like to place themselves, the central question asked of revolutionary historiography today, as in the nineteenth century, may remain the evaluation of how original this revolutionary episode in France was and what it brought to the theory and practice of modern liberty. No one, at least no one since Tocqueville, would doubt that the American Revolution made a decisive contribution to the French conception of democracy. To sum up Tocqueville's thought—at the risk of excessively simplifying it—the incomparable merit of the American synthesis was to have reconciled individual liberties and the rule of the majority. Was it the same in the case of the French Revolution? Tocqueville's answer was much more guarded. For complex reasons the rule of the majority had the greatest trouble in establishing itself, and one may doubt whether the principle is solidly and ineradicably established even today. Public administration and the extent of its competence and prerogatives, even if they are overseen and limited by an administrative law whose increase Tocqueville had not foreseen, reduce the potential for individual initiatives.

Rather than evoking the confusion of historical circumstance that may have changed the nature of the revolutionary legacy, let us try to capture its source, that is, the conception that people had of political order in 1789. This conception is marked by a sharp individualistic orientation. But it is even more worth reflecting on the place accorded the principle of representation and the subtle way in which this principle is defined. The notion of representative government is without doubt the most original of revolutionary demands; at the same time the notion sets out, if not the negation at least strict limits to the principle of representation. But the French revolutionaries, unlike their American counterparts, failed to set forth an acceptable theory of the functions of government. They did specify the rights of man and even of the citizen, but the constitutional instability of France throughout the nineteenth century and until recent times attests that, unlike the Americans, the French have great trouble in establishing the rules for the working of our institutions.

For a long time it was the fashion to mock the Declaration of Rights of 1789. The raillery came from conservatives and from certain sections of the left. For the conservatives, the declaration concerned only an abstract man, an individual, said Renan, who was born an orphan, lived his life as a confirmed bachelor, and died without issue. Joseph de Maistre and then Bonald denounced the abstract turn of revolutionary individualism. On the left, the values of liberty and equality proclaimed by the Declaration of 1789 were denounced as an imposture and a cover-up. It was not only the pseudo-universality of individualistic values that Marx denounced. For him and the neo-Marxists those values were also a cloak for the interests of the ruling class.

But the individualistic values proclaimed by the Declaration of 1789 stand up very well to this twin-pronged attack. It is sufficient to note that they do not refer only to an abstract man, but they also concern the citizen and, more precisely, the citizen of today.

Right from the opening lines of the declaration, the individualistic orientation is marked: "Ignorance of, forgetfulness of, or contempt for human rights are the only causes of public misfortunes." It is underscored in article 2: "The aim of every political association is the preservation of the natural and inviolable rights of man." The allusion to the notion of a contract is made palpable by the use of such words as *aim* and *association*. Political association has aims other than its own preservation. Even if the safety of the state is a great boon to the individual, this safety is valid only because it guarantees us the enjoyment of these natural rights: liberty, equality, property, security, and resistance to oppression (articles 1 and 2). As a result, the state is not in itself a commanding power; it merely brings together the citizens who make it up. The state lives only thanks to the consent of those same citizens.

French public law has departed from those principles only during the time of the Vichy government. It appears that today these principles form the most solid basis for our political consensus. In what way can these principles be called individualistic? Obviously they refer to attributes that are essential to every person, namely, liberty, equality, security, and property. What is not always emphasized clearly enough is that these attributes qualify relationships and not substances. That is manifest in the case of liberty. Literally, I am equal only in regard to another. Liberty consists in being able to do anything that does not harm others (article 4).

The case of property is like that of equality. Indeed, the owner has a private relationship with certain objects, but those rights are relative. The owner may be deprived of property in the name of public necessity, on the twofold condition of a "public, legal, and obvious" observation and a "just preliminary indemnity" (article 17). Thus, property is not an absolute right because, to be effectively protected, it needs a judge and sometimes public strength (presented in article 12 as a guarantee of the rights of man and the citizen), and because it has to be appreciated in the light of "public necessity."

The "relational" nature of human rights is further underscored by article 10 (on freedom of opinion, especially in religious matters). It is confirmed by article 11 as far as concerns "the free communication of thoughts and opinions," which for every citizen entails the right to speak, write, and print freely. Freedom of communication is widened and confirmed a little later on by the recognized freedom of citizens to "assemble peacefully and without arms"—on condition, naturally, that they "satisfy police laws." This right is of a piece with the right to move about, to stay in one place, and to go away without being subject to arrest or detention except according to the conventions outlined in the constitution.

I have emphasized the coherence of these rights associated with the freedom to communicate. Their identity and structure must be noted: at their core, we find an initiative linked with an individual's energy or natural power, such as the power to speak, to move about, and to meet with others. The second group of rights is defined by the response of those to whom the initiative is addressed and for whom it may constitute a hindrance or a help. Finally, public power remains in the background, ready to intervene particularly to right those wrongs that might result from the unilateral use of his power by an individual.

Such a conception of rights may be said to be individualistic because it aims to ensure everyone the exercise of our liberties—I am tempted to say, our *physical* liberties: coming, going, speaking, printing, demonstrating. This individualism is obviously interactional, because it concerns the relationships of individuals to one another. But contrary to what is often said, these rights are not strictly private. They are not exercised only in an impossible "bourgeois" civil society in which the individuals would simply be exchangers, producers, or consumers. Nothing is more foreign to the spirit of 1789 than the strict separation of civil society and the state. Between the two, it is obvious that distinctions must be drawn. "A Frenchman's home is his castle," but to protect himself effectively against possible attacks, he must be able to count on "public strength" in the service of the law. The rights guaranteed by the Declaration of 1789 are, above all, rights of access to public property: liberty, equality, security, resistance to oppression. It is quite improper to reduce these rights to real rights to goods or commercial services. The first section of the constitution of 3 September 1791, which concerns "the fundamental dispositions guaranteed by the Constitution," states "that all citizens may be admitted to places and positions without distinction other than that of their virtue and talents; that all contributions will be shared out proportional to their faculties; that the same crimes will be punishable by the same penalties."

Equality in respect to places and positions, equality in fiscal matters, equality in the eyes of the law—it is a dual question of public property. First, because of the universal nature of the process of its distribution, this property is held in common; second, it is, so to speak, issued by public power itself according to the modalities of law, the expression of the general will. A few lines further on, it is even more obviously a question of public property when there is mention of organizing the "general establishment of public succor to bring up abandoned children, bring comfort to the poor, strong in body" or again, of creating "public instruction . . . free concerning those aspects of learning indispensable for all men."

Three types of rights can be discerned. One type consists of those that appear as mutual obligations, for instance, between buyer and seller in the exchange of property. But the contract is not just an arrangement between private individuals. Public power intervenes in two ways: if one of the contracting parties defaults, public power has a duty to ensure that the engagements agreed are respected; if the engagements themselves are incompatible with the law, public power may break the contract. At the basis of the contract is the freedom to contract (what jurists were later on to call "the autonomy of the contracting parties"), but this freedom is framed by a law that is the condition for liberties belonging to individuals insofar as they are free and equal. As for the rights to public succor and public instruction, they require the support of a public power, a state, even more explicitly than the protection of our rights to contract, to speak, to write, and to print, and just as obviously, they have their source in the power of individuals, envisaged from the point of view of the expansion and development of that power.

The rights mentioned in the 1789 text are not those of man *and* the citizen, but rather those of man *as* a citizen. The rights of 1789, contrary to what is often written, are not "bourgeois" ones—even if they are favorable to bourgeois interests. In the eyes of Siéyès, what ensures the eminent dignity of the Third Estate (the expression used at that time to designate what was later to be called the middle class or bourgeoisie) is not at all, as in the famous Saint-Simonian apology, that its members alone are the "producers," the bees that distill the honey the hornets will devour; it is that the Third Estate, and it alone, is the nation.

In a way, the church depends on foreign authorities, and the nobility is formed by the heirs of the Germanic conquerors. But it is important not to use the term *nation* in the way that modern nationalists understand it. The Third Estate is the state, or something like the "universal class" in the state. The bourgeoisie in 1789 had no special rights, or privileges. The members of the Constituent Assembly did not legislate for the head of the household or the company manager, shut up in the circle of the "small society" formed by his relatives, his associates, or his customers. Above all, the law concerned the universal attributes of free and equal individuals, that is, citizens.

It is by comparison with those two attributes of liberty and equality between individuals that the quality of citizenship is defined. Being a citizen means having fellow citizens with whom one finds oneself to have ties of liberty and equality. But, naturally, this does not mean that everyone is able to do everything, or that everyone is equal to everyone else in every respect. Such is the tenor of the famous restriction in the article that qualified men as "free and equal in *rights*."

For the men of 1789, rights were therefore something other than a sum of economic interests and much more than an abstract ideal. The reproaches leveled against them by conservatives after the manner of Joseph de Maistre as well as by radicals in the style of Marx are without foundation. In fact, for the members of the Constituent Assembly of 1789, the difficulty did not stem from their conception of the rights of man. Along with Paul Bastid, one can even consider this conception as both central and stable within the architecture of French public law: "Since the Revolution, the principles of French public law have to a certain extent remained constant. Although perpetually moved around, the base has not changed in nature: individualism and a representative nature . . . have continued to form its basic elements."[2]

The contribution of 1789 is decisive concerning the first principle identified by Paul Bastid, individualism, provided that its nature is correctly understood; it can even be maintained that the horrors of

1793–4 and the subsequent turbulence were not sufficient to disqualify its message. But it is with the second principle, "the representative regime," that the problems begin. Contrary to what is said, the difficulties of 1789 stem less from the theory of the rights of man than from an insufficient analysis of the "representative regime." The constitutional failure of modern France is not to be ascribed to the "philosophy" that nourished the members of the Constituent Assembly in 1789. Beyond the fact that this philosophy was also that of the Americans who were able to derive a generally satisfactory practice from it, the French never really moved away from the theory of the rights of man after the Revolution. This is shown by the drawing up of the Civil Code at the end of the nineteenth century and the development of administrative law, which extended the competence of the state while limiting its arbitrary powers and increasing its responsibilities. French political organization fails less on account of its ideals and philosophy than on account of its theory and practice of the functions of government. Thus, the second "principle" identified by Bastid, that of representation, calls for a special study, for it is this that governs the organization of public powers.

In article 4, the Declaration of 1789 defined the law as "the expression of the general will." This same article stipulated that all citizens had the "right to contribute to its formation, either personally or through their representatives." This definition does not concern itself with the object of the general will, as was the case with Malebranche, who saw in the "general will of man, the will that bears us towards indeterminate and general well-being."[3] It concerns, rather, the way the general will is formed—from the contributions of all citizens. What is essential is that the general will (in other words, the law) is not the will of any one individual in particular. The "sic jubeo, sic volo, sit pro ratione voluntas" is proscribed in every case. Unable to be the exclusive will of one person or even a few, the law—or the sovereignty it proceeds from, as article 3 says—can only be a collective will. The principle of all sovereignty resides basically in the nation.

This unassailable conclusion, however, raises two difficulties. The universality of will is quite apart from unanimity. Let us concede that all citizens have the right to contribute to the formation of the law; for there to be a law, is it necessary for all citizens to agree on what the law prescribes for them? This difficulty is circumvented by an argument that has been the traditional one since Locke: once the social pact has been sealed, the individuals, becoming citizens by this convention, implicitly agree for the functioning of their association to reach decisions by the application of majority rule. This arrangement may be presented as a sort of consequence of the social contract itself. The legality of this consequence is dubious, to say the least. What can force a person to wish a type of association in which he risks finding himself on the wrong side? And if he accepts this stipulation, to the advantage of the majority, does he not of his own will place himself in a situation in which he refuses to find himself, compared with the will of one person? Does not the will of the majority stand the chance of being as despotic as the will of a dictator or a king?

This question, which was to preoccupy Benjamin Constant as much as Tocqueville, was not openly broached by the men of 1789. For them, the "nation" in which they placed sovereignty constituted the nation of nineteenth-century nationalists; it was not the "people" of the Jacobins and the radicals. The nation was defined by the members of the Constituent Assembly of 1789 in strictly negative terms. It does not allow itself to be confused with "any individual." But quickly we reach the limits of this negative approach. Because the nation is no one and it is to be found nowhere, because it is a sort of Arlésienne (the character in Bizet's opera who is never seen but who is the driving force behind the action), and because all authority that a body of men or an individual could take advantage of is legitimate only if that authority emanates from the body or individual by special delegation, the political problem boils down to knowing how the majority of citizens express the general will, that is, the will of the nation, and whether they are the only ones to express it.

Paul Bastid emphasized the "constancy of the principles of French public law." No doubt he was right as far as the individualistic "principle" is concerned. The principle of representation is a different matter. Roughly speaking, the representative principle has prevailed in the history of French political institutions, but this predominance has been contested since Rousseau. Behind the debate concerning representation is the relationship between those who govern and those who are governed. This relationship is extremely ambiguous, and perhaps its nature prohibits a fully satisfying elucidation.

Two theses lie behind Jacobin and radical ideology to which the supporters of the left adhere today. According to the first thesis, set out in the preamble to the 1848 Constitution, sovereignty resides in all the citizens of France collectively. The upshot of this is that no counterpower may be set up against this "universality" in the name of which the majority of electors have the right to speak. It is this situation that Tocqueville described in chapter 7 of the second part of the first edition of *Democracy in America*, devoted to the omnipotence of the majority in the United States, which he crudely qualified as "tyranny."

The radicals founded their claims in favor of the "omnipotence of the majority" on arguments of unequal worth. In the first place, sovereignty belongs only to the individuals who make up the body politic. Moreover, these individuals, when considered from the point of view of their natural state, are independent entities entitled to their rights because of their will for independence. "At the moment," said Rousseau, "I wish what such and such a man wishes. But I cannot say, 'I shall still wish what the same man will wish tomorrow.'"[4]

This is a radical conception of individualism, which is no longer a capacity or power of initiative working within a network of interactions, as in the Anglo-Scottish variant of individualism. Individualism is defined as an innate and arbitrary will, which can commit itself only in respect of itself, because it depends on no will to consent to anything contrary to the well-being of the person who wishes.[5]

This radical individualism borders on solipsism. No individual is lastingly obliged to any other. In the strictest sense, no one can *represent* anyone else. Rousseau conceded that an individual may transfer his power to another individual, but no one can transfer to another his indeterminate capacity with respect to his will. This innate capacity of the individual is inalienable.

From a philosophical point of view, Rousseau's argument was not devoid of influence. It is at the basis of all *volontariste* conceptions—I am tempted to say from Descartes to Sartre via Nietzsche. But from the political standpoint, is it pertinent? Montesquieu, for instance,[6] who made representation an essential cog in modern political regimes, saw in it nothing more than a transfer of power, possibly widespread and justified by the great disparities in the distribution of political talent. He never made it into an alienation by which the one represented would yield to the absolute discretion of the representative. The debates on the imperative mandate made it clear that those who upheld the representative mandate intended less to protect the represented against the representative than to ensure the fully "national" (that is, nonregional and non-sector-based) nature of this representation. First and foremost, representatives were to represent the entire nation lest they simply become the stooges of selfish or factious interests. The representatives of the nation are not satraps. Even if they have no scores to settle with their electors, they are responsible to the nation.

It is all too easy to say that this responsibility is quite meaningless, because the nation, as distinct from the individuals who make it up, is a mere fiction. Did the radicals provide the proof that all representation is an alienation? At any rate, they found themselves in a very delicate position when, on the basis of an individualism of a strictly "atomic" nature, they had to move away from the solipsism and build up a concept of law and general will. After having made of the individual a sovereign atom, they were led to affirm the sovereignty of the whole in which they dissolved the individual.

Rousseau believed he could get around this predicament by declaring that the sovereignty of the whole resulted from the renunciation by all individuals of their own special sovereignty. "The condition being the same for all," Rousseau reasoned, "it is in no one's interest to render it onerous."

According to Tocqueville, the risk of tyranny, implied by the preponderance of the majority, would thus be controlled by the calculation of interest well perceived. But was "the condition" really equal for all? The condition Rousseau was really thinking of was the alienation by each associate of all his rights, to the benefit of the association. But once this contract is signed, do the associates really find themselves equal with regard to all the conditions the association may impose on them? Or are they not exposed to an unequal treatment by virtue of the engagements they have subscribed to in that first contract? Do not the majority risk being despotic toward private individuals, just as the representatives do with regard to those they represent? And in both cases, does not the risk of despotism spring from the same source, not the metaphysical difficulty of relinquishing wills but the poor control of the relationships between governors and governed?

As for the men of 1789 whose views on representation stand in such marked contrast to those of the radicals, the disciples of Rousseau whom I have just evoked, the fundamental difficulty for them came from the fact that they had sought to construct a normative notion of representation without binding the latter to the empirical conditions of representativeness. The representative is the one who is legitimately empowered to speak in the name of the nation. Max Weber has emphasized[7] that the attribution of responsibilities leads, through the individualization of power, to the identification of persons and representative roles, the embodiment of the group.

In all societies there are people who receive or who are recognized as having a distinctive authority or particular excellence by virtue of their birth or status, or, conversely, their talents and merits. According to the type of society concerned, old men, priests, fakirs, scholars, and judges form part of the category of wise men who have the power to settle conflicts, to engage the whole group, and to pronounce the law in its name. Without being consecrated as representatives at the end of some explicit, public procedure, they are treated as representative authorities. For the men of 1789, the influence and prestige attached to traditional authorities were unfounded privileges. "There are no longer Rights, nor nobility, nor peerage, nor hereditary distinctions, nor distinctions of order . . . nor any superiority other than that of the public functionaries in the exercise of their functions," said the Declaration of the Rights of Man. In other words, there was no longer anything but the nation, in its inaccessible transcendency, and the body of citizens, which should not be confused with it.

With regard to traditional authorities, the embarrassment of the men of 1789 is nowhere better expressed than in the debate on the royal person. The Constitution of 3 September 1791, in article 2 of its third section, made the king a representative of the Nation, alongside the Legislative Assembly. The discussion of this article afforded Roederer and Robespierre the chance to present their views on two essential points. First, on the nature of the executive power: both were willing to acknowledge the king as its "supreme head." The executive power was not a representative power, it was a committed power, subordinate to the legislature, which alone expressed the general will. The executive was charged with taking particular, contingent decisions, but the king was not the representative of the nation because, according to Roederer, "the essence of Representation is that each individual may merge his individual will in the will of his representative. Thus, without elections, no representation. A hereditary king is not a representative."[8]

The Constituent Assembly did not follow Roederer, but affirmed the representative character of the king and granted him a right of suspensive veto and the initiative in negotiating and concluding treaties. In both these capacities, the king was expected to "desire for the Nation," which is the exclusive feature of every representative. For the men of 1789 this feature is what distinguished the king from the functionaries, who were but servants, and from the judges, who, although elected, were also deprived of representative power and had to content themselves with executing simple judiciary *functions*.[9]

The notion of representation that Paul Bastid justifiably made a "constant principle" of French public law claims to link the defense of individual rights with a general will that guarantees their achievement. But the nature of this mediation is not clear. Obviously these rights would not be protected if the will inspiring the law were arbitrary. But is the general nature of this will guaranteed if the legislator, who, by virtue of being elected, ought to be the representative of the nation, is no more than the representative of the majority of the citizens? In the formation of this will, what weight must be attributed to authorities who, without being elected, may nevertheless be qualified as *representatives*?

Around the time of World War I, as resolute a defender of the representative system as Carré de Malberg qualified the French régime as "semi-representative."[10] In his eyes, the relationship between the governors and the governed—which is not to be confused with the relationship between the electors and the elected—was well on the way to profound change. In the doctrine set out by the members of the Assembly in 1875, the electors chose men who did not represent them but who represented national sovereignty. As Carré de Malberg himself recognized, this fiction loses all its credibility as interests of all sorts exercise a growing influence on those elected, thanks to the proliferation of pressure groups and to the various electoral reforms that claim to bring electors and elected closer together, placing the latter under the control of the former. The mutual reinforcement of these two tendencies leads to what our author calls a "régime of opinion" that transforms the functions of elections.[11] As in this model, which is representative in the strictest sense of the word, elections are no longer held to "appoint representatives" who, independent of their electors, speak and wish "in the name of the Nation." "They allow the country itself to determine the main directions of national policy."[12] Elections are nothing more than occasions on which two sorts of decisions are taken, some relative to the choice of policies, others relative to the choice of governors.[13]

It is evident that the notion of representation has greatly changed since the French Revolution. Considering what it has become, it could be said that it deserves neither the "excess of honor" paid it by Siéyès and the men of 1789 nor the excess of reproach by the radical democrats. It is simply an artifice, making the exercise of governmental responsibilities possible. Yet it is also better than that. In fact, it lends support to another fiction of higher rank, absolutely essential for the smooth running of our modern democracies: the notion of the law as the "expression of the general will." What gives consistency to the rights of man and the citizen is the idea that the law is not, or at least should not be, the expression of one particular will—not that of one man, or of one party, or of one class.

Following Carré de Malberg and in keeping with his theory of the "semi-representative" regime, to the twin functions of choosing between rival government teams and choosing between concurrent policies, a third must be added, invested with a sort of axiological supremacy. The representatives elected by a nation are supposed to watch over the rights of man and the citizen, but their doing this is fully ensured only if the "semi-representatives" who govern are prevented from acting arbitrarily and obliged to act in accordance with the common will. The difficulty is not where people are most naturally tempted to look for it; it is not entirely impossible to set up barriers to caprice and ambition or to stir up incitements to public-spiritedness. It amounts to making these "semi-representatives" servants of a law that is the general will only because it is not exclusively the will of anyone, not even of the majority.

The evolution toward "semi-representative" regimes may be considered a tendency common to most Western countries. The "semi-representative" regimes to be seen in different forms almost everywhere in the Western world may be characterized by a combination of ideological principles and institutional arrangements. Those principles are, first, the notion of a law that does not proceed from a special will, or even from a private will, but a law in which all citizens may recognize themselves. The second principle is that the governors who must act in accordance with this law must, one way or another, be answerable to those they govern.

The two propositions stayed independent of each other for a long time. Louis XIV could refuse to be answerable to his subjects. On his deathbed, however, he submitted himself in advance to the judgment of God, the only true sovereign. The sovereignty of the king was therefore limited by the sovereignty of God. By secularizing the sources of legitimate power, the modern democracies made the notion of law and the notion of the general will contingent on each other.

Even if those who govern cannot be held to be the representatives of those governed in a precise way, one may see, in the governors, the representatives of the law who speak—or are supposed to speak—in the name of the entire political community. But this representation is doubly fictitious, because the law exists only as something that must be, and because those who govern exercise their power only in those forms prescribed by the constitution. Under these circumstances, representation is implemented through elections, which make it possible to settle two questions at the same time: the appointment of governors and the orientation of their policies. Unlike the notion of representative government, this theory worked out by jurisconsults and jurists, that of the "semi-representative" regime, of polyarchy or democracy as Schumpeter understands it, does not aim for normative coherence. Giving its place to History, it does not refuse to record the weakness of the joints and links that after a fashion make the various odd pieces in the French political edifice hold together.

The main difficulty encountered in France by the notion of a "semi-representative" regime (and this can be seen from Carré de Malberg's embarrassment in putting forward the conception) is that spontaneously the French imagine sovereignty in a unitary form. Royal sovereignty and then popular sovereignty—the imagery has for long hidden from us the modus operandi of government. As soon as we are forced to recognize that there are several principles of legitimacy, we are tempted to conclude that there is no legitimacy at all. The Americans are in a different situation: the distinction between the federal government and the state governments, the separation of powers and perhaps even more so the *equality* of those powers (in France the question of the priority of the legislative over the executive has scarcely ceased to be posed), the eminent position given by the Americans to judges (in France, judges see themselves enjoined not to interpret the law and limit themselves to its strictest application), the complexity and relatively democratic administrative system (in France, civil servants, in the name of a highly ambitious conception of "public service," seek to pass for a sort of "universal class")—these various elements point up the marked contrast between American and French methods of government, even if both belong to the same tradition. Perhaps they will be called to draw closer to each other—especially if the institutions of the Fifth Republic were to consolidate their position—in particular, concerning the cooperation between equal but differentiated state powers and the importance of various jurisdictional controls. If such were the case, the basic stability of the principles of French public law asserted by Paul Bastid and with it, the importance of the legacy of 1789, would have a chance of being better recognized.

NOTES

1. "Cotraditions et traditions chez Tocqueville," *Tocqueville Review*, 2, no. 1 (Winter 1980): 25–39.
2. Paul Bastid, *Siéyès et sa pensée* (Paris: Hachette, 1970), 15.
3. Nicholas Malebranche, *De la recherche de la vérité*, I, chapter 1.
4. Jean-Jacques Rousseau, *Du contrat social*, II, 1.
5. Ibid.
6. Montesquieu, *L'esprit des lois*.
7. *Economie et Société* (Paris: Plon, 1971) I, "Les concepts fondamentaux de la sociologie", section 11.
8. Roederer's text is quoted by R. Carré de Malberg in *Contribution à la théorie générale de l'Etat* (Paris: Sirey, 1922) 2, p. 270.
9. Ibid., 279.
10. He also uses the word *parliamentary*, making of the direction of the executive by a cabinet and a prime minister in the British fashion, not modeled on Walpole but on Gladstone or Disraeli, the distinctive feature of the system.
11. Ibid., 370.

12. Ibid.
13. This conception of elections is remarkably close to the one defended by Schumpeter in the fourth part of *Capitalism, Socialism and Democracy* (New York: Harper and Brothers, 1942).

3

Liberty and the Illusions of Individualism in Tocqueville

Jean-Claude Lamberti

In 1850, Tocqueville wrote to his friend Kergolay, "I have no traditions, I have no party, I have no cause, except that of liberty and human dignity. Of that I am certain."[1] Had he broken with his ancestral traditions as much as he claimed? His entire life's work was one great effort to imbue democracy, for its own benefit, with aristocratic values, especially the taste for human excellence, mutual respect, and the proud affirmation of personal independence. But better than anyone else in his time he realized that liberty could no longer be founded on inequality or aristocracy. Given this premise, his hierarchy of political values was very clear. Accepting equality because no other possible foundation for liberty was left, he became a democrat because he was a liberal—a democrat as a matter of reason, but a liberal from passionate commitment.

In the course of his research in the Tocqueville family archives, Antoine Redier discovered an unpublished page, a leaf from a sort of private journal, titled, "My instinct, my opinions." The text, which is tantamount to a personal confession, reads as follows:

> Experience has shown me that almost all men, and certainly myself, usually return more or less exactly to their fundamental instincts and that one does well only those things that conform to these instincts. I should therefore make a sincere effort to find out where my fundamental instincts and my serious principles lie. . . . My taste for democratic institutions is in my head, but I am an aristocrat by instinct, that is to say, I despise and fear the mob. I passionately love liberty, legality, respect for individual rights, but not democracy; that is how I feel deep down. . . . In truth, liberty is the foremost of my passions.[2]

His own family had provided Tocqueville with the model of aristocratic liberty and instilled in him the religious idea of a free and responsible soul. His experience in the United States and the philosophical inquiry he pursued between 1835 and 1850 while studying Pascal, Montesquieu, and Rousseau led him to adopt the democratic idea of liberty. But he has not left a precise, complete theory of what he meant by "liberty."[3] It is well known that he had no penchant for pure speculation; whatever the question confronting him, he always approached it by the comparative method. Rather than meditating on the essence of liberty, he painstakingly compared American liberty with French liberty. And he never ceased to contrast liberal democracy and the civic consciousness of the Americans with the democracy bequeathed by the French Revolution and the errors of Rousseau, by the Jacobin myths, and by the corruption of public spirit that had arisen under the Old Regime's administrative monarchy.[4]

To bring out the elements of a theory of liberty in Tocqueville's thought, it seems necessary to begin by setting up what might be called the theoretical framework of his inquiry. Then it is important to give a thorough account of what he considered to be the illusions of individualism, for this critical dimension sheds light on the originality and the profundity of his thought. On this basis it will be possible to show why Tocqueville placed political liberty at the pinnacle of the political values.

THE FRAMEWORK OF TOCQUEVILLE'S THEORY OF LIBERTY

Tocqueville had an aristocratic sense of and love for liberty, yet he also defended the democratic idea of liberty. He had divorced, as it were, his heart from his mind, keeping his personal tastes and feelings separate from the conclusions to which he was led by his political acumen and his sense of justice. Let us apply to an analysis of Tocqueville himself the distinction he so often made between liberty and liberal sentiments.

In his *Histoire de la civilisation en Europe*, Guizot paid tribute to the Germanic barbarians for having introduced into European civilization "the attachment to the personality, to the free development of human spontaneity." As Guizot noted, "This desire for individual independence is a noble and moral sentiment that draws its power from the moral nature of man."[5] This Germanic idea of liberty is at the core of the aristocratic sense of liberty in Tocqueville, and if, as is likely, he attended Guizot's lectures in 1828, he must have found in them confirmation of some of his own penchants. Let us listen to Tocqueville, then, as he speaks of liberty:

At all times, what has so strongly attached the hearts of certain
men to liberty are its very attractions, its sheer delight, quite aside
from the benefits it affords; it is the pleasure of being able to
speak, to act, to breathe without constraint, solely governed by
God and the law. Those who seek anything other than liberty in
liberty are born to serve. . . . Do not ask me to analyze this sublime yearning; it has to be experienced. It simply comes into those
great souls that God has prepared to receive it, filling them and
setting them afire. There is no use trying to explain this to medi-
ocre souls who have never felt it.[6]

Tocqueville here emphasizes the yearning for independence for its
own sake, a feeling that only the best souls will experience. This text
reflects the Germanic idea of liberty, "the noble system that was in-
vented in the forests," as Montesquieu had put it, of which modern
liberty is a distant legacy.[7]

Tocqueville was well aware, of course, that most of his contemporaries did not demand liberty as a valid end in itself, but merely as a
means. But he believed that when liberty becomes nothing more than
a means to equality or to prosperity, it will soon degenerate. In an
original and perspicacious article, Seymour Drescher showed how
much the second half of *Democracy in America*, published in 1840, differed from the work published in 1835.[8] Fear of the tyranny of the
majority was superseded by fear of general apathy, and anxious reflections on the weakening of liberal sentiments and on the decline of
public life became a major theme. Also in the second part of *Democracy*, Tocqueville saw the main threat no longer as the abuse of power
but as the breakdown of civic-mindedness, which would reduce life to
nothing but its private dimension and absorb the citizens in what
Tocqueville called "a sort of virtuous materialism." If this situation
came to pass, the most pernicious effect of democracy would be to
reduce the energy of liberal aspirations so much that the citizens,
satisfied with their prosperous tranquillity, would no longer even feel
the absence of liberty. A new leviathan could then arise without violence, even leaving intact some of the outward forms of liberty.[9]

This distinction between the idea of liberty and the desire in an
individual or a society for liberty will prevent us from imagining contradictions and will permit us to reconcile Tocqueville's abiding love of
aristocratic liberty with his disposition toward equal liberty for all.

Despite his strong attachment to aristocratic liberty, Tocqueville felt
that democratic liberty was better suited to his time. Indeed, he asserted in his *"Essai sur l'état social et politique avant et depuis 1789"*
("Essay on the Social and Political State of France before and since
1789") that democratic liberty was just:

> According to the modern notion—the democratic and, I am not
> afraid to say so, the just notion of liberty—every individual, pre-
> sumed to have received from nature the necessary wisdom to con-
> duct himself, brings with him at birth an equal and inviolable
> right to live independently of his fellows in matters that concern
> him alone and to regulate his own fate as he sees fit.[10]

The moral dimension of this definition lies in the idea of equal rights
for all, which Tocqueville believed to be justified by the Christian
notion of equal moral responsibility for everyone. He also believed
that the Gospel has given human beings the moral strength needed to
temper Germanic liberty and to extend the aristocratic liberties to all.

Certain commentators have seen contradictions in Tocqueville's
thought, noting that he affirms both human liberty and the irresistible
advent of democracy. How is it possible to profess simultaneously the
liberty and the responsibility of the individual on the one hand, and
historical determinism on the other? In fact, Tocqueville never accepted the notion that history is totally determined, and his severe
judgments on Thiers and Mignet, whom he accused of historical fatal-
ism, are well known.[11] There is no contradiction, and the appearance
of one rests largely on a misunderstanding of Tocqueville's vocabulary,
in which the word *democracy* is sometimes used to designate a social
environment characterized by the equality of conditions, and at other
times is used to refer to the political regime of democracy. What Tocqueville asserted was simply that the movement toward the equaliza-
tion of conditions is irresistible, not because some law of history so
dictates, but because this tendency has been gaining in strength for
seven hundred years and has profoundly changed social mores, even
in Europe, notwithstanding some appearances to the contrary. A
movement of such strength cannot suddenly shift direction and reverse itself before it has produced all its effects. But, Tocqueville adds,
such a movement is not brought about by cultural, economic, or political factors. He also warns that the social democratic state is as likely to
lead to despotism as to liberal democracy. Thus, "within vast limits,"
man is "powerful and free," and the last lines of *Democracy in America*
alone should be enough to enlighten the reader of good faith:

> The nations of our time cannot prevent the conditions of men
> from becoming equal, but it depends upon themselves whether
> the principle of equality is to lead them to servitude or freedom,
> to knowledge or barbarism, to prosperity or wretchedness.[12]

Social democracy gives to individuals both equality of condition and
independence. But independence, as Montesquieu observed, is not yet

a complete form of liberty; it must be associated with the idea of the rights and duties of responsible individuals, which is not necessarily a consequence of social democracy.

In a famous speech delivered in 1819, Benjamin Constant had contrasted the liberty of the ancients with that of the moderns: "The aim of the Ancients," he declared, "was the sharing of social power among all the citizens. That is what they called liberty. The aim of the Moderns is to provide security for private enjoyment, and they call liberty the guarantees that institutions accord that enjoyment." Like Constant, Tocqueville demanded respect and guarantees for individual rights, but he wanted more: he also tried to preserve what Constant seemed to relegate to the past without regret, namely, the feeling of civic obligation and the joy of public action. Tocqueville, like Aristotle, saw political life as a means of human fulfillment, and the exercise of political liberty seemed to him necessary to counteract the imbalances and illusions fostered by equality.

Taken in its entirety, Tocqueville's idea of liberty comprises three elements: the desire for individual independence, inherited from the Germanic notion of liberty that was preserved by the aristocracy; the idea of participation in political life, a legacy from the ancients; and the idea of equal rights for all people, as demanded by Christian morality. If all three of these elements are combined, it becomes evident that liberty is not only a right but also the most complete form of duty, that is, an obligation to oneself, to the community, to one's fellow human beings, and to God.

And what would happen if it were forgotten that liberty is a civic as much as a moral duty? Why not, as Benjamin Constant advocated, simply enjoy the right to be free and neglect one's civic duties?[13] As Tocqueville saw it, the principal danger resided precisely in what Constant touted as "the individual's proud and jealous seclusion in the fortress of his rights." For Tocqueville, it was of prime importance to rouse the public spirit, to extend the interests of people beyond their own affairs, and to correct the individualistic illusions spawned by democratic societies.

Absent from the first half of *Democracy in America*, the concept of individualism is the fruit of the prolonged philosophical studies that had occupied Tocqueville between 1835 and 1850. As many commentators have noted, the concept plays a central role in the second volume of *Democracy*; what has not been pointed out, however, is that Tocqueville increasingly came to consider individualistic illusions a threat to democratic liberty.[14] "Individualism," Tocqueville wrote, "has its origin in democracy and threatens to grow as people's conditions become more equal." Unlike the aristocratic societies of the past, which organically linked people to one another in an immense network, democracies are made up of citizens who are more and more alike, yet isolated, and who tend to take little interest in public affairs. Defined in Tocquevillian terms,

> Individualism is a mature and calm feeling which disposes each member of the community to sever himself from the mass of his fellows and to draw apart with his family and his friends, so that after he has thus formed a little circle of his own, he willingly leaves society at large to itself.

Beyond a certain threshold, the deleterious effects of this attitude become obvious to all: "Individualism, at first, only saps the virtues of public life; but in the long run it attacks and destroys all others and is at length absorbed in downright selfishness." In principle, nonetheless, Tocqueville defines individualism as a lack of civic-mindedness and distinguishes it from selfishness: "Selfishness originates in blind instinct; individualism proceeds from erroneous judgment more than from depraved feelings." At the root of individualism, therefore, Tocqueville sees both a sociopolitical structure (in which individuals are alike yet isolated) and an intellectual structure (erroneous judgment), which he evokes in a general formula at the end of the chapter devoted to individualism: "They are apt to imagine that their whole destiny is in their own hands."[15]

TOCQUEVILLE'S ANTIDOTES TO "INDIVIDUALISTIC ILLUSIONS"

One of the principal aims of the "new political science" that Tocqueville wanted to create was to correct the individualistic illusions and the "erroneous judgment" from which they proceed. If there is nothing to thwart the illusion of individual self-sufficiency, people will fall prey to an excessive taste for material well-being; the person who prefers being a consumer to being a citizen will soon become a mere subject once again. Individualists are mistaken to believe that they will be able to enjoy their rights to independence and equality if they do not fulfill their obligations as citizens or, more exactly, if they limit the exercise of their political liberty to a minimum, as Benjamin Constant had advocated. The most serious consequence of the "erroneous judgment" that has spawned individualism is an inadequate idea of liberty, one that considers participation in civic life solely a right and never a duty. Such a conception is bound to lead to democratic despotism. Tocqueville did not believe that it was necessary to provide a systematic listing of the illusions that arise spontaneously in democratic societies, but throughout *Democracy in America* it is obvious that he had in mind three main forms of the individualistic illusion.

The first of these consists in imagining that the individual and private interests of everyone can be defined and permanently safeguarded without reference to public interests and public order. This form of illusion is in fact a crude understanding of the theory of interest, which the Americans were able to expand considerably, thanks to a wider vision of what they called "self-interest rightly understood."[16] The most effective means of correcting this form of illusory self-sufficiency is to get people involved in local affairs and the life of associations, for, as Tocqueville wrote, "As soon as man begins to treat of public affairs in public, he begins to perceive that he is not so independent of his fellow men as he had at first imagined and that in order to obtain their support he must often lend them his cooperation."[17]

Tocqueville recommended encouraging the citizens to participate widely in political life, as was done in the United States. "In civil life every man may, strictly speaking, fancy that he can provide for his own wants; in politics he can fancy no such thing."[18] In France, unfortunately, the July Monarchy was determined to construct local liberties, the right of association, and political activity within extremely limited bounds.

A second form of the individualistic illusion consists in believing that the economic order is autonomous and sufficient unto itself and that people can safely place economic interests above civic duties. Whereas the Americans happily combined a taste for private business with civic-mindedness, Guizot appealed to the economic appetites of the French in order to divert them from participation in public affairs. To quote Tocqueville:

> When the taste for physical gratifications . . . has grown more rapidly than their education or experience of free institutions, the time will come when men are carried away and lose all self-restraint at the sight of the new possessions they about to obtain. . . . The discharge of political duties appears to them to be a troublesome impediment which diverts them from their occupations and business.

To this he added, "And the better to guard what they call their own business, they neglect their chief business, which is to remain their own masters."[19] This text goes to the core of the major weakness of the July Monarchy, a bourgeois regime in which the citizens did not participate.

The third form of the individualistic illusion, the belief that the individual mind is self-sufficient, is the most pernicious of all, for it is at the root of the two other illusions justifying them and preventing them from being corrected. "Everyone shuts himself up tightly within himself and insists upon judging the world from there."[20] According to Tocqueville, such is the essence of intellectual individualism, and there is nothing wrong with it as long as it is used to work out a method of research and individual critical examination; indeed, it can be viewed as the philosophical method naturally suited to democratic societies. Yet the individual mind must retain an exact feel for the limits of its capacity to know. The Americans have been able to achieve this; always having conducted their public affairs on their own, they have learned to correct their ideas in the light of their shared experiences. The French, by contrast, long deprived of political liberty, have taken to indulging in abstract political speculation; they wanted to wipe clean the slate of the past and to rebuild the world on the basis of a few general ideas.

The comparison drawn here by Tocqueville is close to the distinction made much later by Hayek between what he called the two individualisms. One is that of the Anglo-American tradition, which takes into account the role of customs, traditions, and experiences; the other is an individualism inspired by a Cartesianism so extreme that it is likely to forget the limits of reason and would no doubt have horrified Descartes. On the one side are David Hume, Adam Smith, and the Americans; on the other are the physiocrats and Rousseau. In the end, however, Hayek seems to have added nothing to Tocqueville's schema; indeed, Tocqueville was more successful in highlighting the decisive role played by the presence or absence of political liberty in the genesis of the two kinds of individualism.

An exaggerated view of the powers of individual reason leads to the denial of all authority other than itself. This view would destroy any society, wrote the author of *Democracy in America*, were it not for the fact that individuals, however self-sufficient, do consent to submit to the least legitimate of the forms of authority, the power of numbers, the tyranny of public opinion. The corrective to this situation can come only from the moral and religious convictions of the community. Human liberty cannot be total. Tocqueville wrote, "For my part, I doubt whether man can ever support at the same time complete religious independence and entire political freedom, and I am inclined to think that if faith be wanting in him he must be subject, and if he be free he must believe."[21]

If Tocqueville always wanted to unite the "spirit of religion" with the "spirit of liberty," it was above all because he believed that liberty is God-given and that religion, like political liberty, counteracts the worst effects of individualism, namely the isolation of human beings, their excessive taste for material pleasures, and the proud illusion of the self-sufficiency of the individual mind.

Although Tocqueville wanted to correct the illusions and the excesses of individualism, he was an individualist himself, in the sense that he believed the aim of society to be the well-being of individuals, and not vice versa. Unlike such counterrevolutionaries as De Maistre and Bonald, Tocqueville did not view the *Declaration of the Rights of Man* as a cause of social disintegration; he also professed that a certain dose of individualism is bound to result from the democratic structure of society. He denounced the dangerous forms of individualism only in the name of the principles of 1789 and because of his love of liberty. Unlike Balzac, Saint-Simon, and Auguste Comte, Tocqueville was not at all haunted by the fear that society would crumble and that equality would lead to anarchy.[22] Individualism does not ruin sociability, nor does it threaten civil society; as defined by Tocqueville, it only corrodes political society.

The author of *Democracy in America* was as concerned as anyone about order and legality, but he refused to allow order to take precedent over liberty. "A nation," he wrote, "that asks nothing of its government but the maintenance of order is already a slave at heart."[23] Although liberty was the foremost of his political values, he did not conceive of it as total independence but rather, in the manner of the ancients and of Montesquieu, as a liberty subject to just laws. Like all liberals, he refused to grant limitless sovereignty to a monarch or to the people. The law cannot be based on power alone; to be sure, it expresses the sovereign will, but it must remain subject to justice and reason.[24] Moral order, as well as social and political order, has objective norms that humans must respect. But, as Tocqueville understood it, this idea of order by no means excludes liberty, for many decisions leave a considerable margin of uncertainty and error as to what is demanded by justice and reason. In this conception of the relationship between liberty and order, there is ample room for debate and political action; at one point Tocqueville even declared that the institutions that we consider necessary are perhaps only those to which we are accustomed.[25]

A well-tempered individualism is thus compatible with liberty, as is shown by the American example. But as soon as the community falls prey to illusions of individual self-sufficiency, the chimera of total independence ruins order as well as liberty. Order is destroyed because, obviously, total independence for the members and order for the whole group are mutually exclusive. It is more difficult to show how individual claims to self-sufficiency ruin liberty. Yet Tocqueville, in the second volume of *Democracy*, was able to trace the secret path that may lead a society from equality to servitude. As he wrote, "[Equality] predisposes [men] not to consider their fellow creatures."[26] Equality has given rise to individualism, which in turn can foster a new kind of despotism. "I seek to trace," Tocqueville continued,

> the novel feature under which despotism may appear in the world. The first thing that strikes the observer is an innumerable multitude of men, all equal and alike, incessantly endeavoring to procure the petty and paltry pleasures with which they glut their lives. Each of them, living apart, is as a stranger to the fate of all the rest. . . . Above this race of men stands an immense and tutelary power, which takes upon itself alone to secure their gratifications and to watch over their fate. That power is absolute, minute, regular, provident, and mild. . . . Such a power does not tyrannize, but it compresses, enervates, and stupefies a people, till each nation is reduced to nothing better than a flock of timid and industrious animals of which the government is the shepherd.[27]

Unlike the tyrannies of ancient times or revolutionary despotism, this power does not need to impose itself by violence; it grows slowly in response to the demands, or rather the shortcomings, of society. Equality is not the only cause of this abdication on the part of individuals; the weakness of liberal convictions contributes as much to it when it takes the form of civic apathy. Tocqueville explicitly cites the most dangerous forms of individualism, which may well be compatible with an incomplete exercise of political power, "with some of the outward forms of freedom,"[28] and particularly with the free election of national representatives. But whenever the citizens no longer avail themselves of their political freedom to unite for the common good in associations or local groups, it is no longer possible to contain their tendencies toward isolation and indifference within reasonable limits. The central power will take over when people no longer want to work together or even recognize their common responsibilities.

It is therefore not sufficient to say, as many Tocqueville scholars still do, that he believed that a strong egalitarian passion could lead democracy to a new form of despotism by developing an omnipotent administration. In the corruption of democracy, the weakness of the desire for liberty is as important a factor as equality. True, Tocqueville declared that "democratic nations show a more ardent and enduring love of equality than of liberty,"[29] but he placed this statement at the beginning of the chapters devoted to individualism—a place that attests to the importance he attached to keeping individualism firmly under control in order to safeguard the balance between liberty and equality.

In the United States he observed a harmony between liberal and egalitarian sentiments that was sadly lacking in the France of his time. Even though this difference can be attributed to the violent impact of the French Revolution and the failure of the first French Republic, the role of the excesses and illusions wrought by individualism must not be overlooked. Significantly, Tocqueville titled one of his chapters "Individualism Stronger at the Close of a Democratic Revolution Than at Other Periods."[30]

ACHIEVING A BALANCE BETWEEN EQUALITY AND LIBERTY

In the final analysis, the proper balance between equality and liberty that is so fundamental to democracy is achieved by finding a good way to keep individualism under control. On this point, the second part of *Democracy* affords a theoretical schema that goes beyond the ideas of the first. Recall that Tocqueville presents equality as an essentially ambiguous value. It may be defined as the equality of rights in a mobile society—what Tocqueville called *equality of conditions*—but it may also assume the form of an invidious and insatiable passion. In a democracy, equality of conditions must prevail, of course, but it is impossible, and indeed would be unjust, to establish de facto equality. The success of democracy is predicated on giving to citizens who in many respects remain unequal the feeling that they are equal. According to Tocqueville, this can essentially be achieved through social mobility and political freedom.[31] He emphasizes, however, that the forms of political freedom offered to the citizens must not be limited to choosing national representatives, and that it is vital to create structures for bringing people together on the local level, in local government and in associations, as a means to combat public indifference and individualistic illusions. If this effort is not made, and if the demand for freedom is reduced to the defense of individual rights, the level of attachment to liberty and civic-mindedness will fall so low that judicial and civic equality will no longer satisfy people's egalitarian aspirations.

For Tocqueville, liberty was foremost both among political values and in his personal scale of values. A negative liberty with a moral foundation, it implies responsibility for and pride in personal independence. But in individualistic, democratic societies, liberty is threatened by the illusion of total individual independence and self-sufficiency. Liberty would be destroyed if we were to forget that human freedom can be achieved only by the exercise of political rights, among them in particular the right to association. John Locke, and, in France, Benjamin Constant, asserted that the individual is endowed with reason and with the desire for liberty. Less optimistic but more lucid than these founders of liberalism, Tocqueville argued that the sense of freedom must be carefully nurtured if it is to stand up to the competing desires for order and equality in democracies. "Feelings and opinions are recruited, and the human mind is developed, only by the reciprocal influence of men upon one another," he wrote.[32] Troubled about the future of liberty, Tocqueville set out to create a new "political science" that would safeguard the delicate but essential balance between equality and liberty. A tireless proponent of the need for civic-mindedness, he wanted above all to develop a sense of political liberty in his contemporaries.

NOTES

1. O.C. XIII, 2, p. 233. References to Tocqueville's works are to the Gallimard edition of the *Oeuvres complètes (Complete Works)*. O.C. V, 1, p.120, should be read as *Oeuvres complètes*, tome V, volume 1, p. 120. Quotations from *Democracy in America* are from the Reeve translation: *Democracy in America by Alexis de Tocqueville. The Henry Reeve Text as Revised by Francis Bowen, Now Further Corrected and Edited with an Historical Essay, Editorial Notes, and Bibliographies by Phillips Bradley* (New York: Vintage Books, 1958). D.A.II, 4, XI, p. 141, should be read as *Democracy in America*, Part II, Fourth Book, chapter XI, p. 141.
2. Quoted from Antoine Redier, *Comme disait M. de Tocqueville* (Paris: Perrin, 1925), pp. 46–8.
3. His commentators deplore this fact and sometimes try to provide a complete picture of his doctrine, from remarks made by the master in different contexts. See for example, Redier, *Comme disait M. de Tocqueville*, chapter 4, and Jack Lively, *The Social and Political Thought of Alexis de Tocqueville* (Oxford: Clarendon Press, 1965), chapter 1.
4. See Jean-Claude Lamberti, *Tocqueville et les deux démocraties* (Paris: PUF, 1983).
5. François Guizot, *Histoire de la civilisation en Europe* (Paris: Hachette, Collection "Pluriel," 1985), pp. 90–1.
6. O.C. II, 1, p. 217.
7. Montesquieu, *L'Esprit des lois*, Book XI, chapter 6, *in fine*.
8. Seymour Drescher, "Tocqueville's Two Democracies," *Journal of the History of Ideas* (April–June, 1964).
9. D.A. II, 4, VI. The expression "virtuous materialism" is to be found in D.A. II, 4, XI, p. 141.

10. O.C. II, 1, p. 62.
11. On historical constraints and liberty, see D.A. II, 4, XVIII, p. 253; on the tendencies of historians in democratic ages, see D.A. II, 1, XX, pp. 92–3.
12. D.A. II, 4, VIII, p. 352.
13. For an in-depth comparison, see Jean-Claude Lamberti, "De Benjamin Constant à Tocqueville," *Revue France-Forum* (April–May 1983): No. 203–04, 19–26.
14. The analysis of "erroneous judgment" and individualistic illusions that follows was only touched upon in my book *La Notion d'individualisme chez Tocqueville* (Paris: PUF, 1970).
15. All the passages quoted in this paragraph are taken from D.A. II, 2, II, "Of Individualism in Democratic Countries."
16. See D.A. II, 2, VIII, "How the Americans Combat Individualism by the Principle of Self-Interest Rightly Understood."
17. D.A. II, 2, IV, p. 109.
18. D.A. II, 2, VII, p. 123.
19. D.A. II, 2, XIV, p. 149.
20. D.A. II, 1, I, p. 4.
21. D.A. II, 1, V, p. 23.
22. D.A. II, 4, I, p. 304.
23. D.A. II, 2, XIV, p. 150.
24. Tocqueville found this theory in the *doctrinaires*, particularly in the writings of Royer-Collard.
25. See *Souvenirs*, Part II, chapter 2, O.C. XII, p. 97.
26. D.A. II, 2, IV, p. 109.
27. D.A. II, 4, VI, pp. 336–7.
28. D.A. II, 4, VI, p. 337.
29. D.A. II, 2, I, p. 99.
30. D.A. II, 2, III, pp. 107–8.
31. See the last sentence of D.A. II, 2, IV, p. 113.
32. D.A. II, 2, V, p. 117.

4

Tocqueville and Some American Views of Liberty

James T. Schleifer

In this chapter I examine some of the connections between Tocqueville's ideas about liberty and a few classic American views of liberty symbolized by John Winthrop, Thomas Jefferson, James Madison, Joseph Story, and Andrew Jackson. What did Tocqueville learn (or fail to learn) from these American spokesmen for liberty? In what ways, if any, did they influence his notion of freedom?

For analytical convenience I distinguish rather sharply among several American understandings of liberty and link each symbolically with a specific person. Let me hasten to say, however, that the particular American ideas and persons discussed here are neither totally distinct nor mutually exclusive. Some do stand far apart; others run closely parallel. Nor should we forget that these ideas may be found in the writings of many other New World republicans.[1] In one sense, each man's viewpoint simply represents part of a much larger cluster of ideas that define an American vision of freedom; each reflects a different emphasis within a broader area of agreement. As we shall see, Tocqueville was perhaps most influenced by the shared themes that helped to define an American approach to liberty.

TOCQUEVILLE'S FUNDAMENTAL IDEAS ABOUT LIBERTY

Let us begin with some fundamentals.[2] Central to *Democracy in America* is Tocqueville's attachment to liberty, which drew him not by interest or sympathy, but by passion. He wrote about "the holy cult of freedom,"[3] which he described in almost mystical language:

> Do not ask me to analyze this sublime sentiment [of liberty]; it must be felt. It enters of itself, into the great hearts of those God has prepared to receive it; it fills them; it enraptures them. We cannot give understanding to those mediocre souls who have never felt it.[4]

For his readers his book poses a key question: How may "this sublime sentiment" be preserved in times of equality?

Yet, curiously, Tocqueville is not commonly known (at least on first reflection) as a theorist of liberty. Instead, we associate him primarily with his sweeping interpretation of history as advancing equality, or with his chilling visions of despotism.[5] But when, in *Democracy*, Tocqueville so brilliantly explored the consequences of the democratic social condition for modern nations, liberty quickly became a central theme. He taught us that democratic people love both equality and liberty, but that, if forced to choose, they will always prefer the first:

> [Nations whose social condition is democratic] have an instinctive love of [liberty]. But liberty is not the chief and constant object of their desires; equality is their idol; they make rapid and sudden efforts to obtain liberty and, if they miss their aim, resign themselves to their disappointment; but nothing can satisfy them without equality, and they would rather perish than lose it.[6]

He warned that equality of conditions breeds three dangers: first, consolidation of power in the hands of, among others, legislatures, demagogic leaders, majorities, public opinion, the people as a whole, and the bureaucratic state; second, *individualisme*, a turning inward to private interests and those of a small circle of family and friends as traditional social ties are dissolved;[7] and third, materialism, the single-minded pursuit of physical well-being.[8] And Tocqueville demonstrated that, because of this trio of evils, democracy favors tyranny more than freedom. Equality of conditions, he lamented, will always slide more easily toward despotism than toward liberty.

What did liberty mean to Tocqueville? His mental habit of constantly reconsidering the same concept and examining it over long periods of time from a number of perspectives often led him to new insights. Painstaking reconsiderations also encouraged, however, lists of concepts with not always compatible meanings, imprecise usage, and nagging confusion. It is a commonplace that Tocqueville never clearly defined some of his major concepts, including *démocratie* and *égalité*. The same is true for *liberty*; no single meaning emerged from the pages of *Democracy*. Instead, the term is used in a variety of ways.

Most profoundly, Tocqueville assumed a moral or theological liberty. God had created human beings as free and independent, and in human liberty was the "source of all moral greatness."[9] The morally free and responsible person stood at the center of Tocqueville's thought. His most fundamental moral objective was to foster the personal independence and dignity that would permit the fullest possible development of individual capacities and spur each person to his best efforts. "I have," declared Tocqueville, "no traditions, no party, no cause, if not that of liberty and human dignity."[10]

For him, liberty, in perhaps its most crucial sense, meant protection from whatever might erode individual independence. And here was an important part of Tocqueville's originality and contribution to modern political science, for he exposed new democratic threats to the individual. In ages of equality, liberty faced not only traditional challenges from governmental or political institutions, but also unexpected assaults from a variety of social forces, the majority, public opinion, the mass, or even society as a whole. These threats, Tocqueville noted, were even more insidious and invasive than more familiar ones, for they eventually destroyed the very desire to resist the will of the whole and the very imagination to think differently from the crowd.

The democratic assumption that only the people speaking as a whole (or as a majority) constituted a legitimate source of authority encouraged "the maxim that everything is permissible for the interests of society," which Tocqueville called "an impious adage."[11] For him, such nearly automatic deference to the whole would spell the total subjugation of the individual. Against this democratic nightmare he counseled a course of action:

> To lay down extensive but distinct and settled limits to the action
> of the government; to confer certain rights on private persons,
> and to secure to them the undisputed enjoyment of those rights;
> to enable individual man to maintain whatever independence,
> strength and original power he still possesses; to raise him by the
> side of society at large, and uphold him in that position; these ap-
> pear to me the main objects of legislators in the ages upon which
> we are now entering.[12]

Here was still another of Tocqueville's definitions of liberty. When he considered what could be done, he envisaged universal rights, granted and guaranteed by law. Only "liberties," he asserted, could protect freedom in the modern democratic age. And he proposed a long list, including personal liberty; political and civil rights;[13] self-government; private property rights; local liberties, and freedom of the press, of association, of thought and expression, and of religion.

Tocqueville also believed in what might be called historical liberty.[14] Although his leveling trend ordained by Providence raised the specter of determinism, he insisted throughout his book that human beings had to make choices. Humanity faced the alternatives of liberty or servitude, civilization or barbarism, prosperity or wretchedness; and by deciding whether to make the best or the worst of democracy, people would shape the course of history and the future of society.[15]

The moral and historical liberties presented by Tocqueville were both individual and social. Each person was morally independent, worthy of self-determination, and free to choose. And so was each society or nation.

> In the United States the sovereignty of the people is not an isolated doctrine, bearing no relation to the prevailing habits and ideas of the people; it may, on the contrary, be regarded as the last link of a chain of opinions which binds the whole Anglo-American world. That Providence has given to every human being the degree of reason necessary to direct himself in the affairs that interest him exclusively is the grand maxim upon which civil and political society rests in the United States. . . . When extended to the nation, it becomes the doctrine of the sovereignty of the people.[16]

(In this context, sovereignty of the people, as liberty, meant nothing less than a nation's right to self-government and self-determination.)

Despite Tocqueville's emphasis on most of the liberties of traditional liberalism, he did not see liberty solely in negative terms.[17] For him, it signified more than simply freedom from outside constraints; it also had positive implications. Freedom meant active participation in public life. Merely to be left alone (negative liberty) without being engaged in civic activities (positive liberty) did not at all fit Tocqueville's full understanding of freedom. Purely negative liberty shaded into the triumph of *individualisme*, the peculiarly democratic form of selfishness so corrosive to public life. Freedom also meant the positive action of civilized discourse, the exchange of ideas, and cultural progress. And most of all, liberty stimulated the full moral, emotional, psychological, and intellectual flowering of each person; it allowed a person to *become*, not just to *be*.

So Tocqueville's freedom signified much more than just the absence of constraint; positive liberty entailed public obligation, intellectual advance, and personal development. This unusual effort to blend limitations of power and protections for the individual, measures favored by traditional liberalism, with essentially spiritual concerns and the moral obligation of public participation explains why Tocqueville called himself a liberal of a new kind.

A particularly difficult question remains: How is liberty related to equality? Here is the nub of the problem of democracy. In his book

Tocqueville argued that democracy as equality of condition, despite its disadvantages and dangers, is essentially more just than aristocracy, *but only if liberty can be preserved.* Otherwise, he warned, humanity was headed toward equal servitude for all. Men could have equality with or without freedom. As we have seen, their choice was between universal rights or despotism.

But Tocqueville also presented an alternative of a somewhat different sort. He recognized two additional kinds of liberty: the freedom to be equal and the freedom to become unequal. The first was neutral, perhaps meaning nothing more than the destruction of aristocracy and the coming of equality of conditions. (Only when it meant shared political and civil rights did this freedom to be equal side with liberty against despotism.) The second freedom—to become unequal—also was essential to democracy, for it implied a mobile, fluid society where some degree of equality of opportunity prevailed. (Here was one of the fundamental definitions that Tocqueville gave to democracy.[18]) A *free* democratic society required both liberties: to be the same and to become different. Freedom demanded not only equal rights but also the right to create distinctions of wealth, power, and status. Here was still another democratic dilemma posed by Tocqueville.

JOHN WINTHROP'S INFLUENCE

Having now summarized some of Tocqueville's basic ideas about liberty, let us now consider what he learned from our American spokesmen for liberty. John Winthrop (1588–1649), a perennial governor during the early years of Massachusetts Bay Colony, on 3 July 1645 delivered a speech before the General Court in which he addressed his long-standing dispute with the deputies about the prerogatives of the governor and other magistrates.[19] Did broad prerogatives mean arbitrary government, as the deputies argued, or, as Winthrop maintained, did wide discretion simply grant to government leaders the flexibility required by the evolving political and social situation of a new commonwealth? Where did the best safeguard for liberty reside, in specific rules of procedure, duties, and rights or in interpretive latitude?

Winthrop in his oration focused on the meaning of liberty:

> Concerning liberty, I observe a great mistake in the country about that. There is a twofold liberty, natural (I mean as our nature is now corrupt) and civil or federal. The first is common to man with beasts and other creatures. By this, man, as he stands in relation to man simply, hath liberty to do what he lists; it is a liberty to

evil as well as to good. This liberty is incompatible and inconsistent with authority, and cannot endure the least restraint of the most just authority. The exercise and maintaining of this liberty makes men grow more evil, and in time to be worse than brute beasts. . . . The other kind of liberty I call civil or federal; it may also be termed moral, in reference to the covenant between God and man, in the moral law, and the political covenants and constitutions, among men themselves. This liberty is the proper end and object of authority, and cannot subsist without it; and it is a liberty to that only which is good, just and honest. This liberty you are to stand for, with the hazard not only for your goods, but of your lives, if need be. . . . It is of the same kind of liberty wherewith Christ hath made us free.[20]

In the 1835 *Democracy* Tocqueville quoted Winthrop with approval; the governor, Tocqueville declared, had offered a "fine definition of liberty."[21] And for the young Frenchman, Winthrop's remarks symbolized much of what he admired about the New England Puritans.[22] One praiseworthy feature, the sense of community, of a society bound together by moral law and by what Winthrop called "the politic covenants and constitutions among men," was exemplified by local self-government and political liberties. In colonial New England, Tocqueville wrote, "we find the germ and gradual development of that township independence which is the life and mainspring of American liberty at the present day."[23] In the New England town was born the "spirit of locality" so essential to American attitudes and behavior.[24]

A second laudable characteristic was the commitment to moral purposes and spiritual values grounded in religious belief. Winthrop's words, like other writings of early New England cited in Tocqueville's book, breathed the spirit of profound Christian faith. The governor proposed nothing less than the sovereignty of the people *under* the sovereignty of God. Together these two features brought Tocqueville to a striking discovery. The Americans, from the first years of Massachusetts, had achieved a unique and harmonious blend of what he called "the spirit of liberty" and "the spirit of religion." In America,

Religion perceives that civil liberty affords a noble exercise to the faculties of man and that the political world is a field prepared by the Creator for the efforts of mind. . . . Liberty regards religion as its companion in all its battles and its triumphs, as the cradle of its infancy and the divine source of its claims. It considers religion as the safeguard of morality, and morality as the best security of law and the surest pledge of the duration of freedom.[25]

Winthrop's message focused specifically on "civil liberty" or "liberty in the moral law" (liberty safeguarded by the moral standards taught by religion). But more broadly, his message reflected a sense of liberty tempered by human authority and divine law. True liberty, he argued, was paired with restraint. In *Democracy*, Tocqueville repeated this message. During the first decades of colonial New England, political and social innovation, although advanced (even radical), was constrained by moral and religious beliefs that prevented excesses of freedom. And the heritage of nineteenth-century Americans included these same remarkable "habits of restraint."[26] Religion, Tocqueville observed, not only facilitated the use of liberty; in times of equality, it was indispensable. "Despotism," he declared, "may govern without faith, but liberty cannot."[27]

THOMAS JEFFERSON'S INFLUENCE

During the writing of his book, Tocqueville carefully read Thomas Jefferson's *Notes on the State of Virginia* and *Mélanges politiques et philosophiques*, a two-volume selection from the Virginian's letters and memoirs, edited and translated by L. P. Conseil.[28] And in the pages of *Democracy* several quotations from Jefferson would finally appear, along with praise for Jefferson as "the most powerful advocate democracy every had."[29]

For Tocqueville, Jefferson, as the moving force for the abolition of entail and primogeniture in Virginia, symbolized the end of inherited artificial privilege in America; and Jefferson reinforced Tocqueville's fears that power gathered in the legislatures constituted a major threat to freedom in the United States. But a recent examination of what Tocqueville learned form "the great democrat" has revealed more parallel ideas drawn from shared Enlightenment sources and more affinities of tone and personality than direct influences of the American on the Frenchman.[30]

The two theorists shared several important opinions about liberty, however. Both believed in the natural liberty of human beings who were created free, independent, and with certain inalienable rights. Both thought that all human beings, endowed with freedom, possessed a moral sense, or innate knowledge of right and wrong as well. "If we consider the human species as a whole," commented Tocqueville in discarded drafts of *Democracy*,

> we will discover that to live and prosper the species must obey certain moral laws which are derived *necessarily* from the nature and needs given by God to every man without distinction. . . .

[These] moral laws . . . are found wherever men are found and . . . cannot be modified by time, political constitutions or place. These laws are indicated to each man by individual conscience. They are proclaimed by the *raison publique* of all. What we call virtue is exact and willing obedience to these laws which all men instinctively acknowledge.[31]

For Jefferson and Tocqueville, such morality, reinforced by faith in God, was an essential foundation for liberty. Here, despite a diametrically opposed concept of "natural liberty," the two later writers echoed Winthrop's concept of freedom restrained by moral law.

But if all men were created equal, neither Jefferson nor Tocqueville assumed absolute human equality; each saw a natural aristocracy of virtue, intellect, and talent,[32] which, in order to develop and emerge, required a free society (meaning absence of artificial privilege and equal rights for all, especially access to education and intellectual freedom). In essence, Jefferson and Tocqueville shared the conviction that liberty's most precious benefit was to affirm the moral value of each person.

JAMES MADISON'S INFLUENCE

The ideas of James Madison and his coauthors, Alexander Hamilton and John Jay, became familiar to Tocqueville in December 1831 when he began his study of the *Federalist Papers*, which he later declared to be "an excellent book, which ought to be familiar to the statesmen of all countries, though it specially concerns America."[33] From the *Federalist* Tocqueville drew the fundamentals of his astute interpretations of the Constitution and of the nature of the American Union.[34] The authors of the *Federalist* praised the proposed Constitution as a wonderful and necessary safeguard for the freedom and prosperity of the republic. They carefully explained the originality and significance of the new federal system and lauded the framers of the new instrument for their efforts to balance, first, the independence of the states with necessary vigor for the central government, and second, the competing natures of the three branches of government. The *Federalist* particularly stressed the need for an independent judiciary capable of resisting the voracious legislative appetite for power. The federal courts, Tocqueville learned, would also occupy the crucial position of arbiter in both the tug between states and central government and the perennial effort to restrain legislative abuses: the American judiciary possessed the unique power to declare laws unconstitutional. All these ideas would find their way into *Democracy*, which ultimately reflected the viewpoint of the *Federalist* perhaps even more than Tocqueville himself realized.

From Madison, however, Tocqueville learned something more. In Papers No. 10 and No. 51 of the *Federalist*, the Virginian developed what Tocqueville in drafts of *Democracy* described as Madison's *belle théorie*.[35] The danger to liberty in America, Madison asserted, came not from anarchy and social disorder, not from insufficient authority, but from the excessive concentration of power. Madison's remedy was distinctive. To preserve liberty, power in society had to be as widely dispersed as possible. Only interest checked by interest would assure that decisions made and actions taken by government would reflect not the narrow interest of majoritarian factions but the wider interest of the common good. Madison's vision of a pluralistic society evoked, however, more than a variety of self-interested groups, engaged in political struggle, finally reaching some mutually acceptable and advantageous compromise. Pluralism as he described it also meant, more broadly, the widest possible distribution of power; power concentrated anywhere inherently threatened freedom.

To Tocqueville, this *belle théorie* was a revelation. He—like Madison— would make diversity one of the foundations of liberty.[36] In *Democracy* he described how Madison's concept worked through federalism, with the states serving as barriers to possible national abuses, and through administrative decentralization, with local governments acting as hurdles to oppressive state actions.

> However the predominant party in the nation (*la majorité*) may be carried away by its passions, however ardent it may be in the pursuit of its projects, it cannot oblige all the citizens to comply with its desires in the same manner and at the same time throughout the country. . . . The townships, municipal bodies, and counties form so many concealed breakwaters, which check or part the tide of popular determination.[37]

Yet Tocqueville failed to embrace the most original part of Madison's idea. Paper No. 10 had argued that the sheer size of a nation, by multiplying interests, would increase pluralism and discourage despotic majorities. Tocqueville could not bring himself to accept this reasoning. Nonetheless, from Madison and the *Federalist*, Tocqueville gained significant lessons about liberty, especially the protections placed around freedom by the Constitution, by the courts, and by a pluralistic society characterized by the dispersal of power. Each protection, let us note before moving ahead, was once again a restriction on how far men could push their freedom.

JOSEPH STORY'S INFLUENCE

Joseph Story's *Commentaries on the Constitution of the United States* closely echoed the authors of the *Federalist*, and Tocqueville found on nearly every page of Story's book a reflection of what he had already read in the *Federalist* or in the *Commentaries on American Law* of James Kent, or had already heard in conversations with John Canfield Spencer and others.[38] But Justice Story, who wrote his *Commentaries* in part to refute Jefferson's condemnation of the increasing role of the courts and fears of judicial tyranny, presented a special message, which Tocqueville apparently took very much to heart. For the justice, the influence of lawyers and judges was crucial to restraining the excesses of popular democracy. The justice constantly stressed the "moral and educative potential" of the law and its interpreters, especially through the persuasiveness of the judge as he instructed jurors and wrote opinions.[39] To avoid abuses in democratic society he looked to the corporate role of a "legal aristocracy," whose distinctive methods of thought and analysis and whose approach to society and politics were shaped by the demands of judicial functions and by the peculiarities of the common-law tradition.[40] In a free society, Story argued, lawyers and judges had to lead if the people were to be properly guided in the exercise of power. A legal mentality and a judicial establishment— what Tocqueville called the *corps légal* and *l'esprit légale*—were essential to the preservation of liberty in an age of popular democracy. Story's philosophy of liberty tempered by men of the law would be faithfully reflected in *Democracy*.[41]

ANDREW JACKSON'S INFLUENCE

Andrew Jackson, as symbol for his age, stood for political liberty not simply as the right to vote and to hold office, but also as participatory democracy in its broadest sense.[42] "Universal" suffrage (meaning at that time the right for all adult white males to vote) had developed by the 1820s, and from that decade into the 1840s political interest and activity quickened remarkably, with new habits and expectations, new structures and procedures, and new social groupings claiming their voice and position in government. Popular democracy, the politics of the masses, had arrived.

Fundamentally, however, Tocqueville felt ambivalent about popular participation. He approved of most involvement in public life, whether informal (through associations or other private enterprises) or formal (through local institutions or other levels of government). For him, liberty, let us remember, meant civic participation. Yet he also worried about a tendency in the United States toward too much direct, popular, political intervention, what he and some Americans called "excessive democracy." He criticized certain manifestations of Jacksonian politics: movements toward popular mandates (to instruct representatives), the election of judges, and direct rather than indirect election of various officials. More broadly, he recognized that "sovereignty of the people" in Jacksonian America threatened liberty, for where were the effective limits of popular power?

> In the United States . . . society governs itself for itself. All power centers in its bosom, and scarcely an individual is to be met with who would venture to conceive or, still less, to express the idea of seeking it elsewhere. The nation participates in the making of its laws by the choice of its legislators, in the execution of them by the choice of the agents of the executive government; it may almost be said to govern itself, so feeble and so restricted is the share left to the administration, so little do the authorities forget their popular origin and the power from which they emanate. The people reign in the American political world as the Deity does in the universe. They are the cause and the aim of all things; everything comes from them, and everything is absorbed in them.[43]

Tocqueville reminded his readers that unlimited power—no matter where centered—was dangerous.[44] Once again, liberty, as popular sovereignty (and the will of the majority and public opinion), needed limitations. From Madison, Story, and other Americans, Tocqueville knew of institutional and legal restraints. But the Jacksonians repeated an earlier lesson drawn from the Puritans: liberty could best be preserved by patterns of belief and behavior, by mores. Winthrop and other New Englanders had established the spirit of locality and had preached the necessity of morality based on religious faith. In the United States of the 1830s Tocqueville found still other safeguards: the science of association,[45] habits of freedom, and the concept of enlightened self-interest.[46]

He found that the Jacksonian invigoration of politics paralleled a remarkable tempo in public life more generally. Liberty meant the right to initiate or to get involved in the issues and activities of the day; it implied the freedoms to assemble, to organize, to speak, to write. Private associations (and their voice, a free press) embodied these rights for Americans. So the age resounded with the buzz of private groups and enterprises of all sorts. Tocqueville found this civic energy one of the most attractive features of the American Republic:

> No sooner do you set foot upon American ground than you are stunned by a kind of tumult; a confused clamor is heard on every side, and a thousand simultaneous voices demand the satisfaction of their social wants. Everything is in motion around you.[47]

> If an American were condemned to confine his activity to his own affairs, he would be robbed of one-half of his existence; he would feel an immense void in the life which he is accustomed to lead and his wretchedness would be unbearable. I am persuaded that if ever a despotism should be established in America, it will be more difficult to overcome the habits that freedom has formed than to conquer the love of freedom itself.[48]

Tocqueville found himself converted:

> The most natural privilege of man, next to the right of acting for himself, is that of combining his exertions with those of his fellow creatures and of acting in common with them. The right of association therefore appears to me almost as inalienable in its nature as the right to personal liberty.[49]

The American sense that public involvement constituted "one half of [one's own] existence" captivated Tocqueville:

> How does it happen that in the United States, where the inhabitants have only recently immigrated to the land which they now occupy, and brought neither customs nor traditions with them there; where they met one another for the first time with no previous acquaintance; where, in short, the instinctive love of country can scarcely exist; how does it happen that everyone takes as zealous an interest in the affairs of his township, his country, and the whole state as if they were his own? It is because everyone, in his sphere, takes an active part in the government of society.[50]

The Americans had apparently discovered a novel way to blend private and public interest.

> The principle of the republics of antiquity was to sacrifice private interests to the general good. In that sense one could say that they were *virtuous*. The principle of this one seems to be to make private interests harmonize with the general interests. A sort of refined and intelligent selfishness (*égoisme raffiné et intelligent*) seems to be the pivot on which the whole machine turns. These people do not trouble themselves to find out whether public virtue is good, but they do claim to prove it is useful. If the latter point is true, as I think it is in part, this society can pass as enlightened but not as virtuous.[51]

The doctrine of enlightened self-interest assumed that private and public ends ultimately harmonized and could be pursued simultaneously, that private interests were best served by a healthy public life, and that, in turn, the common good was best promoted by the multiplication of individual efforts. As Tocqueville discovered, in Jacksonian America this calculated service to self and others flourished.

The Jacksonians stood for still another variety of freedom: economic opportunity or entrepreneurial liberty. They worked diligently to end monopoly and entrenched economic privilege and to open the way for new commercial and industrial enterprises and other material pursuits. Liberty meant the right to chase "success," to pursue the "American Dream." Tocqueville recognized this dimension of the American Republic, noting especially the benefits of the peculiar American "system" for internal improvements and economic undertakings.[52] The Americans looked not to the central government for initiative and execution, but to a marvelous blend of private (associational and corporate) and public (local, state, and federal) efforts. Pluralism once again brought forth wonders. The refusal to allow a uniform system of centralized direction resulted in impressive material accomplishments, economic prosperity, and remarkable social energy. This multiple approach would remain in marked contrast to what Tocqueville saw in Europe by 1840: the sinister links being forged between industrial development, centralization, and despotism.[53]

Free enterprise also had its weaknesses, however, and, especially in the 1840 *Democracy*, Tocqueville laid them bare. He noted, for example, the essential hollowness of the open economic race cherished by the Jacksonians. Unrestricted competition meant that all were rivals for the same rewards. The track seemed open, but in reality it was clogged by contenders.[54] False hopes, always receding objectives, and abrupt social and economic reversals exacted an emotional and psychological price: increased frustration, anxiety, and restlessness. Worse, the unending pursuit of physical well-being encouraged the self-centeredness of democratic *individualisme* and undermined higher moral purposes. Materialism (in tandem with *individualisme*) threatened the traditional values, the "habits of the heart" that helped to protect liberty in America. Finally, Tocqueville foresaw, arising from industry, the possibility of a new manufacturing aristocracy—"one of the harshest that ever existed in the world"[55] —and the brutalization of industrial workers.[56]

For these and other reasons, Tocqueville did not fully endorse unrestricted capitalism or classic economic liberalism; he refused to be an advocate of the economic doctrine of *laissez-faire*, agreeing with

Lamartine that *laissez-faire* often meant *laissez-souffrir*. By the late 1830s he was advocating subsidized hospitals and other institutional safeguards for the poor and, by the mid-1840s, was proposing tax relief and free education and legal aid for the poor, support for mutual insurance companies that would provide various kinds of social security, and new public institutions to aid the widowed and orphaned, the disabled, and others in difficult or impoverished circumstances.[57] So Tocqueville could not fully support one common American view of liberty: the private economic free-for-all, loser beware.

But before leaving our discussion of Tocqueville's reservations about "free enterprise," we should note that the Jacksonians, too, were ambivalent about their economic and material goals. They, too, wondered whether their hungry pursuit of prosperity and material improvements might not undermine traditional values and habits. As Marvin Meyers demonstrated in his classic study, they tried to overcome their own anxieties by stressing the moral standards of the Old Republic even as they rushed headlong, even greedily, into a new economic age.[58] Their banners read "Tradition," but their feet followed the path marked "Change."

We should also observe that Tocqueville visited and analyzed the new republic just when Americans were first merging both "liberty" and "equality" in their understanding of democracy or American freedom. The Revolutionary generation had almost always distinguished sharply between liberty (usually associated with republicanism) and equality (usually associated—more negatively—with democracy).[59] But since the Jacksonian Era, Americans have tended, somewhat carelessly, to blend the two; in thinking of democracy, we usually assume both liberty and (at least some varieties of) equality. Tocqueville, however, reflected the sensibilities of the older generation and, in his book, carefully delineated the libertarian and egalitarian impulses of democratic peoples and explored the ties and tensions between liberty and equality in the modern age. Here, too, he dissented from the inclinations of most Jacksonian Americans.

CONCLUSION

So the New World republic, where freedom was old,[60] demonstrated for Tocqueville the value of certain legal, political, or institutional safeguards for liberty in democratic society. These included specific mechanisms developed out of the American experience and established by the Constitution (such as indirect election; the veto; bicameralism; checks and balances; judicial independence); civil and political rights (including personal liberty; widespread suffrage; freedom of assembly, association, speech, and press); and principles of decentralization, or, more broadly, the diffusion of power or pluralism (notably, local self-government; federalism; and, once again, private associational initiatives). These mechanisms, rights, and principles Tocqueville lumped together as *les lois*, one of the principal agents for preserving liberty in the United States. From another perspective, these elements represented the accumulated labor of statesmen, legislators, and framers of fundamental law who had long practiced the "art" of freedom.

The United States also showed the visiting Frenchman a second and even more valuable category of protections for liberty: morality, religious faith, the spirit of locality, practical experience, a legal mentality, respect for rights, enlightened self-interest, and habits of restraint. These characteristics of belief, opinion, values, and behavior Tocqueville called mores (*moeurs*). These were not the "art" but the "habits" of freedom, and they constituted the essential means to sustain liberty.[61] "In America," he wrote, "free *moeurs* have made free political institutions; in France, it is for free political institutions to mould *moeurs*."[62]

A few other shared themes also emerge from the several American considerations of liberty we have examined. Central to much of the traditional American approach was individualism, by which Americans, especially in the nineteenth century, meant the capability of a rugged, self-reliant person, responsible for himself, free from anything more than minimal governmental and social intervention to pursue his own goals (especially economic). The object of this pursuit Jefferson named "happiness" and others have called "success." The assumption, as Tocqueville had quickly realized in 1831, was that the individual should be allowed to do as he wished in all that concerned himself alone. This American individualism was not at all Tocqueville's *individualisme*, let us hasten to note. Instead, it paralleled what he meant by individual independence, the essence for him of moral liberty.[63]

For Tocqueville, the American spokesmen for liberty whom we have surveyed carried still another message, one that was not new but was powerfully reinforced by working examples. Liberty demanded the hedging of power. This the Americans did with all the art and habit they could muster. They circumscribed power with morality and faith (Winthrop), with respect for the natural liberty and personal endowments of each person (Jefferson), with legal and constitutional mechanisms and with pluralism (Madison), with law and the judicial establishment (Story), and with minimal government and widespread public participation (Jackson).

Tocqueville's love of liberty was absolute, but, in one sense, it is possible to argue that liberty itself was not. In the *Democracy*, informed by what he had seen in the New World, Tocqueville stood for what we might call "liberty paired." He always joined or balanced liberty with a companion value: liberty and morality; liberty and religion; liberty and law; (popular) liberty and justice; (economic) liberty and the common good; (individual) liberty and civic responsibility. Each of these matched values checked liberty's perennial tendency toward excess and self-destruction. "Liberty paired" meant liberty well regulated and enduring. This sense of liberty restrained by other values was perhaps the fundamental lesson about freedom that Tocqueville learned from the Americans.

NOTES

1. For the classic study, inspired by Tocqueville, of the American consensus, see Louis Hartz, *The Liberal Tradition in America* (New York: Harcourt, Brace, 1955).

    My focus on certain symbolic persons as sources of influence on Tocqueville's ideas about liberty is in no way intended to deny the many other voices and experiences of his American journey; consult the foundation study by George Pierson, *Tocqueville and Beaumont in America* (New York: Oxford University Press, 1938), hereafter cited as Pierson, *Tocqueville in America*; and Tocqueville's travel diaries, published in English as *Journey to America*, translated by George Lawrence and edited by J. P. Mayer (New Haven: Yale University Press, 1960), hereafter cited as *Journey to America*.

    Nor should an emphasis on American sources be taken as a denial of important English lessons or the obvious influence of the French tradition of social and political theory and of contemporary events and politics of Tocqueville's contemporary France. For these connections, see especially, on England, Seymour Drescher, *Tocqueville and England* (Cambridge, Mass.: Harvard University Press, 1964), hereafter cited as Drescher, *England*; and on France, Jean-Claude Lamberti, *Tocqueville et les deux Démocraties* (Paris: PUF, 1983), hereafter cited as Lamberti, *Deux Démocraties*; André Jardin, *Alexis de Tocqueville: 1805–1859* (Paris: Hachette, 1984), hereafter cited as Jardin, *Tocqueville*; and François Furet, "Naissance d'un paradigme: Tocqueville et la voyage en Amérique, 1825–1831," *Annales* 39, no. 2 (mars-avril 1984): 225–39, hereafter cited as Furet, "Paradigme."

2. Several works contain especially fine discussions of Tocqueville's concept of liberty; see Pierre Birnbaum, *Sociologie de Tocqueville* (Paris: PUF, 1970); Drescher, *England and Dilemmas of Democracy: Tocqueville and Modernization* (Pittsburgh: University of Pittsburgh Press, 1968), hereafter cited as Drescher, *Dilemmas*; Lamberti, *Deux Démocraties*, especially 74–90, and *La notion d'individualisme chez Tocqueville* (Paris: PUF, 1970); Jack Lively, *The Social and Political Thought of Alexis de Tocqueville* (Oxford: Clarendon Press, 1962), especially chapter 1, hereafter cited as Lively, *Social and Political Thought*; Pierre Manent, *Tocqueville et la nature de la démocratie* (Paris: Julliard, 1982), especially chapters 2 and 3; Albert Salomon, "Tocqueville's Philosophy of Freedom," *The Review of Politics* 1, no. 4 (October 1939): 400–31; James T. Schleifer, *The Making of*

Tocqueville's "Democracy in America" (Chapel Hill: University of North Carolina Press, 1980), hereafter cited as Schleifer, *Making*; and again Furet, "Paradigme."

3. *Democracy in America*, edited by Phillips Bradley, 2 vols., Vintage paperback edition (New York: Vintage, Random House, 1945), I:13, hereafter cited as *Democracy* (Bradley).

4. Quoted from Drescher, *England*, 7; originally from *Oeuvres, papiers et correspondences d'Alexis de Tocqueville, [Oeuvres complètes], Edition définitive* (Paris: Gallimard, 1951–), hereafter cited as *O.C.* (Gallimard), tome II, *L'Ancien régime et la Révolution*, introduced by Georges Lefebvre and edited by André Jardin, 2 vols. (1953), I:217.

5. See especially Schleifer, *Making*, chapters 10–13.

6. *Democracy* (Bradley), I:56; also see in the 1840 portion, "Why Democratic Nations Show a More Ardent and Enduring Love of Equality than of Liberty," II:99–103.

7. See especially *Democracy* (Bradley), II:104–13, the chapters on *individualisme*.

8. See especially ibid., II: 136–60, the chapters on physical well-being.

9. Ibid., I:12.

10. Letter to Louis de Kergolay, 15 décembre 1850, from *O. C.* Gallimard), tome XIII, *Correspondance d' Alexis de Tocqueville et de Louis de Kergolay*, edited by Jean-Alain Lesourd, text established by André Jardin, 2 vols. (1977) II:233; my translation.

11. *Democracy* (Bradley), I:316.

12. Ibid., II:347.

13. Among such rights, Tocqueville emphasized the right to vote and to participate politically, freedom of speech and assembly, freedom of the press, and the right to trial by jury. Strangely, in the *Democracy*, Tocqueville does not cite, so far as I know, the American Bill of Rights. Only in an early draft is there a reference to the amendments to the Constitution added before Tocqueville's American journey, but his point then concerns not rights but limitations on the power of the federal government; see Schleifer, *Making*, 107–8.

14. For elaboration, see James T. Schleifer, "Tocqueville as Historian: Philosophy and Methodology in the *Democracy*," prepared for a conference to celebrate the 150th anniversary of the publication of the *Democracy*, Brooklyn College, October 1985, published with the other conference papers in *Reconsidering Tocqueville's "Democracy in America*," edited by Abraham S. Eisenstadt (New Brunswick, N.J.: Rutgers University Press, 1988).

15. For examples from the 1835 portion of Tocqueville's book, see *Democracy* (Bradley), I:7, 56, 261–62, 338–42.

16. Ibid., I:435–6.

17. On this question, see especially Drescher, *England*, 10, and *Dilemmas*, 44–5; Lamberti, *Deux Démocraties*, 83–4; and Lively, *Social and Political Thought*, 10.

18. Consult Schleifer, *Making*, chapter 19, "Some Meanings of *Démocratie*."

19. On Winthrop, consult Edmund S. Morgan, *The Puritan Dilemma: The Story of John Winthrop* (Boston: Little, Brown, 1958); and Morgan, ed., *Puritan Political Ideas, 1558–1794* (Indianapolis: Bobbs-Merrill, 1965); and Perry Miller and Thomas H. Johnson, eds., *The Puritans: A Sourcebook of Their Writings*, 2 vols. (New York: Harper and Row, 1963), especially chapter II titled "The Theory of the State and of Society," I:181–280. For the full text of Winthrop's speech, see the Miller and Johnson work, I:205–7.

20. *Democracy* (Bradley), I:44–5.

21. Ibid., I:44.

22. For Tocqueville's full discussion of the Puritans, see ibid., I:32–46. His admiration was limited by his rejection of Puritan intolerance and his denunciation of intrusions into conscience and private behavior. Also consult James T. Schleifer, "Tocqueville and Religion: Some New Perspectives," *Tocqueville Review*, IV, no. 2 (Fall–Winter 1982): 303–21.

23. *Democracy* (Bradley), I:42.

24. See especially ibid., I:68–71, and conversation with Jared Sparks, 29 September 1831, *Journey to America*, 58–9.

25. *Democracy* (Bradley), I:46; also see I:45 and I:315–17.
26. Ibid., I:316.
27. Ibid., I:318.
28. Jefferson's *Notes* were first published in 1785; the edition used by Tocqueville remains unknown. The full title of Conseil's work is *Mélanges politiques et philosophiques extraits des mémoires et de la correspondance de Thomas Jefferson* (Paris: Paulin, 1833). Particularly valuable among the vast number of works on Jefferson is Merrill D. Peterson, *Thomas Jefferson and the New Nation: A Biography* (New York: Oxford University Press, 1970).
29. *Democracy* (Bradley), I: 280.
30. For elaboration, consult James T. Schleifer, "Jefferson and Tocqueville," prepared for a conference at the Claremont Institute, January 1985, published with other conference papers in *Alexis de Tocqueville Observes the New American Order: Essays Honoring the Sesquicentennial of "Democracy in America,"* edited by Ken Masugi (Lanham, Md.: University Press of America, 1989).
31. Yale Tocqueville Manuscripts Collection, Original Drafts of the *Democracy*, "Rubish," C V g, tome 4; both quotations are from the chapter "Of Honor in the United States and in Democratic Communities"; see *Democracy* (Bradley), II:242–55.
32. See *Democracy* (Bradley), I:54, and II:39–40 and 146.
33. Ibid., I:119. Concerning the edition read by Tocqueville and his uses of the *Federalist*, see Schleifer, *Making*, chapters 7–9. Note also that Tocqueville had planned to visit Madison in America, but the need to cut his journey short caused him to miss that opportunity; see Jardin, *Tocqueville*, 104–05. For recent studies of the *Federalist*, see especially John Diggins, *The Lost Soul of American Politics: Virtue, Self-Interest, and the Foundations of Liberalism* (New York: Basic Books, 1984), hereafter cited as Diggins, *Lost Soul*; David F. Epstein, *The Political Theory of "The Federalist"* (Chicago: University of Chicago Press, 1984); and Albert Furtwangler, *The Authority of Publius: A Reading of the Federalist Papers* (Ithaca, N.Y.: Cornell University Press, 1984).
34. See especially *Democracy* (Bradley), I:116–79, "The Federal Constitution."
35. Consult Schleifer, *Making*, 139–41 and 217–23.
36. On this point, see Diggins, *Lost Soul*, 25 and 48–52.
37. *Democracy* (Bradley), I:281–2; and compare I:158–71.
38. Tocqueville used the one-volume abridgement of Story's three-volume work (Boston: Hilliard, Gray, and Cambridge, Mass.: Brown, Shattuck, 1833). For what Tocqueville learned from Story, Kent, Spencer, and others about the law and lawyers, see especially Schleifer, *Making*, chapters 7–9 and 10–14. Also see the pertinent portions of Pierson, *Tocqueville in America*, and conversations and notebooks from *Journey to America*. On Story, see R. Kent Newmyer, *Supreme Court Justice Joseph Story: Statesman of the Old Republic* (Chapel Hill: University of North Carolina Press, 1985); and Perry Miller, *The Life of the Mind in America, From the Revolution to the Civil War* (New York: Harcourt, Brace and World, 1965), especially Book Two: "The Legal Mentality."
39. See Newmyer, *Story*, 85.
40. See ibid., 262–3 and 269–70.
41. See especially *Democracy* (Bradley), I:282–97, "The Temper of the Legal Profession in the United States, and How It Serves as a Counterpoise to Democracy."
42. On Jackson and the Jacksonian Era, see especially Marvin Meyers, *The Jacksonian Persuasion: Politics and Belief* (New York: Vintage, 1957), hereafter cited as Meyers, *Jacksonian Persuasion*; Robert V. Remini's three-volume biography, *Andrew Jackson and the Course of American Empire, 1767–1821, Andrew Jackson and the Course of American Democracy, 1833–1845* (New York: Harper and Row, 1977, 1981, 1984); Arthur M. Schlesinger, Jr., *The Age of Jackson* (Boston: Little, Brown, 1945); and John William Ward, *Andrew Jackson: Symbol for an Age* (New York: Oxford University Press, 1962).
43. *Democracy* (Bradley), I:59–60; also see I:264–80, the chapters on the omnipotence of the majority, and II:9–13, "Of the Principal Source of Belief among Democratic Nations."

44. See, for example, *Democracy* (Bradley), I:270.
45. Ibid., I:198–205, and II:114–18 and 123–8, on associations.
46. On enlightened self-interest, see ibid., I:250–3 and II:129–32 and 133–5. Also consult Schleifer, *Making*, chapters 17 and 18.
47. *Democracy* (Bradley), I:259; also see I:258–63.
48. Ibid., I:260.
49. Ibid., I:203.
50. Ibid., I:252–3.
51. *Journey to America*, "General Questions," Sing-Sing, 29 May 1831, Alphabetic Notebook 1, 210–11.
52. Consult Schleifer, *Making*, chapter 6. On the whole question of the connection between commerce and industry, see especially Drescher, *England*, 126–33.
53. *Democracy* (Bradley), II:327–31.
54. Ibid., II:146.
55. Ibid., II:171.
56. Ibid., II:167–71 and 200–201.
57. For elaboration, see Roger Boesche, "The Strange Liberalism of Alexis de Tocqueville," *History of Political Thought* 2:3 (November 1981), 495–524; and "Tocqueville and *Le Commerce*: A Newspaper Expressing His Unusual Liberalism," *Journal of the History of Ideas* 44:2 (April–June 1983): 277–92; Drescher, *England*, chapter 7; Jardin, *Tocqueville*, 286, 334–7, 368–84; and Lamberti, *Deux Démocraties*, 227–38.
58. For elaboration, see Meyers, *Jacksonian Persuasion*, chapters 1 and 2.
59. Consult Michael G. Kammen, *People of Paradox: An Inquiry Concerning the Origins of American Civilization* (New York: Vintage, 1973), chapter 7, "Ambiguities of the American Revolution." Also see J. R. Pole, *The Pursuit of Equality in American History* (Berkeley: University of California Press, 1978).
60. Ibid., II:315.
61. See a recent study, inspired once again by Tocqueville, which also emphasizes the significance of American *moeurs*: Robert N. Bellah et al., *Habits of the Heart: Individualism and Commitment in American Life* (Berkeley: University of California Press, 1985).
62. *Journey to America*, [1 October 1831], Pocket Notebook 3, 150.
63. For elaboration, see Schleifer, *Making*, 245.

5

Liberalism in the Second Empire and the Influence of America: Edouard Laboulaye and His Circle

Walter D. Gray

Edouard Laboulaye is perhaps best known today as president of the Franco-American Union, which raised funds in France for the Statue of Liberty. In fact, the idea for the statue was originally conceived at a dinner party in 1865, at Laboulaye's house in Glatigny-Versailles, attended by Henri Martin, Rémusat, Gasparin, and the young sculptor Fréderic-Auguste Bartholdi.[1] I do not propose to discuss here Laboulaye's activities concerning the Statue of Liberty per se, but to show the intellectual formation of the man who would become the foremost French Americanist and would eventually head the committee that brought to the United States its most revered symbol of liberty. In this chapter I discuss his scholarly writings during the Second Empire, which are permeated with liberal ideas and show a strong influence from America, his work on behalf of the North during the American Civil War, and his relations with prominent Americans during the 1850s and 1860s. I am deeply indebted in the preparation of this paper to François de Laboulaye for permitting me to research the papers of his distinguished great-grandfather.

Edouard Laboulaye (1811–83) was a leading figure in the liberal opposition to the Second Empire until 1870. He was also the leading interpreter of the United States, its history, and its institutions for the generation of the 1850s and 1860s. René Remond writes:

> A man renowned in an exemplary manner for his work and the development of his political thought which centered on (European) liberalism and the American experience and which brought out the profound ambiguities resulting from this union. Edouard Laboulaye, whose name dominated the history of the intellectual relations between France and the United States between 1850 and 1860 as did that of Lafayette before 1830 and that of

Tocqueville during the July Monarchy. All his life he was the image of the ardent defender of the United States and its institutions, publishing book upon book and numerous articles and studies.[2]

Remond captures here Laboulaye's mature thought. A member of the Institut de France, a columnist for the influential liberal newspaper *Le Journal des Débats*, and a professor of comparative law at the Collège de France, he was a savant of almost universal interests (his bibliography, comprising books, pamphlets, essays, children's stories, and articles, exceeds two hundred entries)[3] and he held a place at the center of French intellectual life during the Second Empire. A dominant theme in his scholarly publications during the Second Empire was the United States. For Laboulaye, who was disillusioned with the aftermath of 1848 in France, the study of American history and politics furnished a model of liberty and of a stable political system, which he hoped would inspire his fellow Frenchmen. Furthermore, the course of American history in the 1850s and 1860s illustrated for him the heroic efforts necessary to preserve liberty and a stable government. Indeed, the period of the Civil War and its aftermath brought Laboulaye into active participation in both French and American politics.

EARLY INFLUENCES AND ACHIEVEMENTS

Little in Laboulaye's early training or scholarly interests pointed to his later earnest interest in the United States. His early intellectual training was in legal institutions and their history, and, like so many other scholars of his generation, he fell under the spell of German thought. Donald R. Kelley has described Laboulaye as "the Germanizing legal historian."[4] Laboulaye was particularly influenced by two minor philosophers, Heinrich Ahrens and K. C. F. Krause, both of whom applied the philosophical principles of the German Idealists to politics. The German writer who exerted the strongest influence on Laboulaye's intellectual formation was Friedrich von Savigny, a legal scholar and one of the leading exponents of the historical school of jurisprudence. On one occasion von Savigny acknowledged Laboulaye as his disciple, and von Savigny's influence can be seen in Laboulaye's early scholarly interests: property rights in the West, the condition of women in Rome, Roman criminal law, and a laudatory study of von Savigny himself.[5]

One of von Savigny's key precepts was that law is not made by the caprice of the legislator (for example, Napoleon and his law code), but that law "is produced above all by internal and silent forces."[6] Another disciple of Savigny, J. K. Bluntschli, accurately described the historical school as follows:

> The historical school . . . does not thoughtlessly and servilely honor actual facts, but recognizes, explains, and interprets the inner connection between Past and Present, the organic development of national life, and the *moral idea* as revealed in its history. This method certainly starts from the actual phenomena, but regards them as living and not as dead.[7]

Laboulaye echoed the historical school when he wrote, "All science, all of politics, are separated between the two schools of thought: the school of the absolute, or philosophical school; and the school of experience, or historical school.[8] In succinct terms, according to Kelley, the historical school "provided a modern, expert, and empirical alternative to the rationalist legacy of Jacobism and Bonapartism."[9] In a sense, Laboulaye agreed with Guizot's dictum that "when history speaks, it is well of politics to listen."[10] Laboulaye in Paris formed with Lieber in New York and Bluntschli in Heidelberg what Lieber used to call a "scientific cloverleaf" of the historical school.[11]

The historical school exerted a strong influence on Laboulaye's scholarly works in the 1840s. Later, its influence was one of method rather than of content. What is more important, Laboulaye, unlike most exponents of the historical school in Europe, never became a conservative in politics; instead he drew his political ideas from such French liberal writers as Benjamin Constant and Alexis de Tocqueville.[12] His admiration for Constant is evident in his introduction to an 1861 critical edition of Constant's political writings, in which he quoted approvingly Constant's definition of liberalism, which doubled as his own political credo:

> For forty years I defended the same principle: liberty in all things: in religion, in philosophy, in literature, in business, in politics; and by liberty I mean the triumph of individuality, as much over that authority which would wish to govern by despotism, as over the masses who demand the right to subject the minority to the majority.[13]

In one of his last lectures at the Collège de France, only a few years before his death, Laboulaye reiterated his devotion to Constant by saying, "Liberty, order, and the happiness of people are the end of human associations. Political organizations are only the means."[14] In his scholarly works, Laboulaye's world view was that of a liberal in the tradition of Constant and Tocqueville, while his method followed the canons of the historical school. He saw institutions develop organically over long periods of time, but in studying the United States he noted that the guiding spirit of its history was liberty.

In the closing years of the July Monarchy, Laboulaye's intellectual achievements in legal and historical studies were recognized by his election at the age of thirty-four to the Académie des Inscriptions et Belles-Lettres, one of the five bodies of the Institut de France. He was, however, never to realize his cherished desire to be elected to its most eminent academy, the Académie Française. When he was thirty-eight he was appointed to the chair of comparative law at the Collège de France. With this appointment in 1848, his major intellectual interests began to center on the United States, perhaps fulfilling an early admonition of Victor Cousin, who had urged him to study America.

Although Laboulaye was the Second Empire's chief Americanist, his views on American society and customs were often naive, largely because he never visited the United States, despite numerous invitations. John Amory Lowell invited him to lecture at the Lowell Institute in Boston, and Henry Villard invited him to take a lecture tour under the auspices of the American Social Science Association (of which Laboulaye was a corresponding member). The presidents of two new universities, Daniel Coit Gilman of Johns Hopkins and Andrew D. Dickson White of Cornell, also invited him to lecture at their institutions, and Francis Lieber repeatedly asked him to visit the United States. Laboulaye declined all the invitations on the grounds that his health would not stand the trip.[15]

After his appointment to the Collège de France, Laboulaye announced that his inaugural lectures would be on American history. As a prologue to the series he delivered seven lectures on the theory of law because, as he informed his students, an understanding of the theory of law was a prerequisite for the study of American history. Only after the summer recess did he begin his lectures on American history in which he hoped to contrast France's Constitution of 1848 with the U. S. Constitution and to show how the French erred in failing to transfer the spirit and general ideas of the U. S. Constitution to their own. His introductory lecture was "De la constitution américaine et de l'utilité de son étude," which forms the first chapter of his monumental three-volume *Histoire des États-Unis*.[16]

LABOULAYE'S MATURE WORK

Laboulaye's masterpiece on America, the three-volume *Histoire des États-Unis*, originally a series of lectures delivered at the Collège de

France, was published between 1855 and 1866. Despite the usual professional admonitions and digressions, the clarity of his thought on America emerges. In 1855, Laboulaye published the first volume, comprising lectures given in 1849 and 1850. In preparing his lectures Laboulaye was aided by Robert Walsh, the U.S. consul general in Paris between 1850 and 1856, who supplied Laboulaye with numerous books, including the works of Edward Everett, George Bancroft, William Ellery Channing, and Joseph Tuckerman. Laboulaye was later to correspond with Everett and Bancroft.[17] In this opening volume he traces the history of the thirteen colonies down to the middle of the eighteenth century. The second volume, published in 1866, begins with what he considered the origins of the Revolution and concludes with the Peace of Paris in 1783. The final volume, also published in 1866, analyzed in great detail the Articles of Confederation and the Constitution. These last two volumes, a published version of his lectures given between 1862 and 1864, conclude with the ratification of the Constitution. His lectures on America in the eighteenth century formed a part of a course on the eighteenth-century world and alternated with a series on the legislation and administration of France under Louis XVI.[18]

In the introductory lecture, "De la constitution américaine, et de l'utilité de son étude," he stated clearly his procedure for studying American history as well as his view of France and the United States:

> Thus, historical and scientific importance, immediate usefulness, such are the two principal reasons for seriously studying the American Constitution in detail, so as to penetrate its true character, to appreciate its spirit not only for purely speculative purposes, but in order to draw from it useful lessons, a rule of conduct, an immediate and certain benefit.[19]

He argued that Americans forged a lasting government because they were practical men, not theoreticians. Laboulaye repudiated theoreticians and stigmatized them as "the most dangerous kind of statesmen."[20] Frenchmen, he noted, were prone to become theoreticians, especially when they drew up constitutions and law codes. The Americans, he argued, were men of experience, and they evolved a workable constitution that safeguarded their liberties. Laboulaye did not wish his countrymen to copy the American Constitution uncritically, but to extract what he called "the spirit" of the Constitution. He told his listeners it was important to distinguish

> What is of the essence of a free government from what is purely American; in a word, let us not copy the Constitution of the

United States, but let us profit from the lessons it contains, and while remaining French, let us not blush at following the example or listening to the advice given by a Washington.[21]

The United States, he argued, did not demand of a constitution what it could not give, whereas France was continually demanding the impossible from French constitutions. Laboulaye never ceased to remind his listeners that since 1789, America had had only one constitution, whereas France had had fourteen. Also, the Americans had only undergone one revolution (he was speaking in 1849), while the French had experienced ten. Laboulaye's major aim as a scholar was to aid his countrymen in establishing a stable and liberal constitution. Although he served on the commission that drafted the Constitution of 1848, he deplored the document because its framers had disdained the American experience by having a unicameral legislature and an executive who combined some of the prerogatives of a constitutional monarch as well as those of a chief executive of a republic. He summed up his views by saying that

by studying the Constitution of the United States, we will take a course in comparative constitutional politics, we will openly confront its (the U.S. Constitution) problems, in which we can see our own future and to which a citizen cannot remain indifferent.[22]

In tracing American history down to the Constitution, Laboulaye developed several themes that explained American history. He examined the origin of liberty in America, distinguishing first between liberty in the abstract and liberty in practice and then between religious and political liberty. For Laboulaye, the American concept of liberty originated in Magna Charta. In this view, he was faithful to the historical school in asserting that America was part of a long historical evolution. He said: "The United States is a new empire, but it is an ancient people; it is a European nation whose civilization is counted not in years but in centuries. What we call the nation's youth is on the contrary its virility."[23] The American Revolution did not establish liberty for the colonists because they already had it, but it did give them self-government. He wrote, "The true course of the revolution was that the American people, master of their destiny in fact, wished to be so in law."[24]

A second theme, a counterpart to the liberty motif that runs through Laboulaye's thought, is that religious ideas form the basis of society: the faith of a people mold and determine its political institutions. He discussed religious liberty at length, because he considered it an essential counterpart to political liberty: the two went hand in hand. Central to his thought was the idea that the United States furnished Europe with an example of religious liberty. Although the United States enjoyed both religious and political liberty, its tradition was Puritan and republican. The problem for Laboulaye was whether France, with its Catholic tradition, could ever enjoy these same liberties. In part, the United States itself furnished the answer, for Laboulaye was amazed that Catholicism flourished there and that it flourished in a republic rather than a monarchy. He condemned the antirepublican attitude of most French Catholics, arguing that a republican government and Catholicism were not incompatible. On this point, Laboulaye was far ahead of his contemporaries, most of whom were constitutional monarchists. He did remark that in the future the Catholic church would have to make changes in order to put the church more in harmony with the century.[25]

Laboulaye also saw in Puritanism the origins of democracy. For him, the first document of American history was the Mayflower Compact, which had established absolute equality among the Pilgrims. A precondition for democracy was political liberty, and political liberty had begun in America with the Puritans, who had inherited and transmitted to America the traditions of English liberty rooted in the Magna Charta.[26] The Puritans had also established self-government in the form of the New England town meeting, which contained "both the spirit of order and the spirit of liberty, independence, and respect."[27]

Although the New England town meeting had been important in developing American institutions, Laboulaye considered the Carolinas of almost equal importance, because their lawgiver had been John Locke.[28] In discussing the Carolinas, Laboulaye was soon drawn into a discussion of what he considered the one odious institution in America that was the antithesis of liberty: slavery. His views on slavery were strongly influenced by William Ellery Channing, whom he described as the "American Fénelon." Laboulaye urged his students to read Channing's work on slavery—a work Laboulaye himself translated into French in 1855.[29] From this time onward Laboulaye became active in antislavery movements, an activity that took up much of his time in the 1860s.

Laboulaye's study of American history was interrupted by the political turmoil of the 1850s. The coup d'état of 2 December 1851 and the ensuing repressive measures, especially the censorship, led Laboulaye to lecture on less controversial subjects. He was especially cautious after two of his colleagues, Edgar Quinet and Jules Michelet, were dismissed from the Collège de France because of their views. Although Laboulaye sympathized with them, he did not wish to lose his academic position. Consequently, from 1852 until 1857 he lectured on the noncontroversial topic of Roman legal institutions, and between 1857 and 1862, on the legal and political institutions of pre-Roman Gaul, Roman Gaul, the German tribes, and the Merovingians, and on Salic Law. During these years he also translated Channing's works, published a book of essays on religious liberty as well as one on morals and politics, and contributed regularly to the *Journal des Débats*. Although his lectures were not on American history, many of his articles and essays dealt with subjects related to America. Only in 1862, after Napoleon III introduced some liberalizing reforms, did Laboulaye resume his lectures on American history.

His lectures between 1862 and 1864, which constitute the final two volumes of the *Histoire*, were contemporaneous with the American Civil War. In these last two volumes Laboulaye continued to develop the themes he had established in his first volume. In his lectures on the American Revolution he did not give a detailed chronological history but instead concentrated on the political and diplomatic events leading to the Revolution, merely sketching the main events of the Revolution, devoting five lectures to the events of the Revolution up to 1778 and only two to the events after 1778. George Washington captivated Laboulaye; he described Washington as one who "resembles the heroes of Greece and Rome; in his perfect understanding of liberty, he is the first man of modern times. He understood that liberty was the law of the future." In analyzing the work of Washington, Franklin, Hamilton, and the other Founding Fathers, he said, "They gave liberty, not only to America, but to the World."[30]

His final lectures began with an analysis of the Articles of Confederation and the reasons for their failure, and he continued with a series of biographical sketches of the Founding Fathers: Alexander Hamilton, James Madison, Benjamin Franklin, Rufus King, Edmund Randolph, James Wilson, and Gouverneur Morris. Laboulaye devoted his last remarks to an analysis, in the best traditions of the *explication de texte*, of the provisions of the Constitution. Consistent with his general view of American history, he described the Constitution as the capstone of the long historical development that granted religious and political liberty to Americans. It fulfilled his cherished dreams to write, "We understand that liberty is the law of his (man's) nature, that he is not permitted to renounce it. . . . Despotism cannot give him happiness; man is, so to speak, condemned by God himself to be happy."[31] In his concluding remarks Laboulaye told the French that he did not want them to copy exactly the American Constitution or, as a second choice, the English Constitution, because it would be unwise to introduce American or English customs into France. Instead he told his students and readers:

> It is the spirit which must be seized. Once that spirit is yours, you will find the forms which will adapt to it naturally. Must one be American or English to practice religious freedom, freedom of the press, individual freedom? No, all of these liberties can be guaranteed by very simple institutions of which we already possess the germs, and which our fathers left us.[32]

LABOULAYE'S REACTION TO THE AMERICAN CIVIL WAR

Laboulaye's response to the great test of the Federal Union, the American Civil War, revealed his deep interest in America. He reacted immediately, and, as was usual with Laboulaye, his reaction was protracted and followed the contours of his biases. That he should side with the North, contrary to the official French governmental position, was predictable because of his commitment to liberty and his firm disapproval of slavery. To examine Laboulaye's ideas on the Civil War brings us to the center of the intellectual milieu opposing the Second Empire.

At a time when the government of Napoleon III seriously considered recognizing the Confederacy, Laboulaye was devoted to the Union cause and viewed the American constitutional government as one that had to be preserved for the sake of humanity. His lectures contained numerous references to the Civil War with a pronounced sympathy for the North. Certainly his students were conversant with his articles in the *Journal des Débats*, in which he defended the North as the citadel of liberty and condemned the South as the protector of slavery.[33]

In 1863, Laboulaye was for a brief time, until he withdrew in favor of Thiers, an opposition candidate for a seat in the Corps Legislatif. His writings and his political activities made him a popular and esteemed professor, as is evidenced by the large crowds that patiently waited in line for admission to his lecture hall, where vacant seats were rarely to be found. In a note to one of his printed lectures the editor observed, "One hour before the class, the room, the corridors, the courtyard of the Collège de France are invaded by an eager crowd. The moment the professor goes up to the podium, he is welcomed by a veritable explosion of enthusiasm."[34]

Laboulaye's first major article on the Civil War titled "La guerre civile aux États-Unis" appeared in the *Journal des Débats* on 2 and 3

October 1861. The *Journal des Débats*, the most distinguished opposition newspaper during the Second Empire, had among its contributors an intellectual elite that was openly hostile to the domestic and foreign policies of Napoleon III. Until 1862 the chief columnist on American affairs was Michel Chevalier, a noted economist and advocate of free trade who supported the South. He resigned in 1862, when, as a result of Laboulaye's efforts, the paper's editorial policy changed in favor of the North. The *Journal's* change of policy became evident when it published Laboulaye's "Les États-Unis et la France" on 26 and 27 August 1862.

In "Les États-Unis et la France," Laboulaye amplified his observations on the Civil War. He began by expressing his concern that many individuals and newspapers in France were supporting the South. He observed, "Although the South has many friends in France, and slavery has found more favor than we would have imagined . . . , the North has gathered, however, a host of defenders who have not abandoned the old and glorious traditions of France."[35] In short, Laboulaye linked France's historic role as a defender of liberty with the Northern cause; the South, tied as it was to slavery, was unworthy of France's support.

In raising the question of France's historic role, Laboulaye was indirectly criticizing Napoleon III's sympathy for the South. With Laboulaye, as with most other liberal writers, attacks against slavery must not be interpreted as being motivated solely by their Northern sympathies. Their criticism served a dual purpose: to attack Napoleon III's political system and to support the cause of liberty in the North. We are concerned here, however, not with Laboulaye's references to French domestic politics, but with his statements on the Civil War.

Slavery was central to Laboulaye's position on the Civil War. Like many of his fellow liberals he condemned slavery on moral and humanitarian grounds while often neglecting economic and social factors that made the system unworkable or unprofitable. The great interest in antislavery movements in the late 1850s and early 1860s can only be viewed as an aspect of the liberal opposition to Napoleon III. French antislavery writings of this time always had a double entendre. Initially, Laboulaye differed from Channing, who wished slavery abolished immediately. He wrote, "Channing is not clear enough in the means he proposes to guard against the dangers of a sudden emancipation; this is the only reproach I have for him, the only blemish I find on his work." Laboulaye favored a gradual or progressive abolition of slaves. In 1862 he said that "to demand immediate abolition, is to walk, in my opinion, into the abyss; one compromises the holiest of causes."[36] Slavery, according to Laboulaye, "is a poison that enervates the master; it has corrupted even religion."[37]

Laboulaye believed that the Civil War posed a moral problem, a political problem, and an economic problem for France. The moral problem was the most important for him, as the simple truth was that the North was right and the South was wrong. Just as France could not support a government based on slavery, in politics France could not abandon its old ally and friend of almost a century. The economic problem was more difficult because of the cotton shortage in France, but here Laboulaye said the shortage was a device of the South to force the European powers, especially France and Britain, to aid the South.[38]

The American consul general in Paris, John Bigelow, wrote Laboulaye requesting permission to reprint the articles at his own expense, saying, "If I do not miscalculate their importance, they will place Europe as well as the United States under the permanent obligations to their author."[39] William L. Dayton, the American minister to Paris, also wrote to congratulate Laboulaye.[40] The distinguished orator, Edward Everett of Massachusetts, wrote Laboulaye that his articles "had attracted the notice of members of the government."[41]

Laboulaye's numerous articles during the course of the Civil War were usually reprinted in French and in English in New York by the Loyal Publication Society of which Francis Lieber was the president. In November, Laboulaye published another article in the *Débats* titled, "Pourquoi le Nord ne peut accepter la séparation," a work that was immediately translated into English under the title "Separation: War without End." The Loyal Publication Society issued it in an initial printing of 10,000 copies.[42]

Laboulaye's reputation as a defender of the North brought him many invitations to speak at meetings of societies and public meetings. American history, the Civil War, Benjamin Franklin, Abraham Lincoln, and Horace Mann were his favorite subjects for lectures. His friendship for the United States was dramatically acknowledged by his being the only Frenchman asked to speak at William Dayton's funeral in 1864. Laboulaye also served as president of the French Anti-Slavery League, a society whose membership was comprised of many intellectuals; François Guizot and the duc de Broglie served as honorary presidents, and Augustin Cochin served as its secretary. Agenor de Gasparin, Henri Martin, and Montalembert were also active members of the league. The first public act of the league was a sad one, for it addressed a statement to President Andrew Johnson expressing its sorrow over the assassination of President Lincoln.[43]

Yet another of Laboulaye's activities concerning America should be pointed out. His most widely read book on America, *Paris in America*, a fictional account of a voyage to "Paris," a community somewhere in New England, enjoyed an immense success, going through thirty-four French editions and eight English ones. Secretary of State Seward wrote to Bigelow that he was "infinitely pleased with its humor as well as its spirit.[44] Bigelow remarked in his eulogy on Laboulaye, given before the Union League Club of New York, that *Paris in America* "betrayed about as much ignorance as knowledge of social life in the United States," but that "of all the publications emanating from European sources during our war, none had more effect than this, in weakening the prejudice against the 'Yankee,' which prevailed among what it was the fashion to call 'the better classes of Europe.' "[45]

Edward Everett wrote Laboulaye:

> No foreigner describes American topics with superior *connaissance de cause*, very few with equal intelligence of the subject. Your *Paris en Amerique* discloses an astonishing familiarity with the state of things in this country. We feel that we have no more enlightened friend in Europe than yourself.[46]

Laboulaye, in a letter to Lieber, expressed gratification with the English translation of what he termed his "*extravaganza*."[47]

The best summary of Laboulaye's views on America is contained in a speech he gave on Benjamin Franklin (he had translated and published a four-volume edition of Franklin's works). During the course of his talk he was informed of Lincoln's death, and in his talk he summarized his love for America:

> I have been involved with America and the history of her first revolution for twenty years, and for twenty years I have been living with Franklin and Washington; I declare that I have never known patriots who were less self-interested, more sincere friends of liberty; I love them, and like all lovers, I must speak about what I love, at the risk of boring my listeners.[48]

One monument to Laboulaye's imagination remains: the Statue of Liberty, proposed by Laboulaye as a French expression of admiration for the United States. It stands in New York's harbor as a monument to the vision of that distinguished French interpreter of America and to his love for a country he never saw. He would be gratified to see that the statue has become for Americans the very symbol of liberty, the cherished ideal that inspired the life and work of Edouard Laboulaye.

NOTES

1. André de Laboulaye, "La Statue de la liberté, 1886–1936," *Franco-American Review*, II (1938): 245.
2. René Remond, *Les États-Unis devant l'opinion française, 1815–1852* (Paris: A. Colin, 1962), II, 851.
3. No book-length biography of Laboulaye exists. There are, however, several useful studies of his life by his pupils and colleagues. His former pupil Émile Boutmy, in his *Taine, Scherer, Laboulaye* (Paris: A. Colin, 1901) included a sympathetic essay written shortly after his master's death. The official eulogy for the Institut de France by Henri Wallon, "Notice sur la vie et les travaux de M. Edouard René-Lefebvre-Laboulaye, membre ordinaire de l'Académie des Inscriptions et Belles-Lettres," *Mémoires des l'Institut National de France, Académie des Inscriptions et Belles-Lettres*, XXXV, 286–321, is helpful and contains a detailed bibliography of Laboulaye's writings. John Bigelow's *Some Recollections of the Late Edouard Laboulaye* (privately printed, n.d.) is the brief testimony of an American friend and admirer. A brief work by Alkan Aîné, *Un fondeur en caractères, membre de l'Institut* (Paris: Typologie-Tucker, 1886), contains a useful bibliography and many anecdotes concerning Laboulaye's youth. A scholarly analysis of his political thought is Jean de Soto, "Édouard Laboulaye," *Revue internationale d'histoire politique et constitutionnelle*, V (1955): 114–50. See also, Walter D. Gray, "Edouard Laboulaye: 'Liberal' Catholic and 'Americanist' during the Second Empire," *Cithara*, III (1964): 3–15
4. Donald R. Kelley, *Historians and the Law in Postrevolutionary France* (Princeton: Princeton University Press, 1984), 53.
5. Letter of von Savigny to Bethmann-Hollweg, 2 February 1842, in Adolf Stoll, *Friedrich von Savigny, ein Bild seines Leben mit einer Sammlung seiner Briefe* (Berlin: C. Heymann, 1927–39), III, 199. See Laboulaye's *Essai sur la vie et les doctrines de Frédéric-Charles de Savigny* (Paris: A. Durand, 1843).
6. Friedrich von Savigny, *Vom Beruf unser Zeit für Gesetzgebung und Rechtswissenschaft* (3rd ed.; Freiburg am Breisgau: Mohr, 1892), 9.
7. J. K. Bluntschli, *The Theory of the State* (2nd ed.; Oxford: Clarendon Press, 1892), 7.
8. Édouard Laboulaye, *Histoire des États-Unis* (4th ed.; Paris: Charpentier, 1870), I, 212.
9. Kelley, *Historians and the Law*, 80.
10. Guizot as quoted in Douglas Johnson, *Guizot, Aspects of French History, 1787–1874* (London: University of Toronto Press, 1963), 51.
11. Daniel Coit Gilman, *Bluntschli, Lieber and Laboulaye* (Baltimore: J. Murphy, 1884), 1. The portion of this work devoted to Laboulaye is a long quotation from John Bigelow and is a summary of observations of Laboulaye later published by Bigelow in his *Some Recollections of the Late Edouard Laboulaye*.
12. His reverence for Tocqueville is evident in an essay written shortly after Tocqueville's death and published in *L'état et ses limites, suivis d'essais politiques sur Alexis de Tocqueville, l'instruction publique, les finances, le droit de pétition, etc.* (Paris: Charpentier, 1863), 138–201.
13. Benjamin Constant, *Cours de politique constitutionnelle ou collection des ouvrages publiés sur le gouvernement représentatif avec une introduction et notes par M. Édouard Laboulaye* (Paris: Guillaumin, 1861), I, viii.
14. Édouard Laboulaye, *Trente ans d'enseignement au Collège de France (1849–1882). Cours inédits de M. Laboulaye . . . Préface de M. Dareste . . .* (Paris: L. Larose et Forcel, 1888), xxiv.
15. Laboulaye Papers, Lowell to Laboulaye, Boston, 15 December 1866; Henry Villard to Laboulaye, Boston, 18 December 1865; Daniel Coit Gilman to Laboulaye, Baltimore, 8 April 1875; Andrew Dickson White to Laboulaye, Paris, 28 April 1868.
16. See Édouard Laboulaye, *Considérations sur la constitution* (Paris: A. Durand, 1848). On American influence in the constitution debates of 1848, see Remond, *Les États-Unis*

devant l'opinion française, II, 831–58; and Eugene Newton Curtis, *The French Assembly of 1848 and American Constitutional Doctrines* (New York: Columbia University Press, 1918).

17. The Laboulaye papers contain thirteen letters from Walsh to Laboulaye written between 1850 and 1856. From these letters it is obvious that Walsh was a major source of information about the United States as well as a provider of recently published works. He also opened his library to Laboulaye.

18. Laboulaye's lectures on French administration during the reign of Louis XVII are printed in the *Revue des cours littéraires de la France et l'étranger*, II-V (1865–68) and his lectures on the French Revolution V-VII (1868–71).

19. Édouard Laboulaye, *De la constitution américaine et de l'utilité de son étude. Discours prononcé en decembre 1849 à l'ouverture du cours de législation comparée* (Paris: De Hennuyer, 1850), 7.

20. Laboulaye, *Histoire des États-Unis*, I, 19.

21. Ibid., 23.

22. Ibid., 40.

23. Ibid., 35.

24. Ibid., 34.

25. Laboulaye's views on religious liberty are explained in *La liberté religieuse* (Paris: Charpentier, 1858). See especially his Préface, vii-xxx. Laboulaye gave further evidence of his views on religious liberty when he wrote in *L'état et ses limites*, 28, "La liberté religieuse, c'est l'âme des sociétés modernes, c'est la racine de toutes les autres libertés."

26. *Histoire des États-Unis*, I, 156.

27. Ibid., 256.

28. His essay on Locke forms two lectures in his *Histoire des États-Unis*, I, 328–64. He also published his lectures on Locke in a separate pamphlet, *Locke, législateur de la Caroline* (Paris: A. Durand, 1850).

29. Laboulaye's indebtedness to Channing was profound. He edited and translated *Oeuvres sociales de W. E. Channing, traduites de l'anglais, précédés d'un essai sur la vie et les doctrines de Channing et d'une introduction par M. Édouard Laboulaye* (Paris: Comon, 1854); and *Oeuvres de W. E. Channing. De l'esclavage, précédé d'une préface et d'une étude sur l'esclavage aux États-Unis* (Paris: Lacroix-Comon, 1855). As a measure of his esteem for Channing he reprinted his essays on Channing in *La liberté religieuse*, 210–51.

30. *Histoire*, III, x.

31. Ibid., 31–2.

32. Ibid., 66.

33. Laboulaye's role on the *Journal des Débats* is discussed by his protégé, Émile Boutmy in "Laboulaye," *Le livre du centenaire du Journal des Débats, 1789–1889* (Paris: Plon-Nourrit, 1889), pp. 253–60. Ernest Renan, also a regular writer for the paper, describes the history of the opposition paper in an essay, "Le *Journal des Débats* sous le Second Empire," ibid., 235–43. Renan affectionately described Laboulaye: "Je ne crois pas que personne ait compris et pratiqué mieux que Laboulaye la règle du parfait libéral," ibid., 240.

34. Édouard Laboulaye, "Cours de législation comparée—De la constitution des États-Unis," *Revue nationale* XV (10 January, 1864): 385.

35. A revised and enlarged version was printed as a pamphlet (Paris: E. Dentu, 1862), 324. This version was reprinted in *L'état et ses limites*, pp. 323–75. References are to this later edition.

36. *Études morales et politiques*, 220. See also Barbara Karsky, "Les libéraux français et l'émancipation des esclaves aux États-Unis, 1852–1870," *Revue d'histoire moderne et contemporaine*, XXI (1974): 575–90; and Serge Gavronsky, "American Slavery and the French Liberals: An Interpretation of Slavery in French Politics during the Second Empire," *Journal of Negro History*, LI (1966): 36–52.

37. "Les États-Unis et la France," 338.

38. Ibid., 361–2.

39. Laboulaye Papers, Bigelow to Laboulaye, Paris, 28 August 1862.
40. William L. Dayton to Laboulaye, Paris, 16 September 1862, in the Dayton Papers at the Princeton University Library.
41. Laboulaye Papers, Edward Everett to Laboulaye, Boston, 14 October 1862.
42. Laboulaye Papers, Francis Lieber to Laboulaye, New York, 10 December 1862.
43. Activites of the League are evident in the great exchange of letters found in the Laboulaye papers. An informal address of the society, given before its actual foundation was sent to the Loyal and National League in New York. See *Reply of Messrs. Agenor de Gasparin, Edouard Laboulaye, Henri Martin, Augustin Cochin to the Loyal and National League of New York together with the Address of the League* (New York: Loyal Publication Society, 1864). This pamphlet was also published in New York in German and French editions.
44. Seward to Bigelow, Washington, 31 March 1863, in Bigelow, *Retrospections of an Active Life*, I, 616–17.
45. Bigelow, *Some Recollections of the Late Edouard Laboulaye*, 7.
46. Laboulaye Papers, Everett to Laboulaye, Boston, 19 January 1864.
47. Laboulaye Papers, Laboulaye to Lieber, Paris, 25 September 1863.
48. Benjamin Franklin, *La science du Bonhomme Richard ou le chemin de la fortune par Benjamin Franklin suivie d'extraits de ses mémoires et précédées de la jeunesse de Franklin par Edouard Laboulaye, de l'Institut* (Paris: H. Bellaire, 1872), 10.

6

Bartholdi's *Liberty* in the French Political Context

Maurice Agulhon

What can I say about Bartholdi's Statue of Liberty Enlightening the World that has not been said before? My contribution will not bring any major revelations—only some different, and I hope pertinent, emphases. Writing from a French point of view, I might also shift the spotlight somewhat. After all, the project was conceived in France, its symbolism was elaborated in France, and it immediately met with great success in France. These, then, are the three components of my approach.

THE PROJECT'S CONCEPTION

As we know, the project was conceived in 1865,[1] a date that deserves attention. In a world that clearly seemed to be on the march toward liberty—the monarchies of central Europe had begun to adopt constitutional regimes, Russia was abolishing serfdom, and the United States was abolishing slavery—liberal and republican French citizens were exasperated that since 2 December 1851 they had been saddled with a government that was rowing against the tide of history.

In domestic politics the regime of Napoleon III hesitated to loosen the iron collar of authoritarianism it had imposed from the outset. In foreign policy, the regime—frightened by its own audacity in 1859—decided to defend the pope of the *Syllabus* against the attacks of Garibaldi. Even worse, when it came to the American Civil War, the regime preferred the aristocratic, conservative South to the democratic, liberal North, and it worked to establish Maximilian rather than Juarez in Mexico. Yet to be a liberal in France, and a fortiori a republican, meant to hate the pope and all despots and to side with the Lincolns and the Garibaldis.[2] By 1865 it seemed obvious that a struggle transcending national boundaries was pitting liberty against the forces of the past. A kind of liberal internationalism had come into being, and it was not uncommon for men to cross frontiers to aid causes they had adopted as their own in foreign countries. Thus Frenchmen were fighting with Garibaldi during the Expedition of the Thousand, with the Union Army during the American Civil War, and in Crete against the Turks. Garibaldi, in turn, would come to France in 1870 to fight alongside the French Republic against the king of Prussia and for the "Universal Republic."

If Garibaldi was a legendary hero in his lifetime,[3] all the more so was Lincoln after his assassination. The premature, violent death of the man who had rekindled the American idealism of yore and had accomplished the emancipation of the slaves was the initial impetus for the undertaking being discussed here. Like the medal sent as a token of sympathy to the slain president's widow,[4] the plan to send an effigy of liberty to the American Republic constituted an act of faith in support of progress in the world and a act of moral opposition to the anti- (or insufficiently) liberal monarchy that continued to hold France in its grip. This idea was particularly dear to the republicans, the forward wing of the liberal coalition. In those days before the Internationale, whose "workers of the world" would eventually establish and monopolize a similar idea, the watchword for the future was Garibaldi's "Universal Republic."

As early as 1854, in his great ideological poem "Lux" in the volume *Châtiments* (*Punishments*)—the one that begins,

> *Temps futurs! vision sublime!*
> *Les peuples ont hors de l'abîme,*
> *Le Désert morne est traversé,*
> (Future times! Sublime vision
> The peoples have emerged from the abyss,
> The mournful desert has been crossed.)

Victor Hugo had written this premonitory stanza:

> *Au fond des cieux, un point scintille.*
> *Regardez, il grandit, il brille,*
> *Il approche, énorme et vermeil.*
> *O République Universelle!*
> *Tu n'es encore que l'étincelle,*
> *Demain tu seras le Soleil.*
> (Deep in the heavens, a point of light burns bright.
> Behold, it grows, it shines,

It draws nigh, huge and bright red,
O Universal Republic!
You are yet but the spark,
Tomorrow you will be the sun.)[5]

Was it this sun of the Universal Republic that was to crown Bartholdi's Statue of Liberty? I have no formal proof of such a reminiscence on the part of the sculptor from Colmar, but we can be sure that he had a copy of the *Châtiments*. Under the Second Empire, everyone with any education at all had read this book and everyone on the left had read it with fervor. Moreover, we know that in 1854 Victor Hugo had America on his mind, for he explicitly referred to it twice in this same poem "Lux."

> *L'Europe en rougissant dit Quoi! J'avais des Rois?*
> *Et l'Amérique dit Quoi! J'avais des esclaves?*
> (Europe, blushing, exclaimed, What! I had kings?
> And America exlaimed, What! I had slaves?)

And later:

> *L'arbre saint du Progrès, autrefois chimérique,*
> *Croîtra, couvrant l'Europe et couvrant l'Amérique*
>   *Sur le passé détruit...*
> (The sacred tree of Progress, formerly but a dream,
> Shall grow, covering Europe and covering America
>   On the ruins of the past.)

Clearly, Victor Hugo was ready, even in 1854, to admire Bartholdi, as indeed he did thirty years later. But let us not anticipate. As for Bartholdi, we have no proof that he was a reader of Hugo, but we do know that he was a follower of Garibaldi. In 1870–1 he fought as a volunteer in the defense of France, which was a normal thing to do, especially for an Alsatian. But he fought under Garibaldi, whom Gambetta had appointed head of the army of the Vosges, and the corps of irregulars that Bartholdi commanded had taken the name of "Irregulars of La Plata."[6] Such was the spirit of left-wing France at the end of the 1860s. It is only fair to add that the disastrous events of 1870–1 caused the French left wing to change its tune to some extent.

Post-1871 France was naturally caught up in its own pressing problems and in the uncertainty about its future. It knew that some day it would again have to go to war to reconquer Alsace and Lorraine. That is why after 1871 the republican party was undeniably more patriotic and less universalistic, more militaristic and less pacifistic than it had been before 1870.

This change in tone is also noticeable in the propaganda connected with the statue. The literature circulated by the Franco-American Union, which after 1875 invited the French to subscribe to Bartholdi's project, emphasized French patriotism, and hardly mentioned liberty. The statue was even called "a monument honoring the friendship between France and the United States," while nothing was said about a Universal Republic. This "patriotic work" was to strengthen France's ties with the American people by showing that "the homeland of Lafayette has remained faithful to its old traditions." "Strengthening the bonds that unite us to a friendly nation" was to be a task "profoundly national in character."[7] The crusading spirit was well-nigh absorbed by the spirit of diplomacy; this wording suggests that even though France was terribly isolated in the Europe of the period, it had at least one ally in the world, even if this ally was far away.

But let us avoid exaggeration. To be sure, the climate of the 1870s was not that of the 1860s, but the fact that politicians more readily referred to the military alliance of 1778 than to the ideological alliance of 1865 simply reflected a shift in emphasis and nuance rather than a dramatic change. The republicans actually understood this situation perfectly well, and so it was indeed the France of the left that subscribed for the financing of the statue. Published in February 1879, the first list of municipal subscriptions—unfortunately, we have no knowledge of the subsequent ones—contained the names of 120 towns and cities, including all the major ones.[8] At this juncture (things were to change later), the towns were republican, whereas rural France, with a few exceptions, was not. In fact the left was more clearly urban and the right more clearly "rural" than at any other time in France's history.[9]

It would be a mistake to use this incomplete list of "Bartholdian" towns and cities as the basis of a geographical analysis after the manner of André Siegfried, but the following observation can safely be made: of the eighty-six departments of France at that time, fifty-six municipal councils of the capital towns subscribed, including all the most important ones such as Paris, Lyon, Marseilles, Bordeaux, Lille, Toulouse, and Dijon. The thirty others that were missing, or at least late in subscribing, were small-town prefectures typical of the more remote provinces, such as Digne, Gap, Foix, Privas, Aurillac, or Mende, or of regions still marked by a strong royalist party, such as Angers, Vannes, and Laval in the west and Avignon, Nîmes, and Carcassonne in the south.

The left was republican, and there is probably no need to make the point that, in the nineteenth century, left-wing politics, support for the republic, progress, liberty, and sympathetic interest, even friendship for America, all went together. The notion that the right is favorably disposed toward the United States and the left is not (a simplistic assertion itself) was to gain ground only in the first quarter of our own century—but that is a different story.

THE SYMBOLS

Has everything possible already been said about the statue—its conception, its symbolism, and, more precisely, the choice of its characteristics? It would seem so. In fact, for several of these attributes, the problem is not to discover an explanation (most of them are perfectly obvious), but to choose among several, and sometimes mutually exclusive, explanations. The existence of an association between an image and an idea in the mind of the beholder or commentator does not necessarily mean that the association also existed in the author's mind.

For the most obvious characteristic of the statue, its colossal size, explanations abound. One of them is furnished by the history of art: in sculpture there is a tradition of gigantism which, having produced a series of famous exemplars throughout the history of the world, was experiencing a certain revival in the nineteenth century. There is also a subjective explanation, for we know that Bartholdi had a personal taste for the grandiose (he was deeply impressed by Egypt and had sculpted a mountainside to create his Lion of Belfort). A functional explanation is that, to be visible over a stretch of sea, a statue must be gigantic, as Bartholdi knew from having worked on a project for a statue-cum-lighthouse for the Suez Canal.[10] An ideological explanation (which I have previously emphasized, perhaps too exclusively) is that, dating from the beginning of the century, democratic art is grandiose and bourgeois art is petty—that the former is made for the great outdoors and the latter for stuffy apartments. Moreover, gigantism presupposes advanced technical skills, which at that time were in themselves considered a sign of progressive attitudes. Aside from our statue, the works of Gustave Eiffel, especially his Tower, come to mind.[11] These explanations are by no means irreconcilable, of course.

There is no difficulty about the meaning of the broken chains that Liberty tramples underfoot, the tablets she carries (the Law, the Constitution, Rules for Living), or the torch she holds aloft (an old association of worldwide human progress with a light that dissipates the darkness).

Nor is there much difficulty about the choice of a calm posture, of a woman standing upright, with the merest hint of movement indicated by the bending of one leg. A statue seen from a distance, more or less a lighthouse, is easily understood as a sort of tower. In nineteenth-century French political sculpture, the association of calm bearing with the idea of order, and violent movement with the idea of revolution, was understood by everyone.[12] Bartholdi was firmly entrenched in the camp of the government republicans, along with men like Jules Ferry, who were close to the liberals and hostile to the revolutionaries.

Explanations for the meaning of the sun also abound. Purely artistic explanations have been marshaled in the form of previous works of art showing allegorical figures of women crowned by suns.[13] Some explanations are biographical; we are told, for instance, that as a small child, Frédéric-Auguste Bartholdi was fascinated by a sun carved on the mantelpiece in the house of family friends.[14] The sun has also been found in Masonic symbolism (and Bartholdi was a Freemason) and in the French tradition that used it to express the power of the state, from the sun of Louis XIV to the seal of the republic created by Auguste Barre in 1848.[15] The sun has already been mentioned as the symbol of Victor Hugo's dream of bringing the Universal Republic all over the world.

Do we have to choose? The sun means beauty, power, and majesty; in effect it is the natural superlative of the message with which it is associated. As for its symbolic elements, they are the realm par excellence of polysemy, of multitiered explanations and multiple resonances—exciting to the aesthetic mind but slightly irritating to the scholarly mind. Still, the idea of something universal is the most likely. Because the fact that Liberty sheds light is already indicated by the torch, the sun makes the additional point that she brings light *to the entire world*. This interpretation is underscored by the name given to the work and by its intercontinental history.

Some time ago I suggested an additional, negative explanation: putting a solar crown on Liberty's head was also a way of *not* putting on the Phrygian cap, which was, after all, the traditional attribute of liberty. Not everyone was convinced by this observation. The last time I proposed it in print, it was dismissed by the most recent American specialist, Marvin Trachtenberg, who is aware, of course, that the Phrygian cap was sometimes suspect as a mark of radicalism (as it was in 1831 on the head of Delacroix's *Liberté*). His main argument, however, is that in the last third of the nineteenth century the traditional iconological teaching had gone out of style, that art was completely unfettered, and that all symbols had to be reinvented.[16]

Nonetheless, I continue to believe that the Phrygian cap was still a full-blown issue when Bartholdi worked on the statue: Liberty or the revolutionary-minded republic wore the red cap, Liberty or the well-mannered republic rejected it. Without returning to the facts and texts I cited in *Marianne au combat*, I can bring three others to bear: First, there is the much-quoted speech that Laboulaye himself, the real father of the enterprise, gave on 25 April 1876 in which he exclaimed, "It is Liberty, yes, but the American Liberty. It is not that Liberty who, wearing a red bonnet and carrying a pike, marches over a field of dead bodies. . . ."[17]

Second, there is the analysis of the 1879 competition for the monument to the Defense of Paris made by the American art historian Ruth Butler (independent of my work).[18] This competition was won by Barrias who submitted a properly draped female allegorical figure wearing a crown of towers and standing in a calm, resolute, but purely defensive posture. Among the rejected submissions was the *Appel aux Armes* (*Call to Arms*) of the great Rodin, a vehement, screaming woman, breasts bared, fists clenched, and arms stretched in front of her. Barrias's project was better suited to the climate of moderation, caution, and peace of the early days of the republic, Ruth Butler comments. She could have added that Rodin's exalted goddess was wearing a Phrygian cap, which was another reason to dislike her.

Finally, there is a recently discovered series of letters exchanged shortly before 1880 between Paul Bart, republican deputy for Yonne who was also a friend and future minister of Gambetta, and one of his protégés, the young sculptor Cadoux.[19] Cadoux showed his republican zeal by sculpting busts of the republic. When shown the first one, Bart retorted, "I don't like your emblems. Above all, skip the Phrygian cap!" In its early days, the republic was thus clearly and passionately divided between two inspirations and two strategies, one pledged to moderate, cautious, and legalistic progress (opportunism), the other to energy and intransigence (radicalism). The Phrygian cap, whose initial radicalism had just been reinvigorated, as it were, by the Paris Commune, was a litmus test in the contest of these two republican themes. Surely, Bartholdi was well aware of this. He belonged to the camp of the reasonable republic, which at this point had no use for the Phrygian cap. This situation, admittedly both typically French and highly topical, was one more reason to choose the sun.[20]

DISSEMINATION OF THE WORK IN FRANCE

The work quickly became a great success. Its highly unusual character and its gigantic size, which necessitated spectacular construction work over several years, captured the public's imagination. In 1878, the head alone, a monumental work in itself, was exhibited on the showground of the Universal Exhibition on the Champ de Mars in Paris.[21] Later on, the scaffolding used in the construction rose above the nearby houses; a painter produced a quaint picture of this scene, which can be seen in the Carnavalet Museum in Paris.[22] The statue also became known in the provinces: in Reims, for instance, in 1881,[23] on the occasion of a "historical cavalcade," (a parade of decorated floats), the last vehicle, called the "Chariot of Liberty," pulled by a dozen oxen, consisted of a reproduction of the statue perched atop a globe several meters high. Around the float were horseback riders dressed in costumes of all the countries of the world.

But let us return to Paris, where a visit to the construction workshop had become a popular outing. The aged Victor Hugo visited it on 30 November 1884, not long before his death in May 1885. It was one of his last outings—at any rate, it is the last one mentioned in his *Choses Vues (Things Seen)*: "I have been to see Bartholdi's colossal bronze [*sic*, for copper] statue for America. It is beautiful. When I saw the statue I said: The sea, that tempestuous element, beholds the union of two great pacified lands. I was asked to allow those words to be engraved on the pedestal."[24]

It would hardly have done for the poet not to make an epic declaration in the antithetical form that was second nature to him. Because the ocean was going to be crossed, the contrast between the tumult of the sea and the stability of the continents naturally came to his mind. Note, however, that his comment tallies with the meaning that republicans on both sides of the Atlantic attributed to the statue and to liberty. Both France after the Commune and after the Moral Order and the United States after the Civil War claimed to have found calm in a regime that would endure because it was popular, democratic, and bound by law. After the chaos of the long struggle to establish it, the reign of liberty was perceived as a "pacification." The utterance of the poet, the bearing of the statue, and its sponsorship by an optimistic center-left all convey the same meaning.

As I have suggested elsewhere,[25] there was a considerable demand for statues in public places at the time, and many art foundries were in the business of supplying that demand. Thus the Paris firm of Thiébaut[26] acquired the license to market the model of the Statue of Liberty, reduced to reasonable dimensions. Although I have not yet been able to make a systematic study of this firm's archives, I do know about many of its activities from my fieldwork to establish the number of civic monuments that exist or have existed in France. Thus I know of ten copies of Liberty Enlightening the World.[27] One that was in Hanoi has disappeared without a trace, but the nine others are still to be found in France. Perhaps there are others, but this small selection will be sufficient to show a rather interesting diversity in the ways in which these statues were used.

In Paris there are two, both well known. In addition to the one in Luxembourg Gardens, there is the statue on the Grenelle Bridge. The latter was given by a group of Americans of French origin as a gesture of thanks for France's gigantic gift of 1886. It was unveiled in 1889 by President Sadi Carnot and is graced by an inscription on the theme of Franco-American friendship.[28]

In Bordeaux, the municipality wanted a Liberty statue to replace an old Liberty Tree planted in 1848 on the Place Picard. The statue has been standing since 1889,[29] a solid and lasting symbol that substitutes for an older, more fragile, and less explicit one. There are other examples of such substitution. The Liberty statue in Bordeaux disappeared during the German Occupation. Two others are thought to have been erected in 1889 for no other purpose than to celebrate the centennial of the French Revolution;[30] one still stands in Poitiers, but the other, erected in Lunel (Hérault), was destroyed during the Occupation.

In Roybon (Isère) the Liberty statue decorates a monument honoring the memory of Saint-Romme, a native of the region and an early supporter of the republic.[31] Were it not for the large size of the statue and the modest dimensions of Saint-Romme's portrait in a medallion, this Liberty could qualify as a secondary allegory in a monument commemorating a great man, a form in which it was frequently used. The choice of Bartholdi's Liberty rather than any other image of the cause served by Saint-Romme can probably be accounted for by personal contacts between the sculptor and the republican from Dauphiné.[32]

Saint-Cyr-sur-Mer (Var) is an even more curious case, for there the Liberty statue was erected over a water fountain, the base of which is inscribed, "In commemoration of the collection and distribution of water in the commune of Saint-Cyr-sur-Mer under the administration of A. Berton, Mayor. Donated by M. A. Ducros."[33] Celebrating the advent of public water supply takes us quite some way from the hymn dedicated by Victor Hugo's fatherland to Lincoln's, but we know of a hundred monuments in the French provinces that explicitly associate the display of a political image with the construction of useful municipal facilities. After all, hygiene, too, is part of that great category called Progress! Like the statue in Roybon, the statue in Saint-Cyr-sur-Mer is still standing.

Finally, two other statues were apparently put up by private individuals. At Izon (Gironde) the Liberty statue that was erected in 1926 and disappeared during the Occupation resulted (or so I have been told) from the initiative of a local resident on his return from the United States.[34] In Barentin (Seine Maritime), a Liberty statue is one item among dozens of others in the motley collection of statues with which a former mayor, the prominent politician André Martin, enhanced the streets, squares, and crossroads of this town, which thus became a curious shrine to the art of sculpture.[35]

The uses to which the liberty statues were put in French provinces are not particularly different from those of other types of statues. Hundreds of allegorical figures were substituted for old Liberty Trees under the Third Republic; statues of goddesses were erected to celebrate the centennial of 1789, and statues of the republic—Marianne— were associated with monuments to great men or used to decorate and add a political note to a water fountain. The fact that Bartholdi's work sometimes fulfilled these same functions clearly shows that the French considered it part of the large and diverse collection of republican figures available to them. It was more striking and more costly, perhaps, than the ordinary run of bronze-covered cast-iron pieces produced by the factories in the Champagne country,[36] yet it belonged to the same category.

In all fairness, it must be said that if France knew Bartholdi's great lady, it was not so much from the few reproductions set up in public squares as from the image of the prototype in New York, which was disseminated in a thousand different ways. But this image was of great importance in France's own history, as well as in the history of the United States and the rest of the world.

Bartholdi's compelling achievement firmly implanted in French culture his association of the idea of liberty with the figure of a tall woman, crowned with the sun and holding aloft a torch.[37] By the same token it also separated the idea of liberty from the image of the Phrygian cap—or at any rate completed this dissociation. As a result, the latter became available for specifically French uses, whether it be the red cap as an evocation of the sansculottes or the cap that became obligatory and commonplace for plaster busts in town halls or on coins. Bartholdi's Statue of Liberty, then, has had a twofold effect: in universal iconology his image of liberty became a firmly rooted tradition, while in French political iconology it ushered in a new era.

NOTES

1. Jacques Betz, *Bartholdi* (Paris: Editions de Minuit, 1954); Willadene Price, *Bartholdi and the Statue of Liberty* (New York: 1959); Marvin Trachtenberg, *The Statue of Liberty* (London: Penguin Books, 1976).
2. On French liberalism in the nineteenth century, see A. Jardin *Histoire du libéralisme politique* (Paris: Hachette, 1985); L. Girard, *Les libéraux français* (Paris: Aubier-Montaigne, 1985); not to forget the older yet rich works by P. Guiral, *Prévost-Paradol, pensée et action d'un libéral sous le Second Empire* (Paris, PUF, 1955); and G. Weill, *Histoire du parti républicain en France, 1814–1870* (Paris, 1928; reprint Geneva: Slatkine, 1980).
3. *Giuseppe Garibaldi e il suo mito: atti del LI Congresso di storia del Risorgimento italiano, Genova, 10–13 novembre 1982* (Rome: Istituto per la storia del Risorgimento italiano, 1984). I contributed the article on Garibaldi's myth in France (pp. 259–304) to this volume.
4. Taxile Delore, *Histoire du Second Empire* (Paris: Germer-Baillere, n.d.), IV, 85.
5. *Châtiments* (Paris, 1854). "Lux," is the last poem in Book VII of the volume and serves as a conclusion.
6. A special point was made of this detail during the symposium *La Révolution américaine et l'Europe* (Paris: Editions du Centre National de la Recherche Scientifique, 1979), 179.
7. The letter addressed to all the mayors of France to solicit subscriptions under the letterhead of the Franco-American Union and signed by Laboulaye, Rochambeau, and Henri Martin, is dated 14 February 1879. I quote from the file kept in the Municipal Archives of Vichy.
8. The list is appended to the document cited in note 7.
9. See, most recently, Maurice Agulhon, "Les citadins et la politique," chapter 4 of G. Duby, ed., *Histoire de la France urbaine*, vol. 4 (Paris: Seuil, 1983).
10. See Maurice Agulhon, *Marianne au combat: l'imagerie et la symbolique républicane de 1789 à 1880* (Paris: Flammarion, 1979), chapter 3; see also Agulhon, "La Statue de la Liberté," delivered at the symposium *La Révolution américaine et l'Europe* (see note 6), 169–78.
11. For these findings, see the thoroughly documented studies of Betz, *Bartholdi*, and Trachtenberg, *The Statue of Liberty*.
12. *Marianne au combat*, passim.
13. Among others, Canova's statue of *Faith* on the tomb of Clement VII, and *La Patrie* by David d'Angers over the entrance of the Panthéon, cited by Trachtenberg. In the church of Santa Croce in Florence, I saw a *Liberty* crowned with the sun on the tomb of Niccolini; this statue must be contemporary with Bartholdi's.
14. Price, *Bartholdi and the Statue of Liberty*, 12–13; Trachtenberg, *The Statue of Liberty*, 75.
15. See note 6.
16. Trachtenberg, *The Statue of Liberty*, 75.
17. Speech delivered at the Paris Opera, 25 April 1876, reproduced in *L'Evénement* of 1 May 1876. (From the documentation assembled under the direction of A. Desvallées for the C.N.A.M Exhibition in Paris.)
18. Ruth Butler, "Rodin and the Paris Salon," *Rodin Rediscovered* (Washington, D.C.: National Gallery of Art, 1981).
19. For details and texts, see the catalogue of the exhibition "Edme-Marie Cadoux," prepared by M. C. Garderet, Auxerre, Musée Leblanc-Duvernay, 1983.
20. This dislike was soon to cease, for reasons I cannot develop here. They will be treated, however, in my forthcoming *Marianne au pouvoir, l'imagerie et la symbolique républicaine depuis 1880*.
21. Thomas von Joest, "L'Exposition universelle de 1878," *Monuments historiques*, special issue, "La République," Paris, 1986, no. 144.
22. The painting is by V. Dargaud, 1883.

23. *Ville de Reims. Cavalcade de Bienfaisance. Reims à travers les Ages. Programme illustré* (Reims: Justinet, 1881).

24. *Choses Vues*, Hubert Juin, ed. (Paris: Gallimard, 1882), IV, 448.

25. "Esquisse pour une archéologie de la République: l'allégorie civique féminine," *Annales, ESC* (January–February 1973). I shall return to the question at greater length in *Marianne au pouvoir*.

26. Information supplied by Anne Pingeot, curator of sculptures, Musée d'Orsay, Paris.

27. This is a slightly more complete list than that of Betz (*Bartholdi*), who did not know about Roybon, Izon, and Barentin.

28. Betz, *Bartholdi*, 219–20; F. Bournon, *La Voie publique et son décor* (Paris: H. Laurens, 1909), 181. At present the statue is being restored.

29. Betz, *Bartholdi*, 213.

30. The statue in Poitiers is still in place, but the inscriptions have been changed. (Information supplied by Prof. J. Valette of the University of Poitiers.) The statue in Lunel was tracked through the inventory, made during the Occupation, of objects slated to be melted down. These files are in the Archives Nationales. The statue is also known from old postcards.

31. I have seen the statue at Roybon, which was tracked down at the Archives Nationales. Henry Saint-Romme (1797–1862) who was a representative of the people from 1848 to 1851, was proscribed on 2 December of that year.

32. I owe this information to D. Poulot, Maître de Conférences at the University of Grenoble.

33. Personal observation.

34. Information about this statue was found in the National Archives by Mlle. Chardon of Bordeaux, at that time a history student.

35. Personal observation.

36. Tussy at Vaucouleurs (Meuse) and Darenne at Sommeville (Haute Marne) were the most important of these factories.

37. This was the principal conclusion I drew from an examination of commercial and cinema advertising in my 1978 paper (cited above, note 6).

7

The Meaning of Liberty in the Age of Emancipation

Eric Foner

It has now been almost two decades since Edmund S. Morgan, in a brilliant presidential address before the Organization of American Historians,[1] drew attention to what he called "the central paradox of American history"—the simultaneous rise of liberty and slavery in colonial and Revolutionary America. There was, of course, nothing new in observing that the Founding Fathers included some of the largest slaveholders in British America. "How is it," Dr. Johnson had asked at the time, "that we hear the loudest yelps for liberty from the drivers of negroes?" Thomas Jefferson himself, as is well known, owned more than one hundred slaves at the time he penned his immortal lines affirming the inalienable right to liberty; and everything he cherished in his own manner of life, from lavish entertainments to the leisure that made possible pursuit of the arts and sciences, ultimately rested on slave labor.

The dilemma of Jefferson and his generation has often been noted: they were aware that slavery in some sense contradicted the professed ideals of their Revolution, but they were in the grip of an intellectual and political paralysis that prevented them (in the South) from taking effective action against the institution. Where Morgan truly broke new ground was in suggesting that far from being contradictory, slavery and freedom were fundamentally interdependent in Jefferson's America. For black slavery was intimately related to the very meaning of liberty for the men who made the American Revolution.

To advance this arresting thesis, Morgan drew on the work of J. G. A. Pocock and other historians who in the past two decades have completely reshaped our understanding of the republican ideology of the American Revolution and given us a deeper understanding of the meaning of liberty to the nation's founders. Previous historians, most notably perhaps Louis Hartz, had viewed the Revolutionary generation as classic Lockean liberals who understood by liberty Americans' freedom to pursue their self-interest without external constraints. It is now clear that the Founders' conception of polity and society owed as much to a heritage of civic humanism as to competitive individualism. Republican government, the leaders of the American Revolution believed, could rest only on a citizenry that enjoyed personal autonomy and thus was able to put aside self-interest in favor of the public good.

The social bedrock of such autonomy was ownership of productive property, which freed citizens from the economic coercions either of an overbearing employer or of the impersonal marketplace. To the revolutionary generation, the significance of property was as much political and social as economic: liberty depended, in their view, on the widest possible diffusion of productive property throughout the community of citizens. By the same token, certain "dependent" social classes were deemed incapable of exercising the independent judgment that marked the public-spirited citizen. Europe, in the republican view, was replete with dependent social types: fawning courtiers, degenerate aristocrats, privileged monopolists. Most important, there were the poor—the landless lower class of the countryside and the emerging proletariat of the cities. The existence of such classes rendered republican government impossible in the Old World, and the founders seriously debated whether republicanism in the New World could survive the growth of large cities and a permanent wage-earning class.

Thus, according to Morgan, plantation slavery, by defining the body politic so as to exclude irrevocably the black lower class, "solved" the social dilemma that threatened to undermine republican government. The paradox of slavery and liberty is therefore no paradox at all: slavery for the black poor (nearly half the population in Jefferson's Virginia) enabled the white population to enjoy republican liberty. Such an analysis helps explain why, when Jefferson did contemplate the end of slavery in Virginia, he generally coupled abolition with the colonization of the emancipated blacks in Africa. Like slavery itself, colonization would eliminate the problem of the dependent lower class: what Jefferson could not envisage was a republican society's somehow incorporating a large class of landless poor into its citizenry. Indeed, the argument may be carried even further. For Madison, who also agonized over the republican future, the surest guarantee of the American experiment was territorial expansion. So long as virgin land existed to the west, the American dream of a society of free and independent citizens made equal by the bounty of nature could endure. Not only, therefore, did republican liberty rest on expropriating the labor of a subordinate class of blacks, but it also required taking possession of the lands of the original inhabitants of the continent.

Morgan's argument is so ingenious that it may seem churlish to raise one or two objections to it. First, while making sense of the paradox of Jefferson, it can hardly explain the rise of republicanism in the northern colonies, where slavery was a minor institution and a free, propertyless lower class did exist, challenging the image of an independent, propertied citizenry. Second, the argument assumes that the republican definition of liberty was embraced by the entire Revolutionary generation. But, as Joyce Appleby has recently argued,[2] although liberalism may not have been the *only* American ideology, as Hartz insisted, it can hardly be expelled from our account altogether. Alongside the republican definition of liberty as active citizenship in pursuit of the public good arose a more recognizably liberal conception of free persons seeking their own self-interest, unrestrained by outside authority. (Like the republican definition, the liberal understanding of liberty was not necessarily incompatible with slavery; after all, if free persons possessed one undisputed right, it was the ability to acquire private property without interference from government or neighbors.)

Thus the American Revolution gave birth to two distinct but overlapping conceptions of liberty. The liberal and classical republican definitions coexisted in an uneasy harmony in the minds of the Revolutionary generation. During the nineteenth century, they would part ways, and the liberal, individualist view would eventually come to dominate American political culture. The process was long and complex, and its precise chronology has not yet been explored by historians. It does seem clear, however, that, as the older republican definition of liberty was eclipsed, it survived as what the eminent Italian historian Franco Venturi calls a "protest ideal." Increasingly out of date as a description of American social reality, classical republicanism remained, for critics of the emerging order, a powerful vehicle for articulating their dissent. And from evolving republican and liberal definitions of the meaning of liberty would emerge new ways of thinking about the paradoxical place of slavery in American life.

The expansion of capitalism in the nineteenth-century United States posed a profound challenge to a traditional republican ideology that viewed economic autonomy as the essential guarantee of liberty. The rise of a permanent wage-earning class forced large numbers of Americans to reconsider their definition of liberty in a republic. As Karl Marx emphasized, under capitalism the free laborer is "free" in a paradoxical double sense. He is not bound as serf or slave and thus enjoys personal liberty, but he is also "free" in that he enjoys no claims to the means of production. Because he does not own productive property, he must sell his labor in the marketplace. His liberty is thus fundamentally different from that of the independent artisan and small farmer, whose autonomy rests on control of productive property.

Classical republicans in the tradition of Jefferson did not view wage earners as being truly free. Dependent on another for their livelihood, they could not exercise the independent judgment essential for republican citizenship. In the pre–Civil War years, southern defenders of slavery like George Fitzhugh and John C. Calhoun drew on the republican heritage to insist that the liberty of the northern wage earner amounted to little more than the right either to be exploited or to starve. The slave, cared for in old age and in ill health and shielded from the exploitation of the competitive marketplace enjoyed, according to them, more genuine liberty than the "wage slave" of the North.

Much the same type of argument, although motivated by very different concerns, was voiced by a different set of critics of emerging capitalism: the northern labor movement in the 1830s and 1840s, which likewise denied that wage earners enjoyed liberty in the sense guaranteed, they believed, by the American Revolution. Working for wages itself was widely perceived as a form of "slavery," an affront to the ideal of the republican citizen enjoying personal and political autonomy. As Orestes Brownson explained in his influential essay on the "laboring classes" in a republic, "there must be no class of our fellow men doomed to toil through life as mere workmen at wages."[3]

In one of those strange twists of fate that seem to characterize so much of nineteenth-century America, it was the northern critics of chattel slavery who undertook to defend the idea that northern wage earners did indeed enjoy authentic liberty. The abolitionists' motivation is not difficult to discover. To them, the cry of "wage slavery," whether emanating from slaveholders in the South or factory workers in the North, was a grotesque equation of two entirely different systems of labor, which only deflected attention from the singular evil of chattel slavery. Abolitionists did not deny that northern workers stood in need of some improvement in their conditions of life; they refused to acknowledge, however, that the situations of the free laborer and the slave were in any way comparable. Thus, while the labor movement articulated a definition of liberty harking back to the republican ideals of the Revolution, abolitionists embraced the emerging liberal creed that defined liberty not as independence, but as self-ownership: that is, simply not being a slave.

To the labor movement, the liberty to seek employment at wages was a mark of degradation; to abolitionists, it exemplified the difference between a society based on free labor and one that rested on slavery.

As abolitionists understood, the condition of the free laborer appeared very different from the vantage point of the slave emerging into freedom than from the vantage point of the former artisan descending into the wage labor force.

Thus the ideological conflict between two societies based on antagonistic labor systems helped define the meaning of liberty in antebellum America. Furthermore, the contrasting definitions of liberty shaped by the struggle over slavery profoundly affected how Americans, northerners and southerners alike, responded to the social revolution wrought by emancipation. For abolition not only eliminated an institution increasingly at odds with the moral sensibility of the age, but raised intractable questions about the system of economic and social relations that should replace slavery. Above all, answers to these questions rested on how contemporaries, black and white alike, understood the meaning of liberty. "What is freedom?" Congressman James A. Garfield asked. "Is it the base privilege of not being chained . . . ? If this is all, then freedom is a bitter mockery, a cruel delusion."[4] Did liberty mean simply the absence of slavery, or did it imply other rights for the emancipated blacks, and if so, which ones: civil equality, the suffrage, property ownership? The abolition of slavery reopened the question that had obsessed and in some sense paralyzed Jefferson: Could a republican government coexist with a large class of landless laborers? Among other things, therefore, the Reconstruction period witnessed a struggle over the definition of liberty in the aftermath of emancipation.

In the postemancipation South, as in every other Western Hemisphere society that experienced the end of slavery in the nineteenth century, conflicts over the definition of liberty reflected an even more pervasive underlying question: How should the labor system be organized now that slavery had been destroyed? Southern whites, especially those who assumed that the survival of the plantation system was essential to maintaining economic stability and white supremacy, defined black liberty in the narrowest conceivable manner. They rejected the idea that the end of slavery implied civil or political equality for the former slaves, or even those opportunities to acquire property and to advance in the marketplace that northerners took for granted as indispensable to any free society. They insisted that blacks remain as a dependent plantation labor force, subject to strict discipline from their employers, in a work situation not all that different from slavery. As the northern journalist Sidney Andrews discovered during a tour of the Southeast late in 1865,

> The whites seem wholly unable to comprehend that freedom for the negro means the same thing as freedom for them. They

readily enough admit that the Government has made him free, but appear to believe that they still have the right to exercise over him the old control. . . . I did not anywhere find a man who could see that laws should be applicable to all persons alike. . . . They acknowledge the overthrow of the special servitude of man to man, but seek to establish the general servitude of man to the commonwealth.[5]

Certainly, few southern whites believed that emancipation implied the incorporation of blacks as citizens or their transformation into property owners. As Confederate General Robert V. Richardson, treasurer of the American Cotton Planters' Association put it in 1866, "The emancipated slaves own nothing, because nothing but freedom has been given to them."[6]

Here was a conception of liberty as limited as can be imagined. The emancipated slave, a southern newspaper echoed, needed to be taught that "he is *free*, but free only to labor."[7] To justify such a truncated definition, planters drew on a variety of arguments. Some surveyed the experience of previous emancipations in the Western Hemisphere, concluding that wherever former slaves had been able to acquire land, plantation agriculture had all but collapsed because of a persistent labor shortage. Others in effect resurrected the Jeffersonian solution to the problem of liberty and slavery by excluding the now-free black lower class from access to citizenship and property. As one Mississippi planter observed, "Our negroes will have to learn that freedom and independence are different things. A man may be free and yet not independent."[8] To enforce this understanding of the meaning of black liberty, southern state governments during Presidential Reconstruction enacted the notorious Black Codes, denying blacks political rights and equality before the law, and attempting to circumscribe their economic liberty so that plantation agriculture could survive the end of slavery.

Northern Republicans, imbued with a free-labor ideology sanctified by their triumph in the Civil War, obviously could not accept a conception of black liberty that seemed to make a mockery of the struggle for emancipation. Of course, the Republican party was itself divided as to exactly how liberty should be defined. But in 1865 and 1866, most Republicans insisted that liberty meant not simply the end of slavery but something more. In the British Empire, as one historian has noted, "the question, 'does a black man equal a white man?' had little meaning in an age when few thought all white men deserved equality."[9] In the United States, however, where equality before the law was the foundation of the political culture, emancipation led almost inexorably to demands for civil and political rights for the former slaves. As one Republican wrote in 1865, "Negro suffrage is . . . the logical sequence of negro emancipation."[10] By 1866 a consensus had emerged within the Republican party that civil equality was an essential attribute of liberty, and, in the following year, black men were accorded political rights equal to those of whites. The Fourteenth Amendment enshrined the notion of civil equality in the Constitution, overseen by a newly powerful national state. Moreover, many Republicans believed that the Thirteenth Amendment, which decreed nationwide abolition, also empowered Congress to overturn such "badges of slavery" as state legislation discriminating among citizens on the basis of race.

The Republican ideology, which merged elements of the republican and liberal meanings of liberty, thus proved a potent weapon for breaking down the civil and political barriers to citizenship for the freedmen. Republicans, like Lincoln, had insisted before the Civil War that what set the society of the North apart from that of the South was precisely the opportunity it offered the laborer to ascend the social ladder and to achieve economic autonomy. Blacks, most Republicans believed, ought to enjoy the opportunity to advance themselves through self-discipline and hard work. But when it came to defining the economic underpinnings of liberty in the postbellum South, Republicans found themselves divided and confused. All Republicans believed that the Civil War had demonstrated once and for all the superiority of the northern system of labor; all believed that emancipation implied the construction of a "free labor society" in the former slave states, modeled on that of the North. But precisely what all this implied for the economic status of the former slaves, Republicans found almost impossible to define.

The confusion that afflicted virtually all northern policymakers during Reconstruction can be glimpsed in the career of General O. O. Howard, commissioner of the Freedman's Bureau, a man who was deeply committed to guaranteeing the liberty of the former slaves but one whose policies all too often thwarted, rather than advanced, the blacks' aspirations. According to any number of writers in the past decade, the Freedman's Bureau was a racist and paternalist institution that, intentionally or unwittingly, operated in the interests of the planter class. Such an interpretation, however, fails to take account of a more complex dynamic illustrated by Howard's career: the inability of the free-labor ideology, even at its moment of triumph, to construct a definition of liberty fully relevant in the postemancipation South. The essential contradiction between two elements of the free-labor outlook—the one harking back to a definition of liberty based on property ownership, the other stressing individual initiative and advancement through competition in the marketplace—are fully revealed in Howard's own account of his career.

Howard's problem was that he could never decide whether his role was to champion the rights of the freedmen or to stand as an impartial intermediary between the irreconcilable ambitions of former master and former slave. Attempting to do both at once, he succeeded only in disappointing all parties. Freedmen besieged Howard with requests for land, while the planters demanded that the emancipated blacks be forced to labor on the plantations. The Freedman's Bureau refused to sanction the insistence by the planters that they be allowed to exercise authority over the freedmen similar to that exercised under slavery. The republican in Howard initially sympathized with the freedmen's desire to acquire land of their own. Once it became apparent that President Andrew Johnson would not approve any arrangement under which blacks acquired homesteads from the property of their former owners, however, the only alternative to labor on the plantations appeared, in Howard's eyes, to be government support of the former slaves. Such charity, he believed, would stifle the very initiative and self-reliance essential for the truly independent citizenship. Thus, Howard concluded, it was essential for the bureau to encourage and, if necessary, compel able-bodied blacks to sign labor contracts. He was able to convince himself that "wholesome compulsion" would eventually result in "larger independence."[11]

Thus, Howard found himself in the contradictory position of decreeing that labor contracts be "free, *bona fide* acts" voluntarily agreed to by both black and white, while cutting off all other alternatives to plantation wage labor on the part of the freedmen. Republican policymakers like Howard were perfectly willing to exert the power of the federal government in an attempt to guarantee the marketplace liberties of blacks—the rights to choose a livelihood, acquire property, sign contracts, and enjoy access to the courts, all on the same formal terms as whites. But further than this—beyond equality, in David Montgomery's phrase—they were unwilling to go.

There were, however, those in Reconstruction America who continued to adhere to the traditional republican conviction that without ownership of productive property, personal autonomy—the essence of republican citizenship—was impossible. Indeed, in the debates over Reconstruction, the political and social paradigm of classical republicanism reflowered, perhaps for the last time in American history. For those who insisted that without a redistribution of landed property in the South emancipation would remain incomplete, eighteenth-century republicanism remained a powerful tool of social analysis. And in the constitutional clause guaranteeing to each state a republican form of government, Radical Republicans like Charles Sumner and Thaddeus Stevens discovered a reservoir of federal authority to impose liberty in the broadest sense on a society emerging from slavery.

Article IV, section 4, of the Constitution ("The United States shall guarantee to every State in this Union a Republican form of Government"), as historian William Wiecek has written, is a clause "enigmatic, almost Delphic in its quality."[12] What is a republican form of government and how shall the United States guarantee it? On such questions, the Constitution remains silent. "The time has come," Sumner announced in 1865, "to fix a meaning on these words."[13]

For Sumner, whose entire career was devoted to the extirpation of caste distinctions from American life, the guarantee clause conferred on Congress the authority not simply to evaluate state constitutions, but also to eliminate all proscriptions and discriminations based on race as incompatible with equal republican citizenship. As Sumner informed the Senate in 1867, the guarantee clause

> is like a sleeping giant in the Constitution, never until this recent war awakened, but now it comes forward with a giant's power. There is no clause in the Constitution like it. There is no clause which gives to Congress such supreme power over the states.[14]

But what of the social underpinnings of republican liberty? No one, to my knowledge, actually argued during Reconstruction that the guarantee clause (as opposed to the rules of war or the government's right to impose penalties for treason) empowered Congress to confiscate the land of the planter class and distribute it among the former slaves. But those relatively few Radicals who did propose a sweeping program of land redistribution in the South fell back upon the traditional republican ideal of liberty to justify their demand.

The idea of land distribution, of course, is most closely associated with Thaddeus Stevens, the cantankerous congressman from Pennsylvania. Stevens' speeches revealed that the republican definition of liberty still retained considerable vitality in the Civil War era. "Nothing," he informed the House of Representatives,

> is so likely to make a man a good citizen as to make him a freeholder. . . . No people will ever be republican in spirit and practice where a few own immense manors and the masses are landless. Small independent landholders are the support and guardians of republican liberty.[15]

The same outlook was echoed by other leading Radicals of the period, including George W. Julian, the veteran antislavery land reformer from Indiana, and William D. Kelley of Pennsylvania. As Kelley put it, "A landed aristocracy and a landless class are alike dangerous in a republic." Kelley, indeed, went even further. One of the few Republican leaders who enjoyed close ties to the northern labor movement, Kelley told the House that "the system of labor for wages . . . is as inconsistent with an ideal republic as slavery."[16]

Most Republicans, by the time of Reconstruction, do not seem to have believed that wage labor and republican liberty were incompatible, so long as the unfettered operations of the marketplace afforded the laborer the opportunity to advance to eventual economic independence. Thus the pleas by Stevens, Julian, Kelley, and a few others that Congress redistribute land in the South fell on deaf ears. In the end, the demise of slavery did not produce that economic autonomy that republicans ranging from Jefferson to Thaddeus Stevens deemed essential to genuine liberty.

There was, of course, one further protagonist in the story whose voice we have not heard thus far: the freedmen. Not surprisingly, they did not share General Richardson's belief, quoted earlier, that they deserved "nothing but freedom." As the black orator and politician John Langston stated in 1865, "The colored man is not content when given simple emancipation. . . . He demands much more than that; he demands absolute legal equality, he demands the free and untrammeled use of the ballot."[17] Equally insistently, blacks affirmed that with liberty should come the personal and economic autonomy signified by ownership of land. As one group of freedmen told A. Warren Kelsey, an emissary of northern cotton manufacturers in 1865, "What's the use to give us our freedom if we can't stay where we were raised and own our houses . . . and our little pieces of ground?"[18]

For blacks in the aftermath of slavery, therefore, liberty meant far more than simply release from bondage. In articulating and justifying their conception of liberty, the former slaves drew on a broad range of experiences and ideas, some derived from slavery itself, others typically American. During the Civil War and Reconstruction, black political leaders appropriated the political language of the large culture and forged from it an expression of the aspirations of their community. "The North," as South Carolina's black congressman Richard H. Cain later remarked, "has sent forth these leading ideas, which have spread like lightning over the land, and the Negro was not so dumb and not so obtuse that he could not catch the light and embrace its blessings and enjoy them."[19]

The "leading idea" that blacks found most compelling was precisely the traditional republican definition of liberty. Like northern Radical Republicans, blacks found in the Constitution's guarantee clause a reservoir of federal power over the states. John R. Dennett, the *Nation's* correspondent who toured the South in 1865, encountered a black barber, a delegate to the North Carolina state black convention, who "hoped that Congress would declare that no state had a republican form of government if every free man in it was not equal before the law."[20]

To blacks, republican liberty implied the right to vote, to obtain an education, to exercise their religion freely, to enjoy access to the courts, and to enter all avenues of economic enterprise—all the rights, that is, already enjoyed by whites. As the black lieutenant governor of Louisiana, Oscar J. Dunn, observed,

> It is the boast and glory of the American republic that there is no discrimination among men, no privileges founded upon birth-right. There are no hereditary distinctions. . . . Our country is therefore, one of republican ideas and republican manners.[21]

Continued proscription of blacks would thus undermine republicanism and even, Dunn warned, "open the door for the institution of aristocracy, nobility, and even monarchy."

But above all, republican liberty implied for blacks a right to the land. Black leaders invoked a broad panoply of justifications for this demand—land distribution would be a recognition of the decisive role black troops had played in winning the Civil War itself and a just recompense for centuries of unrequited toil by the slaves. "The property which they hold," declared an Alabama black convention, "was nearly all earned by the sweat of *our* brows."[22] And, like northern Radicals, blacks invoked classic Jeffersonian values, arguing that a society based on a landed aristocracy and a large propertyless lower class could not be considered truly republican. "Small estates are the real element of democracy," said the *New Orleans Tribune*. "Let the land go into the hands of the actual laborers."[23]

In the end, of course, the aspirations of the freedmen were largely thwarted. The land remained in the possession of white planters and merchants. Emancipation, John Langston declared shortly after the end of Reconstruction, had proved to be severely limited, because the freedmen had not been given that "practical independence" so indispensable to real liberty.[24] Many reasons—social, economic, and political—may be advanced for the failure of Reconstruction to move "beyond equality," or, in other words, to return to the broad republican definition of liberty as resting on ownership of property. But I believe that this signal failure of Reconstruction reflected, at least in part, a crisis of the republican tradition itself. Perhaps Reconstruction ought to be seen as the moment when the United States irrevocably turned its back on an older conception of the meaning of liberty and embraced one more in keeping with the realities and constraints of a capitalist economic order. In attempting to come to terms with the emancipation of blacks, white Americans were forced to confront how thoroughly their own society itself had changed.

Let me return once again to A. Warren Kelsey, the young Bostonian dispatched to the South in 1865 to investigate economic and political conditions in the former slave states. From Orangeburg, South Carolina, Kelsey penned a revealing account of how blacks understood the meaning of liberty:

> The sole ambition of the freedman at the present time appears to be to become the owner of a little piece of land, there to erect a humble home, and to dwell in peace and security at his own free will and pleasure. If he wishes, to cultivate the ground in cotton on his own account, to be able to do so without anyone to dictate to him hours or system or labor, if he wishes instead to plant corn or sorghum or sweet potatoes—to be able to do *that* free from any outside control, in one word to be *free*, to control his own time and efforts without anything that can remind him of past sufferings in bondage. This is their idea, their desire and their hope.[25]

Thomas Jefferson would have well understood this desire—to be master of one's own time, free from the coercions of either an arbitrary master or the impersonal marketplace. Here was an ideal of liberty commensurate with Jefferson's vision of a polity resting on the consent of autonomous individuals. But, in post–Civil War America, how many whites enjoyed liberty thus defined? And in a society where most whites no longer enjoyed such sweeping economic autonomy, could blacks reasonably expect the nation to guarantee it for them? The debates unleashed by the end of slavery, in other words, may well have forced Americans finally to appreciate how far they had traveled from the republican definition of liberty.

Emancipation, therefore, settled for all time one American paradox—the simultaneous existence of slavery and liberty—while reopening another: the coexistence of political equality and economic dependence. In the United States alone among the nations that abolished slavery in this hemisphere, equality in legal and political rights was accorded the former slaves within a few short years of emancipation. But by the end of Reconstruction, a large number of northerners were not only willing to abandon the notion of equality for blacks in the South, but were increasingly alarmed by this specter of labor unrest at home. "The days are over," intoned the *New York Times* in 1877,

> in which this country could rejoice in its freedom from the elements of social strife which have long abounded in the old countries. . . . We cannot too soon face the unwelcome fact that we have dangerous social elements to contend with, and that they are rendered all the more dangerous by the peculiarities of our political system.[26]

The *Times* spoke for large numbers of the northern middle class who, faced with the paradox of a permanent wage-earning class in a republican polity, opted for a retreat from both the republican definition of liberty and, in the South and the urban centers of the North, from the very notion that government should rest on the consent of all the governed.

Thus the abolition of slavery did not resolve the debate over the meaning of liberty in American life. Indeed, the historian examining the legacy of emancipation finds it almost impossible to strike a convincing balance between the realms of liberty that opened for blacks and the very real limits of the freedom that followed the Civil War. "If the Negroes have the right to become free," Alexis de Tocqueville had observed in 1843, "the [planters] have the incontestable right not to be ruined by the Negroes' freedom."[27] And here, as in nearly every post-emancipation society, a rigid social and political dichotomy between former master and former slave, an ideology of racism, and a dependent labor force with limited economic opportunities all survived the end of slavery.

The burden of the past, as Marx observed, "weighs like a nightmare on the brains of the living." Former slave societies appear to represent striking confirmations of Marx's dictum. Unless liberty means the simple fact of not being a slave, the abolition of slavery thrust the former slave into a kind of no-man's land, a partial liberty that made a mockery of the American ideal of the independent citizen. In our racial institutions and attitudes and in the social dislocations around us, the unresolved legacy of emancipation remains a part of our world more than a century after the demise of slavery. And the American paradox—the meaning of liberty in a society pervaded by inequality—continues.

NOTES

1. Edmund S. Morgan, "Slavery and Freedom: The American Paradox," *Journal of American History* 59 (June 1972): 5–29.
2. Joyce Appleby, *Capitalism and a New Social Order: The Republican Vision of the 1790's* (New York: New York University Press, 1984).
3. Walter Hugins, ed., *The Reform Impulse* (New York: Harper and Row, 1972), 99–101.
4. *The Works of James Abram Garfield*, edited by Burke A. Hinsdale (Boston: J. R. Osgood and Co., 1882–83), 1:86.
5. Sidney Andrews, "Three Months among the Reconstructionists," *Atlantic Monthly* 17 (February 1866): 244.
6. Mary Wilkin, ed., "Some Papers of the American Cotton Planters' Association, 1865–1866," *Tennessee Historical Quarterly* 8 (March 1949): 49–50.
7. Louisville *Democrat*, quoted in Columbia *Daily Phoenix*, 3 August 1866.
8. Rev. Samuel Agnew Diary, 3 November 1865, Southern Historical Collection, University of North Carolina.
9. Douglas A. Lorimer, *Colour, Class and the Victorians* (Leicester: Leicester University Press, 1978), 15.
10. *The Works of Charles Sumner* (Boston: Lee and Shepard, 1870–73), 9:424–5.
11. [Oliver O. Howard], *Autobiography of Oliver Otis Howard* (New York: Baker and Taylor Company, 1907), 2:212–14, 250, 312–21, 423.
12. William M. Wiecek, *The Guarantee Clause of the U.S. Constitution* (Ithaca: Cornell University Press, 1972), 1–2.
13. Edward L. Pierce, ed., *Memoir and Letters of Charles Sumner* (Boston: Roberts Brothers, 1877–93), 3:258–9.
14. *Congressional Globe*, 40th Congress, 1st Session, 614.
15. Ibid., 205.
16. *Congressional Globe*, 40th Congress, 3d Session, 133–4.
17. John M. Langston, *Freedom and Citizenship* (Washington, D.C.: R. H. Darby, 1883), 99–100, 110.
18. A. Warren Kelsey to Edward Atkinson, 2 September 1865, Edward Atkinson Papers, Massachusetts Historical Society.
19. *Congressional Record*, 43d Congress, 1st Session, 901.
20. John R. Dennett, *The South As It Is: 1865–1866*, edited by Henry M. Christman (New York: Viking Press, 1965), 176.
21. *Proceedings of the Republican Party of Louisiana* (New Orleans: Printed at the New Orleans Tribune office, 1865), 4–5.
22. *Mobile Nationalist*, 16 May 1867.
23. *New Orleans Tribune*, 16 July and 15 September 1865.
24. Langston, *Freedom and Citizenship*, 164.
25. A. Warren Kelsey to Edward Atkinson, 8 September 1865, Atkinson Papers.
26. *New York Times*, 25 July 1877.
27. *Tocqueville and Beaumont on Social Reform*, edited by Seymour Drescher (New York: Harper and Row, 1968), 167.

II

Liberalism and Rival Ideologies

8

The Jacobin and Liberal Traditions

Jean Rivero

An attempt to define the importance of both Jacobin and liberal traditions in the birth of the French republics of 1848 and 1870–5 invites
the question, What do we mean by the terms *Jacobin* and *liberal?* Only
from the analysis of what these terms represent is it possible to evaluate the effects of the Jacobin and liberal legacies on the genesis of the
two republics in the nineteenth century. This search is not easy, and
using the same word—*tradition*—to characterize the two currents in
question does not make the task any easier, because the currents are
quite different.

Every tradition implies the transmission of a set of coherent values
down the generations. Understood thus, there *is* a liberal tradition; at
the outset, a certain idea of man and society, enriched throughout the
nineteenth century by a line of political thinkers who, from Benjamin
Constant to Tocqueville and Laboulaye, qualify it according to their
own genius and their own experience, without altering its basic content. In the same way, is there a Jacobin tradition? At the start, the
"Club breton" which brought together in Versailles a few elected
members of the first Constituent Assembly and which became "Jacobin" when it moved to Paris to the former Dominican convent,
counted no theoretician in its ranks and scarcely had the time to
produce any. Quickly caught up in the whirlwind of events, multiplying all over France the network of popular societies that was to ensure
their power and that, through the constitution, was to guarantee them
total control of power, finally broken on the ninth of Thermidor—it
was not a doctrine that the Jacobins offered to future generations.
Instead, their legacy consisted of a complex and often contradictory
set of practices, texts, and passions from which a variety of men were
to draw only those features deemed suited to particular and transient
circumstances, while ignoring and erasing a great number in the process. The "Jacobin" label was meant to enhance their standing by
attaching them to a sort of republican fundamentalism, so much so
that rather than speaking of a Jacobin tradition one might speak of a

Jacobin myth, an ideal yet changing image, often far removed from the realities of historical Jacobinism.

Let us analyze the components of the Jacobin myth and the liberal tradition in summary fashion before placing them in the context of the genesis of the two republics.

THE JACOBIN MYTH

It is important to emphasize first the diversity of men and tendencies which rose to the surface during the brief existence of the Jacobin Club. At the beginning, in late 1789, the Société des Amis de la Constitution siégeant aux Jacobins was led by Barnave, Lameth, and Duport. These men, considered "advanced" at first, were, at the end of the Constituent Assembly, to be replaced by new, increasingly radical leaders. But in 1791 Saint-Just still used Montesquieu as his authority and defended the monarchical constitution that the Assembly had just set out.

The great turning point came in April 1792 when the Legislative Assembly declared war on Austria. The Jacobin leaders—Robespierre, Saint-Just, Couthon, and Marat, upheld by the Commune of Paris—were to make of this war (and of the fall of the monarchy after August 10, the election of the Convention, and the proclamation of the Republic) the instruments of their gradual rise to power within the Convention. With the ousting of the Girondins in June 1793, this conquest gathered speed. It was the Jacobins who had the 1793 constitution adopted by the Convention; it was they who decided to put off its application until peace had been reestablished and who in the meanwhile assumed the reins of the revolutionary government. It was they who, through Robespierre and the Committee of Public Safety, were to exercise an undivided dictatorship over France until the ninth of Thermidor (July 1794), when their hegemony ended.

From the elements built up during this dramatic period that marks the apogee of Jacobinism, subsequent generations were to draw those features which gave substance to the Jacobin myth. This had a negative side, as a part of the legacy was put into abeyance. It also had a positive side—the glorification of certain component parts of the whole. Finally, for other components, uncertainty remains; have they found a place in the development of the myth or not?

The features most obviously suppressed are associated with what subsequent generations have called the Reign of Terror. It was indeed a totalitarian dictatorship that Robespierre and the Committee of

Public Safety exercised over France, and the analogies with what was to be Marxist-Leninist practice are striking.

As in the Soviet universe, Jacobin liberty was the freedom to think and act according to the truth as defined by those in power. For months on end, the formula "No liberty for the enemies of liberty" was to feed the guillotine. The words of Manon Rolland on mounting the scaffold are well known: "Liberty! How many crimes are committed in thy name!" In such a light, the annihilation of the adversary was the primary condition for the definitive reign of liberty: "Pitilessly crush the exploiters," the Soviet Declaration of 1918 was to say. The Jacobin discourse, for its part, exalted "the holy guillotine" and "its salutary intersection."[1] There is further analogy in the personality cult that grew around Robespierre, "a virtuous Republican, an unshakable column of the Republic," "the Messiah whom the Eternal Being has promised us to reform all things."[2]

The "friends of liberty" were those who were gathered together in the party in power. All over France, the leaders of societies affiliated with the Jacobins blindly followed the directives of the leaders in Paris and placed in their service the weight of their membership. Although the Jacobin Montagnard bloc was never a majority in the Convention, with the help of popular violence, the legislative body came to submit fearfully to the will of those who assumed the management of the state according to the machinery that was to become traditional—that of the single party.

All that could scarcely sustain a myth likely to inspire future generations. But once those bloody liabilities had been eliminated, important assets remained to nourish the myth. The first was a certain relationship between the *patrie* and the republic. It was the Jacobin dictatorship that saw the first victories of the armies of the Revolution over those of the "tyrants" joined in coalition against them. In the collective subconscious what remained was a link, as in the words of the "Marseillaise," between the concepts of "public safety" and "the *patrie* in danger," and the men who assumed the responsibility for saving "the country of liberty." In the words of Clémenceau when he assumed power in the midst of the worst perils faced by France during World War I, Jacobin echoes are to be found. Victor Hugo's glorification of the "soldiers of Year I" and "the great Republic pointing heavenwards" had helped wipe memories of the Reign of Terror from people's minds.

Apart from the war abroad, after ousting the Girondins who challenged the omnipotence of the Commune of Paris, the Jacobins had to cope with provincial uprisings that, from Lyon to the Vendée, and from Normandy to the Midi, mobilized formidable forces against the central power. They triumphed over these as over the foreign invasion, but at the cost of bloody repression and strict centralization. This centralization also remains one of the component parts of the myth. Even today, the epithet "Jacobin" is often attached to the name of those who, while far distant from other aspects of Jacobinism, defend the centralizing tradition it once embodied.

Yet the basic aspects of the myth are to be found elsewhere, in the Constitution of Year I, which, in traditional terminology, remains "the Jacobin constitution." All historians agree on this: for a long time it remained the archetype of republican constitutions. Here, the paradoxes are very obvious. The Jacobin constitution, hastily put together during the weeks following the removal of the Girondins, scarcely departed from the constitution projected by the latter. But the Jacobins' practice of power, as already summarized, was radically opposed to the text that was to govern it. But the text prevailed over historical reality in contributing to the Jacobin myth. Of all the constitutions that succeeded one other in France from 1789 onward, this text was the only one that, although duly passed and promulgated, never was put into effect. But that fact may explain the prestige this constitution has long enjoyed. Experience often reveals the defects and weaknesses of a constitutional text. Unapplied, it remains beyond the reach of attacks on its authority.

The basic features of this constitution should be recalled. Founded on the dogma of the sovereignty of the people and no longer on the abstract nation (as in 1791), it derived the principle of the unity of power. For its authors Rousseau eclipsed Montesquieu. First, the unity of power excluded the duality of the assemblies; a single legislature,[3] elected by primary assemblies in the cantons on the basis of universal male suffrage, stood alone, because the people constituted one whole. Possessing sovereign power to legislate, it also held the power to pass those decrees necessary for their application. But most of all, the legislature kept what remained of the executive in a state of total dependence. The twenty-four members of the Executive Council,[4] collegiate and of sufficient number to avoid the risks that power would fall into the hands of one man, were elected by the legislature and subject to its permanent control in the exercise of their functions, which were, moreover, reduced to the absolute minimum.

Was this, then, the prototype of government by assembly, according to the traditional constitutional patterns, that the Constitution of Year I offered? To so affirm would be to underestimate one essential fact, namely, the great extent to which the representatives of the people remained dependent on the governed. There again Rousseau's authority carried the day. Without going quite so far as a Rousseauistic abolition of the representative assembly, the constitution did give a large place to the direct exercise of power by the people. It reduced the term of office of those elected to one year;[5] it recognized the definitive nature of laws voted by the legislature only if, within a period of forty days, a relatively small number of the primary assemblies, which included all male citizens, had not asked for them to be submitted to a referendum.[6]

All in all, the text follows a strict democratic logic. However, its complete application was to be asked for only by the rioters of Prairial who, after Thermidor, demanded "bread and the Constitution of Year I." At least, as we shall see, a number of its component parts were to haunt the minds of republicans throughout the nineteenth century.

Should we add to this basic element of the myth both a socialist vision of society and a fundamental hostility to all forms of religion? On both points, uncertainty remains. Did Jacobinism embrace a form of socialism? A number of historians have held to this view—some, like Albert Mathiez, to glorify it, others, like the extreme right-wing historian Pierre Gaxotte, to stigmatize "the communist Terror."[7] On the contrary, Daniel Guérin[8] stands within a historiographical tradition that sees the Jacobins as petty bourgeois, doubtless hostile to large fortunes, and concerned with a certain leveling out of means, but deeply attached to personal property.

How can one decide between the two theses, both founded on texts and hard facts? It cannot be denied that among the Jacobins and after them were "distributionists" hostile to all forms of wealth. But the "fanatics" of Jacques Roux were only a minority, and Hébert, who echoed them, perished on the scaffold. As for the "Conspiracy of Equals" by means of which Babeuf tried, during the days of Prairial, to secure the triumph of the rough form of socialism that formed his doctrine, it took place after Thermidor, and thus was not part of the legacy of the Jacobins in power. Nor can we forget the formula of the Declaration of Rights of Year I, giving to property an even more absolute consecration than the Declaration of 1789 had done. "None may be deprived of the slightest portion of his property. . . ."[9] More than a true form of socialism, what perhaps survived of the Jacobin tradition in the economic and social orders was the preference shown, especially by the radicals of the Third Republic, to the "small"—small proprietors, small businessmen—over the "big."

Every bit as ambiguous in the Jacobin myth is the place to be given to the religious problem. One thing appears sure: the idea of total separation between religion and the state is foreign to the Jacobins. If all, or almost all, agreed on the destruction of the Catholic church, they also agreed on the necessity for the state to adopt a clear position on the religious question. It was on account of this position that opposition arose; for some, anti-catholicism extended to a hostility to all religions and to claims that in the name of "reason" the State had to fight against all forms of "superstition." But if Couthon had "Death is an eternal sleep" carved on the entrances to cemeteries, Robespierre set up the worship of the Supreme Being as a state religion and with his own hand burned the statue of atheism. For him virtue, the cornerstone of the republic, was inseparable from faith in God and in the immortality of the soul. Secularism, understood as the refusal of the State to adopt a position in matters religious, thus abandoned to the freedom of individual consciences, was therefore foreign to Jacobinism. At most we can attribute to it the anticlerical tradition that asserted itself in the radicals of the Third Republic.

THE LIBERAL TRADITION

Compared with the ambiguities and vicissitudes of the Jacobin myth, the liberal tradition shows greater coherence. The institutional patterns it offers stem from a basic ideology that also inspires its position in the economic and social orders. The word that sums up the tradition is also the one from which the Jacobins constantly drew their inspiration, but liberty as this tradition understands it has nothing in common with the "despotism of liberty" exalted by Marat. Is it necessary to recall the famous distinction Benjamin Constant drew between "the liberty of the Ancients" and "the liberty of the Moderns"? The liberty of the ancients, the absolute and unconditional reign of the law, the work of the majority, led to the negation of the rights of the individual, free from the moment he was governed by the general will. It was the liberty of Sparta; for the citizen it excluded all autonomy in the running of his private life. The liberty of the moderns was rooted in the tradition of the Declaration of 1789; it recognized that each man had a wide range of choice in his opinions, "even religious," and in their "free communication,"[10] and in his behavior from the time that they "do not trouble others";[11] it extended to the sphere of the economy, reserved for individual initiative and based on property as "inviolable and sacred."[12] It recognized man's control over and responsibility for his acts.

In the liberal tradition, it was this liberty that defined the purpose of the state and the limits of its powers: the state existed to protect and guarantee the exercise of such powers. The limits of its powers were to be found in the reduction to a minimum of its interventions in the life of society and in the guarantees it offered its citizens against arbitrary rule, inherent in the control of sovereign power. The teachings of Montesquieu were at the basis of the liberal constitution: "Any man holding power is in a position to abuse it." Weighted toward the moderns' concept of respect for liberty, liberalism did not, however, totally reject the liberty of the ancients who founded the democratic principle. The two intersect; individual liberty would be in peril if the laws that man is held to obey proceeded from a will totally foreign to his own. But even when founded on the suffrage of the people and the goal of the protection of liberties, power must be organized in such a way that it does not move away from this goal.

The result was that for the liberals, the form of government—monarchy or republic—mattered less than the actual practice. To the Jacobin unity of power, liberalism, faithful to Montesquieu, opposed the principle of separation. When all was said and done, it mattered little whether a hereditary monarch or an elected assembly headed the state; if either were omnipotent, its hegemony would be equally weighty. The main thing was that the legislative function and the executive function remain independent, balanced organs, and that the judiciary maintain total autonomy with regard to both these functions.

The liberal doctrine went even further in its concern to provide brakes and counterweights to the hegemonic temptation lying in the way of all those holding power. To parry the risk of a return to government by assembly, it opted for the division of the legislature into two distinct chambers. To combat the potential hypertrophy of executive power, it advocated that the latter be divided between a head of state with limited powers and a government responsible for the conduct of affairs.

However, the application of these principles common to all liberals left enough room for important nuances. On the social level, the Catholic liberalism of Lacordaire and Montalembert gave to the growing pauperization of the working proletariat, revealed by the famous report by Doctor Villermé,[13] a place unknown to the liberalism of the Orleanist bourgeoisie. The latter view, epitomized by Guizot, was more concerned with economic liberalism—at least when it went in the direction of its own interests—than with the imperatives of political liberalism. As far as institutions were concerned, two models divided the liberals: the British model, that is, the British government, and the American presidential model. The first rested on the experience of the two monarchies that had succeeded the First Empire. The first had seen the British model born in France, and the monarchy of Louis Philippe had confirmed it after 1830. The presidential model benefited from the prestige of American democracy, which memories of the Revolutionary War and the works of Tocqueville and, later, of Laboulaye kept intact in many people's minds.

Thus, on the eve of the Revolution of 1848, neither liberalism nor what survived of the Jacobin legacy imposed a definite form on the practice of power. Moreover, other currents of thought were emerging in public opinion. The progressive industrialization of the economy had engendered a proletariat and a socialism still seeking the ideological coherence that Marx was to give it. Memories of Napoleonic glories—exalted by the romantics, propagated by the songs of Béranger, and vivified by the return of the emperor's ashes—nourished in some people the theory of a Caesarean democracy based on plebiscite. On the morrow of the February Days (1848), all these currents and all the forces they brought together were to find themselves present again in the definition of the new régime.

THE BIRTH OF THE SECOND REPUBLIC

Like that of 1830, the February 1848 Revolution was the work of the people of Paris, laborers and artisans largely worked up by confused socialist ideologies that were born as much of the misery of the proletarian condition in the early days of industrialization as of the still uncertain theoretical reflections of Fourier, Proudhon, Cabet, Buchez, Louis Blanc or Blanqui. Jacobins? Reference to the Jacobin dictatorship was diluted into a global vision of the Revolution, making no distinction between 1789 and 1793 and encompassing the whole in the magic words *Liberty* and *Republic*. Romanticism had passed that way, substituting verbal mysticism for historical accuracy. Indeed, the republic proclaimed on 25 February 1848, by a provisional government whose figurehead was Lamartine, the apologist of the Girondins and hardly suspected of Jacobinism, had not much to do with the Republic of 1793. Not only a spiritualistic republic but also a Christian one, whose "Trees of Liberty" were blessed by the clergy, it won almost unanimous support immediately. Even those middle-class businessmen who had prospered under Louis Philippe rallied to its cause. The tide of "republicans of tomorrow" (as the expression went at the time) joined as one the handful of "republicans of yesterday"; the stress laid on Fraternity excluded all reference to the Reign of Terror.

The provisional government, however, adopted one essential element of the Constitution of Year I: direct, universal male suffrage was to designate the new Constituent Assembly. The paradoxical results of this fundamental reform, which was to prove to be irreversible, are well known. France, for the most part still rural, sent to the Assembly 450 republicans, all the more moderate because many of them had previously been royalists; 200 Orleanists; a handful of legitimists faithful to the heir or Charles X; and only 200 "advanced republicans" tinged with socialism. In Paris, even Louis Blanc, their leader, could muster only 121,000 votes, which gave him twenty-seventh place on the list of those elected, while 260,000 votes went to Lamartine, a moderate republican and an enemy of the red flag.

Despite the diversity of its members, the liberal current overwhelmingly prevailed in the Assembly. The quality of the men reinforced its power; some of the most eminent representatives of the various shades of liberalism had taken their seats there: Duvergier de Hauranne and Thiers among the Orleanists: Montalembert and Lacordaire, the leaders of the Catholic liberals: and Tocqueville, to name only the most outstanding. Paradoxically, these men of the highest caliber, tried and tested jurists like Vivien and Cormenin and those endowed with first-hand knowledge of foreign institutions like Tocqueville, were to adopt a constitution whose implementation was very soon to reveal its weaknesses.

But even before serious work on the texts started, the harsh repression of the June Days crushed the uprising of Parisian workers who, mobilized by the vague Jacobin reminiscences and the socialist aspirations of the February Revolution, protested against the Assembly's closure of the national workshops.

In the wake of the June Days the members of the Constituent Assembly could have totally divorced themselves from the model of Year I. However, on some points at least, a weak, indirect echo of the Jacobin text can be found in their documents, by their use of the same democratic logic. Conversely, the constitution distanced itself somewhat from liberal orthodoxy. This is borne out, first, by the general principles defined in the preamble, essential for defining the spirit of 1848, and, second, in the way the institutions of government were laid out.

From the point of view of general principles, the constitution declared the republic "one and indivisible" and "the definitive form of government." It was democratic, founded on the sovereignty of the people as exercised through universal male suffrage, as in Year I.[14] But alongside these convergences, the 1848 preamble showed how great a distance it kept from Jacobinism. Christian inspiration is present there in the stress laid on fraternity and in the moral concern that gave "family and work"[15] as the bases of the republic, rather than "property and public order." Similarly, the 1848 text is faithful to the liberal tradition, in that it reaffirms the great liberties of 1789 and even renders the contents explicit with the abolition of slavery and the prohibition of censorship.

Yet this constitution also moved away from the liberal tradition in three ways. The liberal tradition stemming from 1789 greatly limited state intervention in the life of society. Although the 1848 preamble did not retain the echo of the opposing socialist aspirations defended by the "advanced republicans," its affirmation of the right to work at least recognized the "duty of the State to procure work for its needy citizens"[16] and, more widely, "to ensure a more and more equitable sharing of social responsibilities and advantages."[17] These duties carried the seeds of an interventionism contrary to the attitude of nonintervention imposed by the liberal tradition.

In the perspective of 1789, conversely, the proclamation of liberties could be reduced to affirmations of principle—"formal" liberties, as Marxist criticism will have it. Anticipating this, the text entered into an indication of the means proper to making concrete the liberties and duties of the state. Freedom of worship was guaranteed "by the paying of a salary to its ministers";[18] the welfare of labor was to be ensured by "free primary education, professional education, equality of relations between managers and workers, the establishment by the state of public works, suitable for putting unoccupied hands to work."[19] In the same concrete perspective, the text envisaged not man in himself, the abstract man of 1789, but man "in his situation" as Georges Burdeau put it: a society of managers and workers, old people and abandoned children.

Finally, the liberal tradition is individualistic. The text of 1848 consecrated, alongside individual liberties, collective liberties— associating, meeting and petitioning.[20] It exalted the family and within the life of society recognized the necessary place of collective organisms, provident and credit institutions, and agricultural institutions.

Compared with the Jacobin and liberal viewpoints, it was all those features that made for the originality of what is justly called the spirit of 1848. The republicans of subsequent generations—liberals or "Jacobins"—were occasionally to smile at the moralizing concern that inspired it. But in it can also be perceived the outlines of welfare-state liberalism with its concern for the least favored and its opposition to the excesses of laissez-faire, thus anticipating a distant future.

As far as government institutions were concerned, however, the experience of 1848 was to prove basically negative: a foil rather than a model. Liberal it certainly was, by virtue of its concern to prevent the omnipotence of power according to the teachings of Montesquieu. But the members of the Constituent Assembly were unable to choose from among the means to this end offered them by historical precedent.

Strengthened by the British and American examples, the liberal tradition seemed to impose the bicameral system, but it was the inverse logic of 1791 and 1793 that prevailed. The fear of seeing two chambers opposed to each other proved greater than that of a return to government by assembly and led to the investment of legislative power in a single chamber.[21]

Conversely, the memory of Jacobin dictatorship made the necessity of a strong executive uppermost in people's minds. Jules Grévy's famous amendment was rejected by a massive majority; directly stemming from the Constitution of Year I, it would have excluded, in the name of the unity of power, any presidency of the Republic. At the head of the executive, it proposed a "President of the Council of Ministers," elected and capable of dismissal by the Assembly. Purely and simply, this would have been a return to government by assembly, which the liberal tradition condemned.

To whom was the strong executive, meant to forestall this danger, to be entrusted? Even after taking into account the historical context and the still-vivid Napoleonic memories that nourished the idea of democracy ratified by plebiscite, it must be said that the main mistake of the members of the Constituent Assembly lay in their answer to this question. Fortified by the sad experience of the two preceding monarchies, the liberal tradition argued for a head of state who, following the example of the British monarchs, would reign but not rule. The real executive function in the liberal formulation would be vested in a government subject to the control of the Assembly but possessing through the medium of the president of the Republic the right of dissolution, thus permitting a balance between the two power bases. There again, abstract logic and perhaps also the prestige of the American model prevailed over the lessons of experience and consideration of historical context. Setting aside the fear of a personalization of power, the members of the Constituent Assembly of 1848, carried along by the rather hollow eloquence of Lamartine, opted against Jules Grévy. Not only did they establish the institution of a president of the Republic but also, despite the wise arguments of Parien, they endorsed his election by universal suffrage, in the name of a democratic logic, which wants all power to proceed directly from the people.[22] As for the ministers, they depended entirely on the president, being appointed and dismissed by him.[23]

The only brake applied to presidential authority would be the president's ineligibility to run again immediately after his term of office, set at four years in accordance with the American model. Again, it was the American model that prevailed in the refusal to grant the right to dissolve to the head of the executive. Between the two powers, the separation was complete. The desire was that both be strong, but nothing was envisaged to resolve the conflicts that might bring them to oppose each other. The system had shown itself to be viable in the United States. But in a totally different historical and psychological environment, affected by the prestige attached to Napoleon's memory and the blunders of the Legislative Assembly elected in May 1849, the ambitions of the *Prince Président* elected by plebiscite on 10 December 1849 led to the coup d'état of 2 December 1851 and to the death of the Second Republic.

THE BIRTH OF THE THIRD REPUBLIC

On 4 September 1870, news broke of the disaster at Sedan and the capture of the emperor. The Paris mob invaded the Palais Bourbon, where the Corps Legislatif was in session, demanding the reinstitution of the republic. The Jacobin mystique seemed to come alive again. A revival of the great revolutionary days when the people of Paris had imposed their will on the whole of the country—revenge for the defeats they had suffered in June 1848, and on 2 December 1851—the republic could be proclaimed nowhere other than at the Hôtel de Ville, the sanctum of popular power. The republic was proclaimed, but by the provisional government hastily formed by Gambetta and not by the "reds" grouped around Blanqui.

Right from the start, therefore, there appeared the ambiguity of Jacobin memories. What Gambetta and his friends retained of these was indeed a passionate attachment to the republic, so fine under the Empire, but also and especially the evocation of the victorious combat that had saved the homeland when invaded. For the time being, and in order of priority, the imperative of public safety prevailed over the drawing up of institutions or social reforms. Admittedly, the Paris mob shared the same patriotic passion, but its Jacobinism was "red" as much as it was tricolor, puffed out with a socialism whose appurtenance to the true Jacobin legacy was, as we have seen, far from obvious.

This ambiguity is of capital importance. A few months later, the red Jacobinism of the Paris mob was going to become exacerbated in the drama of the Commune, with its violence and the fierce repression that destroyed it. The crushing of the Commune was the crushing of this form of Jacobinism. But already the other component of the myth, the theme of public safety, embodied in Gambetta, had been rejected during the election of the Constituent Assembly by a people aware that victory was impossible and eager for peace.

Henceforth nothing remained of the Jacobin myth within the Assembly. During the five years spanning the election of the Assembly and the passing of the constitutional laws in 1875, it was to all intents and purposes absent from political life. Was it, then, the liberal tradition that triumphed in the Assembly? Truth to tell, the question that stirred passions was not that, but in the choice between monarchy and republic. On the institutions to be established within the framework of one form of government or the other, a fairly wide consensus was obvious. The parliamentary model, liberal in its principles, was accepted both by the 214 Orleanists, faithful to the memory of the July Monarchy, and by the majority of the legitimists, excepting some light cavalry men with their nostalgia for the ancien régime. Apart from a handful of extremists who were to disappear during the Commune, the republican minority also accepted the parliamentary model. This was true on the center-left, where names like those of Thiers, Dufaure, and Laboulaye stand out; of the 112 members of the republican left; and even on the extreme left, where the presence of Louis Blanc and some of those who had known 1848 was eclipsed by the figure of Léon Gambetta who showed greater suppleness than did those referred to by their younger colleagues as the "old fogies."

The consensus that thus developed around the parliamentary regime can be explained by history. The clumsy, unfortunate experiment of the presidential regime of 1848 had failed. Both the Bourbon and Orleanist monarchies more or less practiced the British system. When they were running out of steam, even the First and Second Empires had to rally to liberal parliamentarianism, the first with the Additional Act of 22 April 1815, the work of Benjamin Constant, and the second with the reform of May 1870, approved of by Laboulaye. Moreover, it *was* a quasi-parliamentary system that the Assembly itself, through the ups and downs that punctuated its term of office from Thiers to Mac-Mahon, ended up applying until the passing of the constitutional laws in 1875. The return to the values of the ancien régime, to which the Comte de Chambord intended remaining faithful with the symbol of the white flag, proved to be impossible. Consequently the restoration could not come about for the time being. Called on to succeed the last descendant of Charles X, when in the famous saying of the time,

Heaven, which had not deigned to open his eyes, closed them, the Comte de Paris accepted the parliamentary regime against the day when he might accede to the throne.

For the republicans, what mattered was precisely to avoid this accession. The important thing was for the republic to cease being the provisional regime proclaimed on September 4 by a de facto government and become the definitive regime, consecrated by the constitution. They obtained this consecration by a one-vote majority when the Wallon amendment confirmed the title of President of the Republic for the head of state.[24] For them, from then on, the basic essential had been attained. But to obtain this majority, they had sacrificed what little remained of Jacobin tradition and adopted all the forms of liberal parliamentarianism. Of Jacobinism, nothing remained in the constitutional laws: neither the rejection of an individual head of state, nor even his reduction to a symbolic function, because the constitution invested him with important attributions, especially with the right of dissolution;[25] neither the unity of legislative power—in the Senate, Gambetta himself hailed "the great council of the communes of France"—nor the portion of direct democracy written into the Constitution of 1793. The democracy of 1875 was exclusively representative.

In its parliamentary form, this triumph of institutional liberalism admittedly lacked the parallel consecration of ideological liberalism in the constitutional laws. Of all the French constitutions from 1791 onwards, that of 1875 alone, pragmatic as it was, remained absolutely silent on the principles it implemented, on the rights of man and basic liberties. But was it necessary to confirm them explicitly, because, according to the formula already present in the Charter of 1814, evolution had made of them "French public law" and the word *Republic* in this Constitution of 1875 embodied all these values?

All in all, the Republic of 1875, the sensible republic accepted by the most conservative liberals had, at its birth, totally effaced all memories of the Jacobin Republic.

The latter, however, was to know a sort of revenge. After the hapless application of the right of dissolution by MacMahon and the triumph of the republican party on the morrow of 16 May 1876, fate ironically called to the presidency of the Republic the man who, in 1848, had unsuccessfully proposed its suppression. Jules Grévy had not forgotten the Jacobin fervor that had inspired his amendment: "I shall never challenge the will of the nation expressed through its constitutional organs." As soon as he was elected, he announced his refusal to have recourse to dissolution, and expressed his desire to submit himself entirely to the decisions of the parliamentary majority; he set out a line of conduct that was to be adopted by all his successors. While not suppressing the presidency, he did disarm it. To the parliamentary regime of the Third Republic, he thus introduced, to the benefit of the legislature and the detriment of the executive, an element of imbalance. This disequilibrium, if it did not allow a complete return to the dictatorship of the Assemblies, was nonetheless at the root of the ministerial instability that ended up corrupting the regime and has a lot to answer for in the disaster of 1940 that destroyed it.

The Jacobin reference popped up at other times, too: for the worse, as consistently from Gambetta to Edouard Herriot, anticlericalism readily claimed it as its inspiration, and for the better, the fierce willpower that made of Georges Clemenceau "the organizer of Victory" in 1918. But when, in the last years of the Fourth Republic, the young radicals grouped round Pierre Mendès-France called themselves "Jacobins," it was then little more than a label they were using, a historical memory devoid of all precise content. As a final act of sacrilege, it is sometimes evoked in a humorous tone. At the Socialist Party Congress in 1981, when a young deputy with the Christian name of Paul used, to underline the necessity of a certain weeding-out among the top civil servants, a metaphor that to his eyes was stripped of all sanguinary ulterior motives, "Some heads will have to roll," his colleagues, in memory of the father of the Jacobin Terror, were not long in nicknaming him "Robespaul."

A myth had disappeared, but a tradition remains well and truly alive; thus Georges Clemenceau's famous formula, "The Revolution is a single bloc," finds itself invalidated. Successive republics, those of the twentieth century after those of the nineteenth, claimed to be faithful to 1789 and the rights of man; they swept aside 1793 and the "dictatorship of liberty." Is this to be wondered at? Jacobinism was only a moment in history, a confused complex of passions, ideas, and behavior bringing together the best and the worst. As for liberalism, even if it does offer numerous variants, even if its applications in the economic order are not met with universal approval, it does remain a doctrine. The currents of thought that claim it as their source of inspiration would be unfaithful to it if they did not respect its core idea: the value of liberty inherent in man, which is the basis of his dignity.

NOTES

1. See *Rapport à la Convention de la Commission chargée de l'examen des papiers trouvés chez Robespierre*, Paris, Imprimerie Nationale, Nivôse An III, 175, 379, and *passim*.
2. Ibid., 107, 110, and *passim*.
3. Constitution of June 24, 1793, Article 39 and *sqq*.
4. Articles 62 to 77.
5. Article 32.
6. Article 59.
7. P. Gaxotte, *La Révolution Française* (Paris: Fayard, 1928). This is the title given to the chapter devoted to this period, 324.
8. D. Guérin, *La lutte des classes sous la Ière République, 1793–97* (Paris: Gallimard, 1946).
9. 1793 Declaration of Rights, Article 19.
10. 1789 Declaration, Articles 10 and 11.
11. 1789 Declaration, Article 4.
12. 1789 Declaration, Article 17.
13. Villermé, *Tableau de l'état physique et moral des ouvriers employés dans les manufactures*, 1840.
14. 1848 Constitution, Preamble, I and II.
15. Preamble, IV.
16. Preamble, VIII.
17. Preamble, I.
18. Constitution, Article 7.
19. Constitution, Article 13.
20. Constitution, Article 8.
21. Constitution, Article 20.
22. Constitution, Article 43 and *sqq*.
23. Constitution, Article 64.
24. Constitutional Law of February 25, 1875, Article 2.
25. Constitutional Law of February 25, 1875, Article 5.

9

The Jacobin and Liberal Contributions to the Founding of the Second and Third French Republics (with an Epilogue on America)

George Armstrong Kelly

The words *Jacobin* and *liberal* entered the French lexicon long after elements of their "traditions" had been absorbed.[1] No doubt the first French liberal was Vercingétorix and the first Jacobin, Julius Caesar. I have been told that King Philip Augustus, who introduced the earliest *monopole d'état*, was a Jacobin; and I do not doubt that Peter Abelard was a liberal. Closer to our own time, we have the often-cited examples of Cardinal Richelieu and Michel de Montaigne. This approach to our subject is not entirely fanciful: for it has the advantage of showing that traditions are not suddenly created from nothing. Traditions are like albums of ancestral portraits: they display generational differences, but always with an *air de famille*. And so it is with two of the *grandes familles politiques* of France: Jacobinism and liberalism.

There can be no question of presenting a political archaeology of the French race or of French thought. But in keeping with my commission in this chapter, I do try to say something about the significant and often contrasting dimensions of these two doctrines; I also suggest how they joust and combine in the origins, institutions, and *esprit* of the Second and Third republics; I say something about all this in the perspective of liberty; and because this enterprise is comparative, I conclude with some remarks about the very different political experiences of the United States.

THE DIMENSIONS OF LIBERALISM AND JACOBINISM

Liberalism and Jacobinism are necessarily defined in their relationship to each other by the events of the Great Revolution of 1789 and retrospective interpretations of them. The essential mission of liberalism was to reduce and constrain the power of politics over a newly burgeoning "civil society" that raised its standard of "public opinion" against a legacy of *mon plaisir*. The essential mission of Jacobinism was to renew that same power from a totally new ideological base, the *volonté générale*; to control, and even stifle, the liberal experiment in the interest of unity, efficiency, and a common, strict *morale*. It is often said that 1789 was liberal and 1793 Jacobin. But this clash of principles could be perceived from the earliest motions of the Revolution: an absolute claim for individual human rights was in conflict with an absolute demand for incarnating the common will of the nation in sovereign representative institutions. Of all the statesmen of the Constituent Assembly, Mirabeau probably saw this contradiction most clearly. But Mirabeau had no success in his attempt to mediate the politics of freedom with the politics of the clubs and the politics of the Court.[2] This is also to say that he had no success in "closing the Revolution." Thus, although 1789 was certainly liberal in effect, and although Jacobinism achieved its full rhetoric and reputation—its populism, republicanism, virtue, and belligerency—only in 1793, Jacobinism had been at least latent in Siéyès's notion that one should create the integral nation by excising the unhealthy and privileged parts of it.[3] This father of liberalism had some Jacobin tendencies of his own. So did others. As Mounier had written: "It could be said that there are Jacobins of monarchy, aristocracy and superstition, just as there are those of democracy."[4]

It is also significant that both liberalism and Jacobinism, as I have primitively described them, were eminently political doctrines. If their collision course, implicit in 1789, was not made clear until three years later, this fact was temporarily concealed in the Fête de la Fédération. Later there would not be that brotherhood. The political character of Jacobinism helps to explain why, even in the Commune of 1871 and well into the days of the Third Republic, there was a misunderstanding between Jacobinism and socialism. The tradition of *unité* and *indivisibilité* muted the *question sociale* and the idea of class struggle with its broader hostility toward *les grands*, *les riches*, and *les dévôts*. Despite numerous collaborations with socialists under the banners of republicanism and *laïcisme*, despite the *démo-socs* of 1849[5] and a variety of later *cartels des gauches*, the Jacobins sustained their earlier orientations toward the political power and the creation of a specific kind of solidaristic nation, not a different kind of society.

One further matter remains before we get into the heart of our discussion. The weary and somewhat chastened France that emerged from a generation of war and glory, novelty and revolution, in 1814 was in full retreat from Jacobin energy. Liberal publicists—preeminently, Constant and Madame de Staël—persuasively argued that the *jacobinisme d'en bas* of 1793–4 and the *jacobinisme d'en haut* of the Consulate and Empire were types of the same political pathology, an *arbitraire* without rival because it was seemingly reinforced by the power of popular sovereignty. By representing these excesses of political control and manipulation as hostile to modernity—that is as *la liberté des anciens* and *l'esprit de conquête*—Constant sought to banish them from the new repertoire of politics.[6]

The liberals themselves, however, had had calamitous experiences in trying to implant freedom and organize power at the same time, both under the bicephalous constitution of 1791 and in the troubled period of the Directory, when not only Siéyès but also Constant and Madame de Staël had helped prepare the way for Bonaparte. The Empire had added to France's institutions and political mentality an enduring strain of *jacobinisme napoléonisé*, as well as the fateful phenomenon of an individual plebiscitary sovereign. The immense theoretical fertility shown by the liberals during the Restoration is a reflection on their bitter failures of the past, now concentrated on new solutions of organizing power. But there was not exactly a French way of doing this, despite the philosophes and despite a parliamentary and constitutional tradition. For the most part—if I may generalize outrageously—there were Montesquieu and Whig England.[7] That model, admirable in itself but always somewhat foreign, would later reinforce Jacobinism's claim to be a "national" destiny, fortified by its memories of heroism. Thus, in the France of the future, liberalism, inspired from England and, later, the United States, would fail to seem "French" enough. Perhaps it is only in the past twenty years that large numbers of French have felt political liberalism to be genuinely national.

When liberalism, so to speak, came to power in 1830, with a political system that it had largely but not totally constructed, it faced vigorously implanted oppositions. It also failed to show its most generous features. It provided that a quarter of a million men might vote, out of a total population of 30 million. The more it seemed beleaguered, the more it needed to become Napoleonic in practice, to educate the benighted to its advantages and stifle the subversives. It was tied to a monarch who, "bourgeois" as he may have seemed, desperately wished to achieve legitimation through an exercise of the ample personal power left at his disposal. In these conditions, liberal government was not so corrupt as has often been claimed; but it was clannish, formulaic, and ultimately banal, despite the *capacités* of those who ran it or contested for power within its rules. As Lamartine put it, in 1839: "La France s'ennuie."[8] That would be said again, more than eighty years later, by André Tardieu. Indeed, there *was* something profoundly boring about July Monarchy politics in a culture cascading with the works of Hugo, Vigny, and George Sand. Boring, but indescribably free and comfortable, as Ernest Renan would later recall. Although, as Renan said, "jamais on n'a vécu plus à l'aise que de 1830 à 1848," and he implied that one might wait for a very long time to enjoy a comparable regime of "negative liberty," he deplored its outcome. For it had despiritualized freedom: "The whole secret of the intellectual situation," he thought, was that "intellectual work has been degraded to the rank of pleasure. With a time of serious struggles upon us, pleasure now seems paltry and stale."[9] Such was the reflective judgment of a (then) young liberal on a regime run by old liberals. The July Monarchy offended parts of society above and beneath its *juste milieu*; but its days were truly numbered when it seemed to stifle the imagination of its own progeny.

Thus, a fatal quandary and a fatal split occurred within French liberalism itself, one that would have lasting consequences for more than a century. And, by the same token, the submerged spirit of Jacobinism returned in vigor—a Jacobinism powerful not because it would reproduce 1793 in more than a few transient episodes, but because it would be able to unite *jacobinisme d'en bas* with *jacobinisme d'en haut* in a spirit of government that challenged a liberalism with a fragile social base. It is no accident that French liberalism found its great redoubt in the arts and culture, thereby performing an indispensable function for world civilization.

REFINEMENT OF THE DOCTRINAL DEFINITIONS

Before we proceed with our impression of how Jacobinism and liberalism interacted in the creation of the Second and Third republics, each doctrine must be defined more closely. French Jacobinism could be said to have the following major features:

- It is emphatically centralist or centralizing, in this respect heir to a long tradition including the early Capetian kings, Colbert and Louvois: the political science of the Abbé de Saint-Pierre: the *république une et indivisible*, and the institutions of the First Empire. This authoritarian style according to which the capital rules the provinces and the state shapes society—has been compatible with a number of regimes.

- Jacobinism is egalitarian in the negative sense that it seeks to mix or level (*confondre*) the social particles that are placed beneath the will of the state and its agents; as Rousseau wrote, there should be no "partial societies" between the common will that is sovereign and the particular wills that, although creating the sovereign, are subject.[10]
- It is egalitarian in the positive sense, at least since 1789, because the individual wills, taken collectively as a *volonté générale*, do create and legitimize public power and can revoke it. These wills, formally equivalent in value, form a *peuple*, whose collective will, properly expressed, is "always right" and is in theory opposed to all special privileges or interests.
- In such a scheme—and we must remember that the only unambiguous government of *jacobinisme d'en bas* was an emergency government—the "general good" or "conscience du peuple," while, as with liberalism, founded on rights, tends to overbalance them with duties, submerging the rights of particulars and the primacy of the private life.
- Since 1792, Jacobinism either has been staunchly, passionately republican in its regime preference or has favored types of leadership legitimated by the express consent of the people.
- Both representation and lawmaking (the law *is* the general will) are held by Jacobinism to proceed by way of a kinetic and undistorted refinement of will from its source in the nation to its embodiment in the law: for this legislative supremacy is essential.
- While not, according to certain criteria, antireligious, Jacobinism is profoundly antisacerdotal, not so much because it objects to spiritual interference in private affairs, but because it regards all spiritual corporations within the state as potential enemies that might undermine civic solidarity (Gambetta's "voilà l'ennemi"). Its own religion tends to be one of the nation-state, a "civil religion," typically having scientific and positivistic overtones.
- Over time, Jacobinism has appeared to alternate between a will to virtue, a will to democratic inclusiveness, and a will to the efficient organization of the national capacity. These wills are by no means mutually exclusive, but their emphases suit different situations.
- French Jacobinism has also been nationalistic and bellicose, with roots deeply sunk in the tradition of the wars of the Revolution and the Empire. This nationalism achieved cosmopolitan stature (in this respect following the hegemonic cultural pretensions of the old regime) because the Jacobins originally saw France as a pilot-state and a pilot-people for all mankind. Although not a

cosmopolitan ideology in the same sense as economic liberalism or Marxism, it has been an inspiration to numerous new nations in their quest to construct a state on strong, centralized foundations.

By contrast, we can say the following of French liberalism, as its doctrine takes shape from 1814 on. (Here we must acknowledge the fact that if there is a *jacobinisme d'en bas* and a *jacobinisme d'en haut*, there are also important differences among *economic liberalism, doctrinaire liberalism*, and *democratic liberalism* in France: in the period of reference, the second is the most important.)

- In theory, liberalism favors decentralization (one has only to refer to various texts of Constant, Barante, Tocqueville, or Montalembert). However, liberalism was embarrassed by having to share this view with a dispossessed legitimism, and was also, after 1830, faced with its own problems of organizing power. Distinctions were sometimes made between administrative and political decentralization, for example, Lamartine favored the second, but not the first.[11] Some liberals, like Thiers, were rather resolute centralizers.
- Philosophically, liberalism starts from the individual, with individual rights and interests, as the focus of dignity and value. The state is basically conceived as an organization of powers designed to promote the felicity of the individual. However, many nineteenth-century liberals saw the individual as a social and historical product and, almost without exception, they rejected the abstract rationalism of the social contract. Thus, the state was conceived to be the servant of the *forces vives* or *capacités* of civil society.
- Where the Jacobin says *peuple*, the liberal says *société*, conceiving it as an entity subject both to an economic division of labor and a political distinction of *capacités*. Although neither the Jacobin nor the liberal gives weight to class analysis in understanding or organizing political power, the liberal accepts a hierarchy of merit as society defines it.
- Liberals rebuff the principle of absolute sovereignty—whether popular, divine, or legislative—as anarchic or tyrannical, or both; and they seek to render it innocuous in practice. "Sovereignty, constituted of free governments," said Royer-Collard, is distinguished from "popular sovereignty" by its attachment to "rights and interests," rather than to "persons and wills."[12]
- The liberal organization of public powers reposes on a sturdy constitutionalism, accenting the following features: a large, re-

served "private" or "social" sphere guaranteed by the most solemn legal commitment of rulers and ruled; a functional separation of the powers of government, tending to relax its "energy" and its tendency to *arbitraire*; a wide play of personal and civil freedoms; and equality before the law for all citizens, indeed a legal, rather than a legislative, supremacy.

- Liberals are reluctant to choose between liberal monarchy and conservative republic as long as their conditions for freedom are met. We see this in Constant when he writes: "We are no longer in an age when monarchy was declared an unnatural power, nor do I write in a country where one is compelled to state that the republic is an anti-social institution."[13] Also in Rémusat: "What is the best political constitution? It is the one best suited to shed the light of truth on everything and to direct power into the hands of those who know best how to exercise it."[14] Even Tocqueville, in 1855, could tell Nassau Senior: "If Louis Napoleon . . . should ever grant to France, or accept from her, institutions really constitutional . . . the Parliamentarians [meaning his "party"] would eagerly rally round him. . . . They are the friends of liberty, whatever be the form in which she may present herself."[15] In 1870, the preference of Albert de Broglie was for "a monarchy that approaches a republic; a republic that approaches a monarchy."[16]

- Liberalism characteristically fears the power of transparent and momentary majorities in making laws or declaring public policy, preferring instead such filtering devices as restricted or unequal suffrage, bicameralism, or executive participation in legislating. "Property" and "capacities" are critical qualifications of the political class.[17] "Democracy" has a part in the political organization of society, but only a part.

- In religious matters, liberalism is skeptical, tolerant, and secularizing by its nature. But in France it recoiled before the idolatries of the Revolution. Despite important Protestant and liberal Catholic contributions (as represented by such figures as Guizot and Montalembert), it is most accurate to say that French liberalism was "spiritualist" in the style of Victor Cousin and Jouffroy. The "Voltairians," like Thiers, were exceptions, although, more by way of Comte than Voltaire, they later provided a bridge to Jacobinism in writers like Littré. With its catalogue of freedoms, tolerant disposition toward dissenting minorities, notions of parliamentary organization, penchant for free economic enterprise, and optimistic assumptions about civilization, liberal doctrine had pronounced cosmopolitan features. In France, however, it was per-

ceived by its opponents as a rather restrictive set of political ax-
ioms, as "bourgeois" or "elitist."

THE ORIGINS OF THE SECOND REPUBLIC

The Second Republic (1848–52) came unexpectedly. The few republicans who sat in the Chamber of the July Monarchy—Dupont de l'Eure,
Arago, Garnier-Pagès, Marie, Ledru-Rollin, and the more ambiguous
Lamartine—were not embarked on any mission to overturn the monarchy. They were not revolutionaries. They hoped for the republic but
did not really conspire for it. The famous "campaign of the banquets"
(itself an English import) could not have figured in an important way
without the support of the liberal dynastic opposition. Odilon Barrot
and his friends did not want a change of regime; they simply wanted
new electoral laws—at most a doubling of eligible voters—so that they
could win and form the government.
    Liberals do not, in general, or at least unaided, make revolutions.
They preach reforms. Liberals accept revolutions once made, which
they then, more or less well, try to reshape—as their plastic doctrines
teach—into a kind of order with more liberty. Thus it was with the
Provisional Government of February 1848. With the plausible exception of Ledru-Rollin,[18] who has been presented in history as an arche-
typal Jacobin, the core of that government was liberal; but these were
democratic liberals as opposed to doctrinaire liberals, and the source
and the nature of their power were explicitly Jacobin. Lamartine himself, the oratorical aristocrat and hero of the public at large, was a
liberal; but he had come to that position by way of legitimism, Catholicism, and Romanticism—not exactly the prescribed route. For Lamartine, popular sovereignty was a prudent concession, not an axiom: he
preferred, as he put it, "the sovereignty of ideas" or "the sovereignty of
organized society."[19] But the sudden collapse of Orleanism in 1848
had produced a de facto situation in which all had to agree on a form
of democratic republic, created, as in 1792, by a universally elected
assembly. Thiers, Tocqueville, and Barrot all accepted this. The problem was not, then, whether the people should speak, but when. The
Paris Jacobins, seconded by their minister of the interior, Ledru-
Rollin, agitated for delay, believing that a certain "prefectoral" education was needed before the people could properly articulate the *volonté générale* free from the pressures of the *seigneurs* and *grands notables*.
Jacobinisme d'en haut would have to come to the rescue of *jacobinisme tout
court*. But, as one knows, the elections were speedily held, returning a
majority of moderates to the Constituent Assembly.

The origins of the Second Republic may be cursorily described as the merger of a Jacobin event in Paris (guided by legislators and journalists who, on the whole, did not desire a repetition of 1793) and a conservative event in most of the provinces. Between action and reaction there was effective room for liberal compromise, despite the bewilderment of many liberals. ("M. Thiers and M. Barrot," Tocqueville writes, "are half mad."[20]) In the circumstances, unavoidable concessions were made to the *république une et indivisible*, to universal suffrage, and to a Jacobin-inspired executive and populist city government. But radical Jacobinism had to concede most of the parliamentary forms of liberalism in anticipation of the framing of a liberal constitution. Finally, the specter and then the reality of social revolution in June drove the opportunist republicans and the Jacobins into a brief, but significant, entente in defense of their common principle of private property.

I have already said that the Second Republic marked a passage from doctrinaire to democratic liberalism, somewhat checked by a legislature of moderate persuasion and, of course, by the fear of social revolution. A similar distinction must be made within Jacobinism. If the mere fact of being a *républicain de toujours*, like Dupont or Cavaignac, signified a Jacobin ancestry, then such *jacobins de la légalité* should be carefully distinguished from the conspiratorial Jacobins of the Buonarotti or Blanqui type, who organized the clubs, sought to create revolutionary *journées*, and had fond memories of the *Comité de salut public*. The difference is important because it would recur in the scenario leading to the establishment of the Third Republic, where, as it is said, the Paris Commune of 1871, with men like Félix Pyat and Charles Delescluze, was more than half "Jacobin"; but it is equally true that nationalist republicans like Gambetta, Eugène Spuller, and Georges Clémenceau also have a just claim to the title *Jacobin*.

As regards its organization of powers, the Second Republic bore a striking resemblance to the regime declared in the Constitution of 1791, with the substitution for the monarch of a president elected every four years by universal suffrage. As in 1791, the constitution was not submitted to the nation for ratification and, as in 1791, the constitution recognized rights prior to the existence of positive laws. Similarly, there was a complete separation of powers: the legislature was omnicompetent in its domain, with no presidential right of veto or dissolution; the president enjoyed all normal executive powers and was not compelled to choose his ministers according to any parliamentary majority. Finally, again as in 1791, the legislature of 700 members was unicameral (as Marrast put it: "Si la nation est une, la législature doit l'être aussi").

It is thus possible, without stretching the imagination, to refer back to what was said earlier about the relative presence of liberalism and Jacobinism in the foundation of the First Republic. If two models—the brief constitutional monarchy of Louis XVI and the *république à l'américaine*—are proposed, it is clear that the French owed more to the former in 1848. This form of republic must be called liberal, but numerous features of its constitutional spirit bend it in a Jacobin direction: the republic is declared *démocratique, une et indivisible*; popular sovereignty is proclaimed; the suffrage is universal for adult males; the voting is by departmental lists; there is only one chamber; and legislative supremacy is asserted.

As everyone knows, the legislative-executive standoff (and the ban on the president succeeding himself) led fatally to the coup d'état of Louis Bonaparte that ended the republican experiment. It is useless to try to interpret those events in terms of "liberalism" and "Jacobinism"; but the comparative ease with which the *prince-président* was able to reassert the prerogatives of *l'état fort* illustrates, if we turn now to the matter of *esprit*, how fragile liberal government had been in France and how strong the centralizing urge remained. Another point is to be noted: temporarily, at least, the failure of the Second Republic exhausted the last chance the French had given themselves to create any reasonably common standard of legitimacy. Henceforth, the ideal of an allegiant citizenry was fractured; and it would remain so for a very long time. And, if one cannot rally around a regime, the natural tendency will be to cleave to the state, not because it is an *État vache à lait* (which the French state then was not), but because it is the only trustworthy source of public rules and standards. Regimes pass (*dictatures provisoires*, Lamartine called them, taking that word in its Roman sense),[21] but the state remains to incarnate the will of the nation.

With the demise of the republic, it might be said broadly that the liberals with their individualistic principles went into internal migration—they still frequented the academies and the highbrow reviews—and the Jacobins went into a sort of underground opposition (insofar as they were not the kind of *jacobin d'en haut* who found the Empire appetizing). Of course, a few liberals and a few Jacobins found reasons to cooperate with a regime that, simple on its surface, had certain depths of attractiveness (e.g., it negotiated free trade with England, stimulated innovation in French industry, pursued—except for Rome—a Jacobinizing foreign policy, recognized workers' organizations, and in its last year attempted political liberalization).

At about this time, a cultural phenomenon vastly more important than any political quarrel was taking shape with astonishing speed, carrying human expectations along. This was the almost unanimous belief, among the literate, in Progress. Never before had humanity been able to conceive its destiny with such optimism. With aspirations and rhetoric framed by their own traditions, Jacobinism, liberalism, and imperialism could all celebrate the potency of Progress. Their chorus was not harmonious, for the melodies were not the same— their gospels were not synoptic. But the confidence was shared; and in each case it came down to a stress on material technology and education. It was especially in the realm of education—specifically, civic education—that the ideologies collided in France, although this collision was itself masked beneath a greater collision of church and state. It would be the persisting mission of the Third Republic to give life to a civic catechism of education and progress, thereby making Jacobinism conservative and no longer conspiratorial.

In the particular circumstances I have mentioned, the cunning of progress and the resources of the state seemed to cohabit cozily. Although Charles Dupont-White must not be taken as some important and forgotten master of political thought, his work is at least symptomatic. Dupont-White, who was the translator of John Stuart Mill's *On Liberty*, wrote mainly during the Second Empire. His major work, *L'individu et l'État*, was, in its time, accused of having socialist or collectivist leanings; when it is mentioned at all today, it is usually classed as a text of "interventionalist liberalism."[22] Perhaps it would be best to call it a meeting of *jacobinisme d'en haut* with liberalism. "No," writes Dupont-White,

> the State is not just a sterile protector of the existing order that applies and executes pre-existing laws. Its major task is to make new laws, that is, to foresee what will come to pass, to prepare what ought to be, for that is the real work of progress.[23]

Also, "the State is not only physical force; above all, it is moral authority."[24] More striking than these generalities is Dupont-White's view that the French, in particular, need the state because of their past habits and history:

> This greatness and necessity of the role of the State, everywhere visible, is most evident in France, There, progress is, to an unheard of extent, the business of government: neither the country's disposition, nor liberty, nor nature could suffice in this effort.[25]

To put it briefly, the state must prevail, even over liberty, if France is to enjoy progress and prosperity. This is not exactly Danton's "périsse ma vie, que la France soit sauvée," but it is a major strain of Jacobinism.

THE DEVELOPMENT OF THE INSTITUTIONS AND ESPRIT OF THE SECOND AND THIRD REPUBLICS

The most acute critics of the Second Empire had been liberals, by that time somewhat *américanisés, démocratisés,* in the wake of Alexis de Tocqueville. Laboulaye and Prévost-Paradol were their most commanding voices.[26] Their message was, of course, that progress was second to liberty and should, in any case, be guided by individual initiative. But the amazing circumstances of the Prussian victory of 1870 and the emperor's capture and dethronement opened a promising opportunity for ardent Jacobin republicans to weigh on the character of the successor regime. With solid implantation in the major cities and in parts of the country (notably the Midi) that had been agitated by the *démo-soc* network of 1849, they were now free of persecution by Bonapart's prefects. In certain respects, unlike the case in 1848, city and countryside were not antipodal but shared a certain bondedness in the idea of a *république une et indivisible,* especially in answer to the calamitous fortunes of the nation at Sedan.

However, this was not to be. The working out of the nation's new institutions took a long time and remained ambiguous until Marshal MacMahon's resignation in 1877; but it gradually became clear that France would have a republic with liberal forms and Jacobin habits. Several circumstantial episodes helped to determine this outcome. First, there was France's military incapacity and the pressing public desire to make peace with the Germans on the best terms. Unfortunately, the most radical of the Jacobins were also the most belligerent of the French, preaching *la guerre à outrance* to a beaten country. Gambetta, with his courage and great political sense, carried this gospel as far as was wise, reaping a harvest of glory for the future; but he knew when to stop. The vast majority of the French were unwilling to keep on fighting the Germans simply to promote a social revolution. When Thiers and Jules Favre obtained an armistice for the purpose of electing a national legislature qualified to treat with Bismarck, the electors, exposed to only a week's campaign, voted massively for peace and, almost unwittingly, returned a large royalist majority. Because, despite serious attrition, that assembly and that majority remained the government of France until late in 1875, any option of a radical republic was a dead letter. Indeed—against the probable desires of the nation—the question was one of monarchy.

The second major factor was the Commune of 1871. Despite parallel uprisings in a handful of other cities (Lyons, Toulouse, Montpellier, etc.), the Paris Commune appeared to most French to post not only a threat to property, society, and peace—but also to *the state.* Dozens of volumes have now been written (beginning with Lissagaray's powerful *Histoire de la Commune de 1871*)[27] in celebration of the Paris radicals. But from Versailles and most of France the Commune seemed an insane menace. In dealing with the insurrection in the way that history records, Thiers simply added to the popularity he had achieved for making peace with the enemy. If there was any disposition toward radical Jacobinism in France at large, the Commune did much to chasten it; for it placed the most visible Jacobin leaders, almost to a man, on the side of Versailles, just as they had been on the side of Cavaignac in June 1848.

Third, we must mention little old tough Adolphe Thiers, described by Maurice Agulhon in an earlier context as "a chemically pure bourgeois Orleaniste."[28] Voltairian, close to the *peuple* by birth, this liberal from the south of France had always possessed certain Jacobin traits. He was a centralizer, a protectionist, a chauvinist, and, at a respectable distance, an admirer of Napoleon I. Influential in the revolution of 1830, disoriented by the one of 1848, he reserved his destiny for 1870, when events made him France's hero and chief executive. Strongly attached to the Orleans princes, he nevertheless opted, first privately, then openly, for the solution of a conservative republic.[29] His influence among the Orleanists and his reputation as a man of order helped to achieve that result. Curiously enough, in becoming a republican and in insisting on a strong nation-state, Thiers was more a Jacobin than those who, far to his left, like Delescluze, were fighting for municipal autonomy in Paris.

Last, Thiers had to be completed by Gambetta, the congenital Jacobin republican. Although they were political enemies at the start, their interests and views converged. From liberal monarchism, Thiers moved toward the Third Republic; from belligerent Jacobinism, Gambetta became an "opportunist," that is, a conscious agent of the conservative republic, provided that it was fertilized by new elites from below. Eventually they sang each other's praises and fought political campaigns side by side.[30]

Perhaps these vignettes more incisively suggest how liberalism and Jacobinism drew together in the Third Republic than would an arid description of the parliamentary maneuvering that produced it. But a few words need to be devoted to the tenor of its institutions and its *esprit.* In contrast to previous French constitutional regimes, this one had virtually no constitution to speak of. Instead it was created organically out of acts and precedents of the National Assembly and, in its pivotal form, by the three laws of 1875 pertaining to the organization of powers. There is no preamble of principles and no declaration of rights. There is no mention of regimes (leading careless historians to repeat the canard that it was intended to prepare the way for a monarchy; rather, it was intended not to offend wavering monarchists).

In any case, the organization of powers is clear (although some would be changed). Whereas the implementation of the Third Republic was sequential and, for the French, remarkably pragmatic, there is no need to regard the foundation as casual. Indeed, it was far better prepared than the Second Republic. Its constitution provided for a republic founded on universal male suffrage, and for a two-chamber legislature, with each chamber having (à *l'américaine*) equal powers, but here meaning especially that the Senate as well as the Chamber of deputies could overturn ministries. The president had powers comparable to those of a constitutional king, was elected for seven years, and was constitutionally inviolable (because his acts required ministerial countersignature). A ministry summoned by the president was collectively responsible for the acts of government. The deadlocks of 1791 and 1848 should not have been able to occur, for the president (with the advice of the Senate) was given the power to dissolve the lower chamber: but, as one knows, after 1877, this power remained unexercised. Popular sovereignty was the source of government, but in practice it was carefully measured: the deputies were elected directly and all at once; the senators were elected indirectly from a base of local suffrage, heavily skewed toward the rural areas, a third of them every three years; the president was elected indirectly to his seven-year term by the two chambers together.

Formally, this constitution conceded more to French-style liberalism than to Jacobinism, but with all taint of aristocracy removed: first, in its empirical avoidance of abstract principle; second, in its separation of powers and filtration of the *volonté générale*; third, in the *lenteurs* of the whole process by which the popular will was translated into law; finally, in respect to the preservation of certain executive powers. It inaugurated a delicate system of political and social balances that, if finally resulting in a *société bloquée*, nevertheless permitted France a long period—scarcely unperturbed—of ideological healing and national consolidation.

Thus the Third Republic achieved a temporary compromise between Jacobin rhetoric, an essentially liberal practice of politics, and a conservative social order suited both to the exigencies of progress and the comfort of *esprit de clocher*. France not only had a state but an acceptable regime, one that, to speak negatively with Thiers, divided the nation least. Gambetta also correctly perceived that, in accepting the conservative republic, the ordinary Frenchman would have a safe and sure vehicle for advancing his interests in a democratic direction without threat of revolution.[31]

The forms of the Third Republic were always more liberal than much of its political language and many of its governmental practices. For France was not miraculously relieved of its powerful factional energy or serious contests over social power. The new republicans, like all their predecessors in power, moved as quickly as they could to plant their friends in the Conseil d'État, the magistracy, the university, and, generally speaking, in the key positions of a civil society that was by habit *étatisée*. The exercise of police power and even judicial power was not always carried out in a liberal vein.[32] But it might be said that these infusions of authoritarianism and paternalism—of Jacobinism, if one likes—were the dark side of an education to republicanism in a country that, as Tocqueville more than hinted, was not naturally freedom-loving.

THE POLITICAL EXPERIENCES OF THE UNITED STATES

Whatever may be said now about France's failure to grasp "modern liberty" or "negative liberty" or "Anglo-Saxon liberty," the detached observer can only conclude that France sought and achieved liberty in ways that were available to its political culture and to its talent as a nation. Aside from what the English and Americans say about their ideas of liberty, there is also a Jacobin liberty, and it seems twofold. First, and somewhat dubiously, it is a collective liberty of nationhood, often belligerent in form and abstract in entitlement. But it is also a liberty of many smallholders or city dwellers, packed into tight spaces, persons in danger of sinking and in fear of calamity, persons whose independence hinges on the small margin of security and degree of foresight that only the state is in a position to provide.[33] This might seem an inferior freedom to Americans, whose geographical bounty, historical isolation, and Protestant theology have combined to give them a different instruction. But why would one demand of the French that they construct their meanings of liberty according to alien models? If there is today in France some evidence that, after two centuries of ideological struggle over the meaning of liberty, not only between liberals and Jacobins, but among other contestants as well, a revival of faith in "our kind of liberty"—the liberty of society against the state—has occurred, we will not hide our approval. But we should understand that if this is so, France has reached its conclusion by its own means; and we should not take it as France's ideological last word on its contribution to the definition of liberty.

The American sense of liberty also is culture-bound. There is admittedly very little in our historical experience or political consciousness that would incline us toward Jacobinism. Our distaste for it is so strong that, whatever the substance of our debates, our political oratory from all sides is cast in the discourse of individualistic liberalism. We have a state; we do not much like it. But, being a sort of empire and commonwealth at the same time, America is inescapably Jacobin in many of its practices, despite its rhetorical facade. How is this possible? It is possible because, under whatever administration we have or whatever public philosophy it professes, it is necessary to govern a very large and diverse nation, to implement *e pluribus unum*. More significantly, this is a condition of the increasing concentration of populations within minimum space in certain parts of the country. Hegel expressed the rationale for American Jacobinism better than anyone I know, although he had never visited our country. In his last lectures on the philosophy of history, delivered in Berlin at exactly the same time that Tocqueville was our guest, he said:

> A real State and a real Government arise only after a distinction of classes has arisen, when wealth and poverty become extreme, and when it happens that a large portion of the people can no longer satisfy its needs in the accustomed way. . . . North America will be comparable with Europe only after the immeasurable space which that country provides for its inhabitants has been occupied, and the members of the political body have begun to be pressed back on each other.[34]

A second and more important moment came directly after our Civil War of 1861–5. At the conclusion of that bloody struggle, Northern Jacobins—abolitionists and their allies in the Congress (e.g., Thaddeus Stevens of Pennsylvania)—fought an ideological combat with both the moderates and the defeated Southerners, making demands of radical virtue on their adversaries that resembled certain experiences of Europe. Georges Clémenceau, then visiting the United States as a stringer for *Le Temps*, wrote a series of brilliant dispatches that express his sympathy for the Republican radicals.[35] Jacobins recognized each other across the sea at this moment: for the style of American politics was not so different from the aspirations of Gambetta's "nouvelles couches." In fact, despite the success of the one and the failure of the other, it is not difficult to imagine General Grant and General Trochu exchanging places, or indeed Grover Cleveland and Jules Grévy.

The third Jacobin moment was the New Deal of Franklin D. Roosevelt. I do not mean that Roosevelt was especially a Jacobin by temperament; perhaps it might be more appropriate to describe him as our Thiers, even though he had come from a family of privileged ancestry and wealth. Rather, I would say that the New Deal was the point in time when America was first compelled to face the Hegelian scenario mentioned earlier. Thus, a structural setting for Jacobinism was created—and created permanently. In a complex sense, a real State was created; and, far from "withering away," it has grown increasingly more powerful. This may be expected to continue, for—official rhetoric to the contrary—the state now faces demands that were once unknown placed on it by the citizens and it also faces emergencies common to the rest of the Western world. As France, for reasons of its own making or choosing, begins to enrich its repertoire of liberty with a deeper examination of "le moment libéral," it seems likely that the United States will have to come to terms with "le moment jacobin." Our ideas of liberty will therefore have to be rethought. In this strange enterprise, France and America will have much to learn from each other.[36]

NOTES

1. The newest *Robert* (Paris, 1985) defines a political liberal as "favorable aux libertés individuelles dans le domaine politique" and cites the first use of the term in the Marquis d'Argenson's *Journal* (1750), noting "sens répandu, 1799–1800" (vol. V, p. 1028). As for *Jacobin*, it is defined as "républicain intransigeant, partisan d'un pouvoir central fort, dans une république démocratique" (first use, 1790: vol. V, p. 776).
2. Aside from Mirabeau's parliamentary speeches (e.g., on the royal veto and the power to declare war), see especially his "secret letters to the Court," in Adolphe de Bacourt, ed., *Correspondance entre le comte de Mirabeau et le comte de La Marck*, 3 vols. (Paris: Adolphe de Bacourt, 1851).
3. Emmanuel-Joseph Sieyès, *Qu'est-ce que le Tiers Etat?* edited by Roberto Zapperi (Geneva: Droz, 1970), 128: "Pourquoi ne renverroit-il pas dans les forêts de la Franconie toutes ces familles qui conservent la folle prétention d'être issues de la race des conquérants. . . ."
4. Jean-Joseph Mounier, *De l'influence attribuée aux philosophes, aux franc-maçons et aux illuminés dans la Révolution française*; English translation, *Of the Influence Attributed to Modern Philosophers*, etc. (London: J. G. Cotta, 1801), 124.
5. On this, see Edward Berenson, *Populist Religion and Left-Wing Politics in France, 1830–1852* (Princeton: Princeton University Press, 1984).
6. Benjamin Constant, *De l'esprit de conquête et de l'usurpation dans leurs rapports avec la civilisation européenne* (1814); and *De la liberté des anciens comparée à celle des modernes* (1819): both texts republished in Marcel Gauchet, ed., *Benjamin Constant: De la liberté chez les modernes* (Paris: Gallimard, 1980).
7. The English connection was promoted by Madame de Staël, who, far exceeding Montesquieu, wrote, "Après un siècle de durée des institutions qui ont formé la

nation la plus religieuse, la plus morale et la plus éclairée dont l'Europe puisse se vanter, je ne concevrois pas de quelle manière la prospérité du pays, c'est-à-dire, sa liberté, pourrait être jamais ménacée." (*Considérations sur la Révolution française*, 3 vols. [London, 1818], I, 361.)

8. Alphonse de Lamartine, to the Chamber of Deputies, 10 January 1839, cited in Pierre Quentin-Bauchart, *Lamartine, homme politique* (Paris: Plon-Nourrit and Co., 1903), 48.

9. Ernest Renan, "L'état des esprits en 1849," in *Questions contemporaines* (Paris: Calmann-Lévy, 1868), 302–3, 313.

10. Jean-Jacques Rousseau, *Contrat social*, I, vi; II, iii. In C.E. Vaughan, ed., *The Political Writings of Jean-Jacques Rousseau*, 2 vols. (New York: Wiley, 1962), II, 33–4, 43.

11. See Alphonse de Lamartine, *Sur la politique rationnelle* (1831), in *Oeuvres complètes*, 42 vols. (Paris: La Librairie de Charles Gosselin, 1860–1866), XXXVII, 379–80.

12. Prosper de Barante, *La vie politique de M. Royer-Collard: ses discours et ses écrits*, 2 vols. (Paris: Didier and Co., 1861), II, 18.

13. Constant, *De l'esprit de conquête et de l'usurpation* ("Usurpation," chapter 1), in Gauchet, ed., *Benjamin Constant*, 161.

14. Charles de Rémusat, in *Le Globe*, VII, 11 March 1829, cited in Pierre Rosanvallon, *Le moment Guizot* (Paris: Gallimard, 1985), 157.

15. M. C. M. Simpson, ed., *Correspondence and Conversations of Alexis de Tocqueville with Nassau William Senior*, 2 vols. (London: H. S. King and Co., 1872), II, 112. Original in English.

16. Albert, duc de Broglie, introduction to *Vues sur le gouvernement de France* (Paris: Michel Lévy frères, 1872), lxxii.

17. This is exceptionally well treated by P. Rosanvallon, *Moment Guizot*, 107–40.

18. See Robert Schnerb, *Ledru-Rollin* (Paris: Presses Universitaires de France, 1948).

19. See P. Quentin-Bauchart, *Lamartine*, 106.

20. Alexis de Tocqueville, *Souvenirs*, in his *Oeuvres Complètes*, vol. XII (Paris: Gallimard, 1964), 80.

21. See Lamartine, *Politique rationnelle*, 375–76.

22. Well discussed in Georges Burdeau, *Traité de science politique*, vol. V: *L'Etat libéral et les techniques politiques de la démocratie gouvernée* (Paris: Librairie générale de droit et de jurisprudence, 1953), 334.

23. Charles Brook Dupont-White, *L'individu et l'État* (Paris: Guillaumin and Co., 1865), vi.

24. Ibid., xiii.

25. Ibid., 153.

26. Edouard de Laboulaye, *L'Etat et ses limites* (Paris: Charpentier, 1863); and Lucien-Anatole Prévost-Paradol, *La France nouvelle* (Paris: Michel Lévy frères, 1868).

27. Prosper-Olivier-Hippolyte Lissagaray was a radical journalist in Paris who vividly recounted the events of the Commune in a partisan but intelligent vein. He published the work in Brussels in 1876; Eleanor Marx translated it into English from an original manuscript with the advice and approval of her father (new ed., London: Clearwater Publishers, 1976).

28. Maurice Agulhon, *L'apprentissage de la République, 1848–1852* (Paris: Editions de Seuil, 1973), 42.

29. See "Discours de M. Thiers du 24 mai 1873," reprinted in Jacques Chastenet, *Cent ans de république*, vol. I: *L'enfance de la Troisième, 1870–1878* (Paris: J. Jallandier, 1970), 450–69.

30. See ibid., 290, 298–9.

31. See Gambetta, in Joseph Reinach, ed., *Discours et plaidoyers politiques de Gambetta*, 11 vols. (Paris, G. Charpentier, 1881–5), I, 426: "[la démocratie radicale] nous rendra tous politiquement plus libres—intellectuellement plus savants—économiquement plus aisés—moralement plus justes—socialement plus égaux, et elle établira l'ordre sur l'équilibre et l'harmonie des droits et des intérêts."

32. See the excellent comments on this by Jean Rivero, "Le libéralisme à l'épreuve," *Centenaire de la Troisième République: Actes du colloque de Rennes, 15–17 mai 1975* (Paris: J. P. Delarge, 1975), 36–45.

33. See J. Chastenet, *Enfance de la Troisième*, 246, description of Gambetta's *bourgeois moyen*: "Il se rattache plutôt à la tradition jacobine, tantôt sous sa forme républicaine, tantôt sous sa forme bonapartiste. . . . Son idéal, discrètement opposé à celui de l'ordre moral [c'est-à-dire, le parti du duc de Broglie], est celui d'une République centralisée, autoritaire, égalitaire, fermée aux nobles comme aux prêtres, se méfiant des 'gros,' protectrice des 'petits,' hostile en même temps à la démagogie, soucieuse des enterprises modestes et répandant, par l'instruction laïque et obligatoire, les 'lumières' à pleines mains."
34. G. W. F. Hegel, [*Lectures on*] *The Philosophy of History* (New York: Dover, 1955), 85–6, translation slightly altered. I have expanded on this theme in my book *Hegel's Retreat from Eleusis* (Princeton: Princeton University Press, 1978), 184–223.
35. I do not, of course, mean that Hamilton's doctrine of liberty owes anything to Jacobinism or that the events cited here took place while he was in power. However, the involvement of public policy and public finance in the "opening of the West" is a direct consequence of Hamilton's vision of the "Continental System."
36. Clémenceau's articles are collected and translated in Fernand Baldensperger, ed., *American Reconstruction, 1865–1870* (New York, 1928).

10

The Birth of America's Second Bill of Rights

William E. Leuchtenburg

When, as a consequence of the genius of Edouard Laboulaye and the generosity of the French nation, the majestic Statue of Liberty was unveiled in New York harbor in the autumn of 1886, the American people were properly appreciative—but nonetheless regarded the gift as only their due. For had not the citizenry of "the land of the free" enshrined in their Constitution a Bill of Rights that made their country's charter the model for those who treasured liberty throughout the civilized world? In truth, the people of the United States, however exaggerated their view of the uniqueness of their situation, did have more than a little reason for pride. Yet not only were there a great many Americans in 1886 who did not enjoy all the blessings of liberty, but the constitutional order was, far more than was recognized then or is fully recognized even today, in one critical respect seriously deficient.

To illustrate that reality, I like to begin my course on the U.S. Supreme Court at the University of North Carolina with a fictitious scenario. The year, I tell my students, is 1859. The North Carolina state legislature, they are to imagine, has enacted a law stipulating that any criticism of the state government at all, no matter how gentle, is punishable by death. A local newspaper publishes an editorial mildly critical of the governor. The editor is arrested and hauled off to prison to await prosecution for an offense that could cost him his life. What protection, I ask, does he have under the U.S. Constitution?

Because it is the first day of class, students might be expected to be a bit shy about speaking out, but this question seems so easy that they are not at all hesitant, and from every spot around the seminar table answers are called out. "Freedom of the press." I shake my head, no. "Freedom of speech." No. "Right to a fair trial." No. "Habeas corpus." No. "The Bill of Rights." No. "The First Amendment." No. "The First Eight Amendments." No. Finally, they subside in puzzlement and await the answer. And it comes as a shock to them to learn that the answer is that the editor has *no* protection under the U.S. Constitution, none at all.[1]

The students are now baffled. But does the Constitution not provide for freedom of press and freedom of speech, they ask? What about the Bill of Rights? What about the First Amendment? Well, I answer, what does the Constitution actually say? They think about that, and some of them scurry to their books, and before long, one of the quicker students grasps what the problem is. The Constitution says, in the First Amendment of the Bill of Rights:

> Congress shall make no law respecting an establishment of religion, or prohibiting the free exercise thereof; or abridging the freedom of speech, or of press; or the right of the people peaceably to assemble, and to petition the Government for a redress of grievances.

To repeat, "*Congress* shall make no law . . . ." The restrictions apply wholly to the *national* government. The First Amendment says nothing at all about the states, which are free to act as they will.

The U.S. Supreme Court itself had confirmed that the Bill of Rights did not apply to the states, first in a ruling in 1833[2] and again in 1845 in a case that grew out of a dreadful yellow fever epidemic. To curb the spread of the disease, the city of New Orleans confined funerals to one chapel. When a priest carried out funeral rites not in that chapel but in another Catholic church, he was arrested and fined. He appealed to the U.S. Supreme Court on the ground that his conviction violated the free exercise of religion clause of the First Amendment. But the Court denied his claim. "The Constitution," it explained, "makes no provision for protecting the citizens of the respective States in their religious liberties."[3]

That omission left a considerable gap in the guarantees of liberty in America, for, although when we consider the need for safeguarding freedom we think first of the menace of the leviathan national state, liberty has, in fact, been more menaced in localities. To be sure, there have been serious transgressions by the national government: episodes such as the Alien and Sedition Acts in the early republic, the persecution of dissenters in World War I and its aftermath, and the frenzy of McCarthyism in the 1950s come to mind. But the Bill of Rights, as interpreted by the U.S. Supreme Court, has provided little shield at such times. As Henry Steele Commager pointed out in 1943, the record of the Supreme Court discloses not a single case, in a century and a half, where the Supreme Court has protected freedom of speech, press, assembly, or petition against Congressional attack.[4]

Furthermore, the incursions by the national government have usually turned out to be short-lived, limited to a brief war crisis, whereas the denial of rights by state and local governments has not infrequently been endemic. Throughout our history, a black in Mississippi had far more to fear from state than federal authority, and the absence of any provision in the U.S. Constitution to protect his or her rights against abuse by local sovereigns was a grievous shortcoming.

The year 1859 in the scenario, however, was chosen advisedly, for something was soon to happen that had the potential for radically changing that reality by revolutionizing the relationship of the national government to the states. Out of the Civil War and Reconstruction came three constitutional amendments, one of which was eventually to prove of enormous significance for civil liberties in America. Especially encouraging was the first section of the Fourteenth Amendment, ratified in 1868, which reads:

> No State shall make or enforce any law which shall abridge the privileges or immunities of citizens of the United States; nor shall any State deprive any person of life, liberty, or property, without due process of law; nor deny to any person within its jurisdiction the equal protection of the laws.

It was far from clear, though, what Congress had in mind when it approved those words. Did it intend to have all the Bill of Rights, which had bound only the national government before, henceforth be just as binding on the states, so that the New Orleans priest and the hypothetical North Carolina editor would have the same protection of fundamental rights from state action that they had hitherto enjoyed from action by the federal government? That is a question scholars and statesmen have been debating for more than a century, and the question is still unresolved. In actuality, the issue would be decided neither by scholars nor statesmen, although both would be influential, but by the U.S. Supreme Court, for, as Charles Evans Hughes once observed, "the Constitution is what the judges say it is."[5]

And when the Court began to interpret the Fourteenth Amendment, it did so in a fashion that indicated that the amendment had changed virtually nothing. The New Orleans priest and the hypothetical North Carolina editor appeared to be no better off than they had been before the Fourteenth Amendment was ratified. When the Court first explored the meaning of the Fourteenth Amendment, in a major pronouncement in 1873,[6] it construed the meaning of "privileges and immunities" so narrowly that virtually nothing has been heard of that clause from that day to this.[7]

Much more important has been the due process clause of the Fourteenth Amendment, though it, too, got off to an unpropitious start. The Court first took a serious look at the meaning of that clause for civil liberties in a case that arose out of marital infidelity in the capital city of California. In February, 1882, Joseph Hurtado, who had already killed one man in a barroom brawl and gotten away with it, shot and bludgeoned to death on a Sacramento street a Chilean immigrant who had been carrying on an affair with Hurtado's wife. He was tried, convicted and sentenced to hang. Hurtado's lawyers claimed that his rights had been violated because he had not been indicted by a grand jury, a procedure required by the Fifth Amendment of the U.S. Constitution, which, it was said, should now be thought of as integrated in the due process clause of the Fourteenth Amendment, restricting state governments in the same way that the national government was restricted. In 1884, the Supreme Court, in *Hurtado v. California*, ruled against the murderer. Though the states, it said, must respect "fundamental principles of liberty and justice," they should not have rigid procedures imposed on them, for to do so "would be to stamp upon our jurisprudence the unchangeableness attributed to the laws of the Medes and Persians." Despite the Fourteenth Amendment, Hurtado was to hang.[8]

That landmark decision, coming in the very year that Bartholdi and Eiffel were putting the finishing touches on the Statue of Liberty in Paris, defined the constitutional situation in late nineteenth-century America. The Fourteenth Amendment promised a new beginning; the Court in some of its language had indicated it might at some point recognize a new departure; but no one had yet derived any palpable benefit. Not until 1897, a generation after the Fourteenth Amendment was ratified, did the Court first indicate that it was open to the view that the Amendment might incorporate any of the Bill of Rights, and that observation came in a railroad property case that had no immediate consequence for individual liberties. Moreover, as was to be characteristic of such opinions, in spite of that dictum, the plaintiff lost.[9]

Defense attorneys, however, are a persistent lot, and the avenue of the Fourteenth Amendment seemed so inviting that the Supreme Court was given more than one chance to change its mind. In 1900, in a case involving a desperado named "Gunplay" Maxwell who had robbed a Utah bank of more than three thousand dollars in gold coins and taken off in a horse and buggy for a canyon hideaway where he was apprehended by a posse, the Court denied that conviction by an eight-man jury in a state court violated a Constitutional right even though federal practice under the Sixth Amendment required a twelve-man panel. In fact, the Justices went out of their way to say that the Fourteenth Amendment had effected no new curbs on the behavior of the states.[10] Eight years later, in a seminal case growing out of accusations of fraud and deception in the collapse of two New Jersey banks, the Court declared that the question whether the first eight amendments applied to the states via the privileges and immunities clause "is no longer open in this Court," and maintained that the due process clause did not afford a right against self-incrimination, for that right was not fundamental.[11] That ruling—that the U.S. Constitution established no right against self-incrimination in state prosecutions—was to last all the way down until 1964.[12]

The country had now gone through the 1870s, 1880s, 1890s, and would go through the first two decades of this century and more with the situation essentially unchanged with respect to the nationalization of civil liberties from what it had been before the Civil War. As late as 1922 the Supreme Court asserted that "neither the Fourteenth Amendment nor any other provision of the Constitution of the United States imposes upon the states any restrictions about 'freedom of speech.'"[13] It was not, indeed, until 1925, just two generations ago, that the Court first said clearly that some, at least, of the Bill of Rights applied to the states, and even then, the plaintiff lost.

The milestone case of 1925, which took a long time to make its way to the Supreme Court, arose out of the Red Scare following World War I. Early in November 1919, a committee of the New York state legislature dispatched seven hundred policemen on a dragnet raid of radical headquarters. Of the five hundred people they arrested, the biggest catch was a twenty-eight-year-old man, Benjamin Gitlow, a leader of the left-wing faction of the Socialist Party that would soon help found the Communist party. Though the raids caught a number of innocent people, Gitlow was a genuine revolutionary. He was charged with violating New York's Criminal Anarchy Act of 1902, adopted after the assassination of President McKinley in Buffalo, because he had several months before taken part in writing and disseminating a manifesto denying that change could come through the democratic legislative process and saying that it was imperative "to destroy the parliamentary state." Gitlow did not dispute this accusation. Indeed, to the despair of his well-known attorney, Clarence Darrow, he insisted on lecturing the jury on the principles of the Left Wing Manifesto. Under these circumstances, it is hardly surprising that the jury took less than an hour to convict him. In February 1920, he was given the maximum sentence of five to ten years, and he could have no doubt that he would spend a full ten years in the state penitentiary.

To Gitlow's side, though, came a new organization that had emerged from the travail of pacifists and conscientious objectors in World War I: the American Civil Liberties Union. The ACLU's attorney sought to persuade the Supreme Court that the Fourteenth Amendment embraced one of the vital clauses of the First Amendment: the right of free speech. Furthermore, he maintained that Gitlow's activities did not constitute a clear and present danger to the community, for as one historian has observed,

> There had been no showing by the state of New York that the Left Wing Manifesto had induced anything other than massive yawning among the public of New York, and as Zechariah Chafee has said, any 'agitator who read these thirty-four pages . . . to a mob would not stir them to violence, except possibly against himself.'[14]

When the Court finally handed down its decision in the *Gitlow* case in 1925, some six years after the issue of the Left Wing Manifesto, it made a historic statement. "For present purposes we may and do assume," it said,

> that freedom of speech and of the press—which are protected by the First Amendment from abridgment by Congress—are among the fundamental personal rights and 'liberties' protected by the due process clause of the Fourteenth Amendment from impairment by the States.[15]

For the first time since ratification of the post–Civil War amendments some seventy years before, the Court was at last willing to say unequivocally: Yes, the Fourteenth Amendment does include some of the original Bill of Rights, now applied to the states. Not that this acknowledgment did Ben Gitlow any good—since, characteristically, the Court went on, despite these words, to uphold Gitlow's conviction.[16] Three quarters of a century after the adoption of the Fourteenth Amendment, the Court had yet to reverse any conviction or to strike down any state law for violating civil liberties.

That situation changed dramatically, however, in the fertile year of 1931 when, on two occasions, the Court broke new ground. The first of the cases grew out of a raid launched on a Communist party youth camp in the San Bernardino range in California. Arrested were one man and six women, including "the girl Red," as newspapers called her, nineteen-year-old Yetta Stromberg. Like Gitlow, these were no liberal innocents, but bona fide Communists. Each morning at seven the children at the camp, under Yetta's tutelage, participated in raising the flag of the Soviet Union with its hammer and sickle to the top of a flagpole; the children then pledged allegiance to "the workers' red flag, and to the cause for which it stands." Yet having arrested these people, what was the state to charge them with? Nobody could figure that out until someone remembered that in 1919 the California legislature had enacted a law forbidding the flying of a red flag for seditious purposes. The seven were indicted and convicted of violating the red flag statute. The lone man escaped a prison term by committing suicide. The women, though, received stiff sentences with the heaviest sentence meted out to Yetta Stromberg—one to ten years in San Quentin: for displaying a red flag.[17]

With the help both of the ACLU and a Communist front legal association, the International Labor Defense, Yetta carried her case to the United States Supreme Court, and on May 18, 1931, in *Stromberg v. California*, the Court, in an opinion delivered by the new chief justice, Charles Evans Hughes, reversed Yetta's conviction because the red flag law was a denial of the freedom of speech guaranteed by the Fourteenth Amendment.

> "It has been determined," the Chief Justice said, "that the conception of liberty under the due process clause of the Fourteenth Amendment embraces the right of free speech [in the First Amendment]."[18]

Two weeks later came an even more significant decision, this one involving a scoundrel named J. M. Near. Together with an equally unsavory character, Howard Guilford, who, it has been said, "always had one foot in jail," Near ran a scandal sheet, the *Saturday Press*, that accused the foremost public officials in Minneapolis of being in league with a gambling syndicate. The Twin Cities were, in fact, notorious for venality—Lincoln Steffens had once written of "The Shame of Minneapolis"—but the weekly went beyond legitimate exposure to engage in character assassination and was viciously anti-Semitic. It called on "the decent citizens of Minneapolis" to "rid the city of these criminal Jews," and resorted to racial stereotyping. Moreover, the two men may well have been involved in an extortion racket—threatening to publish defamatory stories unless they were paid off. Guilford, in fact, had at various times been convicted of criminal libel, arrested for carrying concealed weapons, and charged with extortion. In short, though the name of Jay Near has a secure place in the annals of freedom of the press, he was no heroic crusading editor.[19] (In that regard, Near was typical, for as a leading authority has noted, the litigants who brought about a second Bill of Rights were "murderers, thieves, bookies . . . , university professors, narcotics addicts."[20])

The case of *Near v. Minnesota* had begun in 1927 when a country attorney and future governor, Floyd Olson—who had been personally attacked by the weekly, and who, having been raised in a Jewish neighborhood, resented the anti-Semitic slurs on his friends—obtained a court order to restrain Near and Guilford from further publication of the *Saturday Press*. He took this step under authority of a law that had been enacted in response to the resentment aroused by scandal sheets plaguing the state. The regular press did not object to this legislation, and the act was validated by the Minnesota Supreme Court.[21] Nonetheless, Near's case was carried to the U.S. Supreme Court—not by liberals or radicals but by the publisher of the arch-conservative *Chicago Tribune*, Colonel Robert R. McCormick, who saw in Minnesota's "gag law," as it was called, a threat to the press everywhere. Early in June 1931, the Supreme Court, in a 5–4 decision, with yet another opinion by Charles Evans Hughes, struck down the Minnesota law for imposing prior restraint upon publication. "It is no longer open to doubt," the Chief Justice declared, "that the liberty of the press and of speech is within the liberty safeguarded by the due process clause of the 14th Amendment."[22]

So after three quarters of a century of silence or denial, the Supreme Court had at long last announced in a two-week interval in 1931 that two aspects of the original Bill of Rights that restrained the national government—freedom of speech and freedom of press—now applied to state governments as well. How did that happen? Why did the Supreme Court so abruptly change its mind? We are not sure. All we know definitely is that the Court first enunciated this principle almost offhandedly in 1925 in *Gitlow*, and by 1931, a majority of five justices, two of them newly appointed, took the *Gitlow* principle for granted and saw no need to offer a well-wrought justification for what it was doing. The whole process has been defined by one scholar as "absent-minded incrementalism."[23] With no satisfactory documentary evidence, we are reduced to speculation, and it is not unreasonable to suppose that, among the many conceivable causes of the change, one may have been the very presence of the Statue of Liberty as a reminder to a new generation of jurists not of promise achieved but of promise unfulfilled.

Once the Court, for whatever reason, accepted the principle, it managed to absorb more and more of the Bill of Rights into the Fourteenth Amendment, with the next advance coming less than six years after the great breakthrough of 1931, in a case that, like *Gitlow* and *Stromberg*, arose out of a red scare. In 1934, a maritime strike led by an Australian-born radical sent a shudder through the American middle class when it tied up the entire Pacific Coast from San Diego to Vancouver and in San Francisco even resulted, however briefly, in resort to the most feared of labor's weapons: a general strike. On July 11, in an effort to break the strike in Portland, Oregon, the police shot four pickets and raided Communist headquarters. Two weeks later, the Communists staged a protest rally, which was again raided by the Portland police who arrested four Communists, one of them Dirk De Jonge, who had been the Communist candidate for mayor of the city. He was convicted of violating the state's criminal syndicalism act of 1919 by organizing the rally, even though nothing unlawful was said or done at the meeting, and sentenced to seven years in prison. But in January 1937, the United States Supreme Court, with Hughes once more writing the opinion, reversed the conviction and struck down the syndicalism law. The "right of peaceable assembly," said the Chief Justice, "is the right cognate to those of free speech and free press and is equally fundamental."[24] So still another provision of the Bill of Rights had been absorbed into the due process clause of the Fourteenth Amendment. What before had constrained only the national government now restricted the states too.

The Court soon demonstrated that it was also prepared to carry what remained of the First Amendment—the religious liberties—into the Fourteenth Amendment, in no small part because of challenges raised by one obstreperous religious sect. It is doubtful that any single organization in our history has brought about more Supreme Court rulings in the realm of civil liberties than the Jehovah's Witnesses, despite the fact that they were unalterably opposed to government and all of its works. Some of their difficulty with the law stemmed from the fact that they were no less hostile to the Catholic church, and many Catholics were understandably offended by a sect that aggressively promoted pamphlets and records likening their church to a "harlot" or calling it "the representative of the devil." When on a spring day in 1938, a Jehovah's Witness named Cantwell and his two teen-aged sons, armed with anti-Catholic tracts and recordings, started their round of doorbell ringing in a neighborhood of New Haven that could not have been more ill-chosen (it was 90 percent Catholic), a Catholic woman on whom they called phoned the police, and they were arrested and subsequently convicted. The main counts against them were breach of peace and violation of a state law requiring a permit to solicit for a religious purpose. In May 1940, the U.S. Supreme Court reversed their convictions and struck down the Connecticut law requiring a permit as a denial of the free exercise of religion. The Fourteenth Amendment, the Court said,

> embraces the liberties guaranteed by the First Amendment. The First Amendment declares that Congress shall make no law respecting an establishment of religion or prohibiting the free exercise thereof. The Fourteenth Amendment has rendered the legislatures of the states as incompetent as Congress to enact such laws.[25]

In sum, the Court had now, as a consequence of *Cantwell* (which would be amplified by a later decision on a religion clause)[26] absorbed all of the First Amendment—the liberty amendment—into the Fourteenth Amendment of the Constitution.[27]

It would require another generation to complete the nationalization of the Bill of Rights, but with a nice sense of fitness, that final accomplishment of the Warren Court, which had hardly let a year pass in the 1960s without expanding further the meaning of the Fourteenth Amendment, was to come on June 23, 1969, Earl Warren's final day as chief justice of the United States.[28] That ruling brought to a climax a generation of fulfillment in constitutional law. For, though on the occasion of the centennial of the Statue of Liberty, our thoughts inevitably return to the birth of the Bill of Rights in the eighteenth century, the most significant developments have come since the gracious gift of the French people first arrived in New York harbor. Indeed, they go back only so far as the case of Ben Gitlow in 1926, or, more properly, to the cases of Yetta Stromberg, the girl Red, and Jay Near, the Minnesota scandalmonger, in 1931, which is to say within the lifetime of many people still alive today. The Statue of Liberty, then, has proven to be not a reward for virtue achieved but an everpresent reminder that the task of maintaining and expanding civic rights is never done.

And it is this rich legacy of liberty that, many fear, is now in danger. For beginning in 1985 the Attorney General of the United States launched an assault upon it so vigorous that it led to unprecedented public rejoinders by two members of the United States Supreme Court. In his addresses, Attorney General Meese used words such as "bizarre" to characterize rulings both of the Warren Court and of the Burger Court, and he categorized the developments I have described to you here—the application of the Bill of Rights to the states—as "politically violent and constitutionally suspect."[29] Some of the response to these remarks strikes me as excessive. We always do well to keep in mind, as my former colleague and teaching partner Benno

Schmidt, the president of Yale University, has pointed out, that a court in a democracy must anchor itself to the Constitution and cannot merely offer "a pretentious gaggle of political pronouncements."[30] But if we were truly to roll back the achievements of the past generation, back beyond the trial of Ben Gitlow, back beyond the misadventures of Gunplay Maxwell, back even beyond the adoption of the Fourteenth Amendment, all the way back to the scenario in North Carolina in 1859 with which this chapter began, we would eradicate a remarkable chapter in the never-ending story of the struggle for liberty that we rightly honor as we commemorate the Statue of Liberty's centennial.

NOTES

1. I hasten to add that there has never been so draconian a law. However, in 1858 in North Carolina a man was sentenced to a year in prison for circulating a book hostile to slavery, and the North Carolina Supreme Court sustained the conviction on the ground that it was criminal conduct to disseminate literature that caused "slaves to be discontented and free negroes dissatisfied." *State v. Worth*, 52 N.C. (7 Jones) 488 (1860) at 492; Michael Kent Curtis, *No State Shall Abridge* (Durham, N.C.: Duke University Press, 1986), 31. Individuals could, of course, invoke the bills of rights in state constitutions, but, Curtis maintains, "too often they proved to be paper barriers." *Ibid.*, xiii.
2. *Barron v. Baltimore*, 7 Pet. 243 (1833).
3. *Permoli v. New Orleans*, 3 How. 589 (1845) at 609.
4. Henry Steele Commager, *Majority Rule and Minority Rights* (New York: Oxford University Press, 1943), 55.
5. For Hughes's explanation of what he meant by that often-misquoted remark, see Merlo Pusey, *Charles Evans Hughes* (New York: Columbia University Press, 1963), 204. The literature on "original intent" is vast. The basic statement denying that Congress intended to incorporate the Bill of Rights appeared in Charles Fairman, "Does the Fourteenth Amendment Incorporate the Bill of Rights?" *Stanford Law Review*, 2 (December 1949): 5–139. Fairman wrote in response to Justice Hugo Black's contrary claim in *Adamson v. California*, 332 U.S. 46 (1947) at 71. Black is rebutted somewhat differently in Frank H. Walker, Jr., "Was It Intended that the Fourteenth Amendment Incorporate the Bill of Rights?" *North Carolina Law Review*, 42 (1964): 925–36. The most extensive response to Fairman is: Curtis, *No State Shall Abridge*, with an arresting foreword by William W. Van Alstyne.
6. *Slaughter House Cases*, 16 Wall. 36 (1873).
7. When the Court invoked the privileges and immunities clause to strike down a Vermont tax law in 1935, it encountered widespread criticism for resurrecting a corpse. *Colgate v. Harvey*, 296 U.S. 404 (1935). That ruling survived for only five years. It was overturned in *Madden v. Kentucky*, 309 U.S. 83 (1940). For criticism of *Colgate*, see Alpheus Thomas Mason, *Harlan Fiske Stone* (New York: Viking Press, 1956), 397–99; Felix Frankfurter to Harlan Fiske Stone, December 16, 19, 1935, Frankfurter MSS, Library of Congress, Box 105.
8. *Hurtado v. California*, 110 U.S. 516 (1884) at 529. As it happened, he did not hang but died of tuberculosis in his cell. The Court did acknowledge that the due process clause of the Fourteenth Amendment safeguarded those "fundamental principles of

liberty and justice which lie at the base of all our civil and political institutions." But it did not indicate what it meant by that statement.

9. *Chicago, Burlington & Quincy Railroad Co. v. Chicago*, 166 U.S. 226 (1897). The decision was significant chiefly in departing from the view in *Hurtado* that "due process" could not include any of the basic rights of the first eight amendments because such a reading would render some of the language of the Constitution superfluous.

10. *Maxwell v. Dow*, 176 U.S. 581 (1900). The Court also dismissed Maxwell's claim that indictment by a grand jury was required by citing *Hurtado*.

11. *Twining v. New Jersey*, 211 U.S. 78 (1908) at 98. *Twining* did, though, hold out the hope that rights similar to those in the Bill of Rights might apply to the states.

12. *Malloy v. Hogan*, 378 U.S. 1 (1964).

13. *Prudential Insurance Co. v. Cheek*, 259 U.S. 530 (1922) at 543.

14. Richard C. Cortner, *The Supreme Court and the Second Bill of Rights* (Madison: University of Wisconsin Press, 1981), 57–58, citing Zechariah Chafee, Jr., *Free Speech in the United States* (Cambridge, Mass.: Harvard University Press, 1954), 319. Cortner's account of this case, as well as of other cases discussed in this paper, is indispensable.

15. *Gitlow v. New York*, 268 U.S. 652 (1925) at 666. That conclusion had been reached individually by several justices before then. Alex B. Lacy, Jr., "The Bill of Rights and the Fourteenth Amendment: The Evolution of the Absorption Doctrine," *Washington and Lee Law Review*, 23 (1966): 43.

16. Before the year was out, though, Gitlow had been pardoned by the governor of New York, Al Smith. He went on to be the Communist party's national vice-presidential candidate in 1928—ironically, on a ticket opposed to Al Smith—and then, after a falling out with Stalin, an implacable anti-Communist for the next generation.

17. Cortner, *The Supreme Court and the Second Bill of Rights*, 73–81.

18. *Stromberg v. California*, 283 U.S. 359 (1931) at 368. A few writers place the dividing line four years earlier with *Fiske v. Kansas*, 274 U.S. 380 (1927). See, for example, John Raeburn Green, "The Bill of Rights, the Fourteenth Amendment and the Supreme Court," *Michigan Law Review*, 46 (May 1948): 869. Most commentators, however, regard *Fiske* as too slender a reed.

19. The most extensive account of *Near* is Fred W. Friendly's lively *Minnesota Rag* (New York: Random House, 1981). The passages quoted appear on p. 31 and pp. 45–48. But see, too, Paul L. Murphy, "*Near v. Minnesota* in the Context of Historical Developments," *Minnesota Law Review*, 66 (November 1981): 95–160.

20. Cortner, *The Supreme Court and the Second Bill of Rights*, p. x.

21. *State ex rel Olson v. Guilford*, 174 Minn. 457 (1928); 179 Minn. 40 (1929).

22. *Near v. Minnesota*, 283 U.S. 697 (1931) at 707. For Hughes's achievements, see Merle William Loper, "The Court of Chief Justice Hughes: Contributions to Civil Liberties," *Wayne Law Review*, 12 (Spring 1966): 535–95.

23. Klaus H. Heberle, "From Gitlow to Near: Judicial Amendment by Absent-Minded Incrementalism," *Journal of Politics*, 34 (1972): 458–83. Curiously, not even the ACLU, despite its role in *Gitlow*, appeared to grasp the historic importance of the case.

24. *De Jonge v. Oregon*, 299 U.S. 353 (1937) at 364.

25. Cortner, *The Supreme Court and the Second Bill of Rights*, 100–108; *Cantwell v. Connecticut*, 310 U.S. 296 (1940) at 303.

26. *Everson v. Board of Education*, 330 U.S. 1 (1947).

27. The emphasis on civil liberties was strengthened by the emergence of the "preferred position" doctrine in *United States v. Carolene Prods. Co.*, 304 U.S. 144 (1938) at 152 n. 4. See Louis Lusky, "Footnote Redux: A *Carolene Products* Reminiscence," *Columbia Law Review*, 82 (October 1982): 1093–1105.

28. The Court had indicated that there were limits to its enthusiasm for absorption in *Palko v. Connecticut*, 302 U.S. 319 (1937). It confirmed that attitude in *Adamson v. California*, 332 U.S. 46 (1947), in a decision in which the restraint of Felix Frankfurter prevailed over the ardor of Hugo Black. But twelve years later, the march resumed in *Mapp v. Ohio*, 367 U.S. 643 (1961). Thereafter, almost every year added a new element:

Robinson v. California, 370 U.S. 660 (1962); *Gideon v. Wainwright*, 372 U.S. 335 (1963); *Malloy v. Hogan*, 378 U.S. 1 (1964); *Pointer v. Texas*, 380 U.S. 400 (1965); *Washington v. Texas*, 385 U.S. 812 (1966); *Klopfer v. North Carolina*, 386 U.S. 213 (1967); *Duncan v. Louisiana*, 391 U.S. 146 (1968); *Benton v. Maryland*, 395 U.S. 784 (1969). Some segments of the Bill of Rights were still not absorbed, but they were insignificant. Yet not even in 1969 in *Benton v. Maryland* 395 U.S. 784 (1969), did the Court, in so many words, embrace Black's view that the Fourteenth Amendment incorporated all of the first eight amendments. Indeed, it has never done so. Roald Y. Mykkeltvedt, *The Nationalization of the Bill of Rights* (Port Washington, N.Y.: Associated Faculty Press, 1983), 2.

29. *Los Angeles Times*, 18 October, 1985, II:5; *Washington Post*, November 3, 1985, C2. Meese's views created so much alarm because the advanced ages of liberal justices such as William J. Brennan, Jr., and Thurgood Marshall increased the likelihood that President Reagan would have a number of opportunities to alter the composition of the Supreme Court, and Meese was his main adviser on appointments to the judiciary. The Reagan-nominated chief justice of the United States, William H. Rehnquist, has said that "not all of the strictures which the First Amendment imposes upon Congress are carried over against the states by the Fourteenth Amendment." *Buckley v. Valeo*, 424 U.S. 1 (1976) at 291.

30. Benno C. Schmidt, Jr., "The Quality of Justice," *Los Angeles Times*, 10 November 1985, IV:1, 2.

11

Liberal Models in France, 1900–1930

René Remond

This chapter deals with France from the opening years of the twentieth century, in the immediate aftermath of the Dreyfus Affair, to 1932 on the eve of the great crisis that was to shake confidence in institutions and liberal values. As the period opens, the Third Republic had surmounted one of its gravest crises, but at what a price in terms of liberal ideas and practices! The upheaval brought in its wake a radicalization of the political debate, an exacerbation of tensions and conflicts, and an intensified polarization. The resulting realignments drew a new ideological configuration that left little room for liberal ideas. Liberalism demands a calm climate and at least a minimal consensus among political groups. But the crisis of the Dreyfus Affair had dashed all attempts to bring the centrists together and had cut short all overtures toward consensus. After 1899 and the formation of a leftist coalition government to defend the republic, the "new spirit" was encouraged. Now in the republic, in the government, and in the majority, there was room only for lifelong republicans.

The three decades under discussion here differ strikingly from the previous era. The nineteenth century saw periodic breaks in the continuity of regimes, but the first thirty years of the twentieth century witnessed a continuity of French political institutions. Thus, these decades take their place between a domestic crisis that was prejudicial to liberalism and another crisis, more general in its repercussions, that was to call into question the postulates of the system of liberal thought.

But was this period a liberal oasis for all that? It was split right down the middle by the ordeal of World War I, which brutally disrupted the regular course of collective existence. What were the consequences for liberalism of those four highly exceptional years? Circumstances imposed the provisional abandonment of certain arrangements that characterize the workings of a liberal society. The imperative of national defense was not a matter to be discussed, because it was a matter of public safety, hence the resurgence of Jacobinism with the setting up of a war government. The presence of the old authoritarian radical Clemenceau at the head of the government after November 1917 was more than a symbol. He presided over a sort of parliamentary dictatorship. But once the peril had been removed, what remained of the innovations dictated by necessity? Was not the war merely a parenthesis that people hastened to close as soon as possible, or were there still traces of this exceptional situation in postwar institutions, practices, and attitudes?

The first three decades of the century not only demarcate a coherent period from the point of view of institutions and political forces, they also have meaning on another level as the beginning and end points that coincide with the publication of two important essays capable of providing some insights into the situation of liberalism in those years. They are the work of two penetrating observers of political life, two sincerely liberal minds. In 1903, Emile Faguet published a book titled quite simply *Le Libéralisme,* which made an essentially negative assessment of its subject. Faguet claimed he had never met a truly liberal Frenchman and concluded that liberalism was foreign to French culture. France, he asserted, was not liberal, and the Frenchman was not made to be liberal.

It is true that Faguet was writing at a time when Jacobinism was triumphant and political passions were reaching their climax. In 1932, Albert Thibaudet devoted a chapter to liberalism in his book, *Les idées politiques de la France.* He also spoke of liberalism elsewhere. Thibaudet's judgment was more nuanced and less pessimistic than that of Faguet. He remarked that, at the time of writing, France was the only major country in continental Europe to have remained liberal, and he concluded from this fact that such singularity was the sign of a sincere attachment to the values of liberalism.

Which of the two observers is to be considered right? Might their judgments differ only in terms of time and situation? If so, the trend from 1903 to 1932 would seem to indicate the progress of liberal ideas and practices. Is this the real meaning of the period?

That in the early years of the twentieth century France was a democratic society is not in doubt, but this does not necessarily mean that France was also a liberal society, as other chapters in this volume make clear. Liberalism was not originally democratic, nor does democracy have liberalism in its genes. So, was France really liberal between 1900 and 1932?

The answer is less obvious than it might appear. In fact, there is no single answer. It depends on whether intellectual activity, political debates, or administrative practices are taken into account. It also depends on whether the political or economic applications of liberalism are considered. Finally, the answer depends on the moment in time.

The period under consideration was not one of the richest for liberal thought. It contained no great names equal to those that had brought fame to liberal thought in the nineteenth century. There was no one comparable to Constant, Tocqueville, or Laboulaye. These men had themselves fallen into oblivion. Tocqueville's reputation remained in eclipse until after World War II. But if liberal thought scarcely renewed itself, it did occupy solid positions in the universities and at the Académie des Sciences Morales et Politiques perhaps even more than in the Académie Française. One of the most significant manifestations of academic liberalism was the petition signed by those who were called the *cardinaux verts*, Catholics who wished to prevent the clash between the lay republic and an intransigent Catholicism and who pronounced themselves in favor of the acceptance of the separation of church and state. Liberalism also dominated within the Faculty of Law as well as at the Ecole Libre des Sciences Politiques, whose director, Anatole Leroy-Beaulieu, was a model liberal. Liberalism was less powerful at the Sorbonne, where it had to come to terms with more advanced opinions and had compromised with republican radicals. The liberal point of view was expressed in periodicals; even if these did not have a large circulation, they enjoyed a reputation that conferred respectability and authority on their analyses and remarks. Among the most prominent were the *Journal des Débats*, *Les Temps*, and *Revue des Deux Mondes*. Finally, if we may risk what is a verbal anachronism for the period, liberalism was the dominant ideology of the traditional social and intellectual elites, with their marked conservative leanings. Between the two attractions that, in contradictory fashion, always seek out liberalism, the progressive and the conservative, it was the latter that unquestionably dominated at the turn of the century. This was an effect of the break with the government ministers who rejected the liberals as too far to the right.

If certain elites widened the circle, it is to be noted that other more advanced and more systematic doctrines challenged liberal ideas and fought against liberal postulates. On the extreme right was the rising star of Action Française, diametrically opposed to liberal thought, both by its stance and by its turn of mind: the criticism of representative institutions in which the liberals saw the guarantee of liberties; antiparliamentarianism; the denunciation of individualism; the imperatives of reason of state in foreign affairs; the exaltation of the nation; anticapitalism; the dogmatic mind and the intolerance that went with it. One minor point could be grounds for a rapprochement: the attachment to decentralization, which at that time was clearly a conservative opinion. Parallel to this movement there appeared in intellectual circles a Catholic renaissance, as attested by the relatively high number of conversions. But this development took place under the inspiration of an intransigent, antimodernist, and counterrevolutionary interpretation of Catholic tradition, which saw in liberalism the source of all present errors and the cause of all the evils devastating society. On this side of public opinion, therefore, no sympathy for liberal ideas was to be expected.

On the extreme left, socialist doctrines also were defined in terms of opposition to the postulates of liberalism, the denunciation of its effects, and the challenging of its consequences. Before 1914, socialism was perceived as a great hope that many people were to identify as much with the aspiration to universal peace as with the construction of a more just and more fraternal society. After 1918, the example of the Soviet revolution, which exalted the memory of the Commune, and the resurgence of Jacobinism and anarchistic aspirations reactivated many currents fundamentally hostile to liberalism. References to what had been tried abroad became infrequent. People scarcely thought of drawing inspiration from the example of the United States. President Wilson himself was very popular, and honor was paid to his contribution to peace and plans for international organization, but not to the U.S. Constitution. As for references to the British model, more frequent on the right than on the left, these concerned the institution of the monarchy, the Crown, and dynastic continuity, more than Parliament.

And what about the republican party? Was not there a liberal majority formed around the desire to protect democracy against reaction? The answer is mixed. The republicans in power were admittedly liberals, if having an individualistic vision of society and wishing to extend civil and political liberties are enough to earn the liberal label. In 1901, the majority established the freedom to associate, previously viewed as suspect. Like all good liberals, they were also sincerely attached to parliamentary institutions and did not intend to abdicate the sovereignty of elected representatives.

But on other issues, they were anything but liberal in their strategy, behavior, and practices, no doubt partly an effect of the division of the country into two ideological camps. Because the legacy of the Revolution remained contested and because democracy was always rejected by a fraction of the right, the defense of the republic prevailed over all other considerations. The republic had to be saved at all costs, even if basic liberties had to be violated. Everything was justified when it was a matter of preserving what democracy had achieved: no liberty for the enemies of liberty. Hence, there was much legislation that was none too respectful of liberties. In his thesis *La République contre les libertés?* Jean Pierre Machelon picks out many examples of violations of this nature, including the scandalous suspension of the irremovability of magistrates so as to purge several hundred judges whom the government suspected of republicanism. Here we are far from our conception of a legal state.

Nowhere was this tendency so blatant as in religious policy. Anticlerical passion inspired discriminatory legislation that disqualified citizens in the eyes of the law just because they were members of religious orders. Thus, from 1904, monks were deprived of the right to teach, a right that was granted to all their fellow citizens. It was a proscriptive legislation that the republicans adopted. In principle, the separation of church and state was a liberal idea, and in other times its adoption could have been a victory for liberalism. For was this separation not the legal expression of the state's recognition of religious freedom and of its refusal to interfere in the field of individual conscience? But the spirit of the majority who voted for separation and the majority's refusal to take into consideration the particulars of church organization made this law an act of combat. Only subsequent application was to change the law's direction and substitute for the legislators' antireligious intentions a more respectful practice of liberty.

One final element of dissension and radical misunderstanding between the majority left and liberalism was a republican integralism. This was an attitude that did not allow the slightest concession; that held democratic realizations to be an indivisible whole; and that, above all, reserved access to power for true-born republican party members. The republicans appropriated for themselves an exclusive right to the republic.

Let us add that the notion of pluralism was quite foreign to the spirit of the times, on the right as on the left. It did not occur to anyone that differences could be a source of strength. The passion for unity, a unity conceived of as uniformity, excluded any compromising between the goal of national unity around the principles of 1789 and democracy. For all those reasons, liberalism was not an honored or a powerful force in the France of the early twentieth century.

World War I brought both gains and losses for liberalism. Immediate needs and war policies intensified the attacks on the liberal economy. After social legislation that had started to curb the applications of liberalism and move the workings of the economy away from partners' absolute freedom to contract, the government imposed regulations and extended the state's scope for intervention. The state rationed, requisitioned, and fixed prices and wages. The state even participated directly in the economy. It became an industrialist and an employer. The planned economy that came into being was the exact opposite of the market economy advocated by liberalism. Of the measures thus taken under the force of necessity, several were to outlive the circumstances and last until the next war and even beyond. One such measure was rent control, which was decided on in the first days of the war to preserve the rights of those tenants who had been called up and to avoid the eviction of their families. Rent control was to remain in force until the present for certain categories of housing, and would gravely affect the real estate market.

But for ideas as well as for political behavior, the changes took place in a way that was rather acceptable to liberalism. French public opinion did not support the reinstatement of anticlerical legislation, the application of which had been suspended since the declaration of war. The cooling of passions formerly stirred up by the religious question made possible the reintegration within the republic of men on the political right who were liberals: André Tardieu, Paul Reynaud, and Pierre-Etienne Flandrin, to name but a few of the more representative ones. The theme of pluralism made a timid appearance under cover of the formula of the "spiritual families" comprising France. From the fiercely unitarian concepts of the republicans of the 1900s to the recognition of a plurality of families working toward the creation of the national community, the shift was a major one. Finally, let us note the beginnings of a regionalization that was to temper centralism and introduce a dose of liberalism into administrative organization and relations between the state and local communities.

What was vital was that a diffuse liberalism should penetrate people's consciences and mores and inspire behavior. The fundamental freedoms of opinion and of expression were respected. The French, who had become used to these freedoms, enjoyed them without thinking much about them. Were they not to be taken as a given? They forgot the price at which they had been obtained and the long road they had had to traverse before such freedoms were durably implemented. In 1932, Thibaudet, a lucid observer of political manners and a connoisseur of the sensitivity of his contemporaries, believed that liberalism had won the day. If liberalism no longer roused great devotion or sparked enthusiasm, the reason was that it had become part and parcel of reality. It was the victim of its own triumph. Even if liberal theses did not enjoy the favor of intellectuals, liberalism in France had become a common practice.

Almost immediately, all this was to be called into question by the upheavals of the 1930s, the rise of perils abroad, the fascination with foreign models, and the imminence of fresh conflict. Thus the situation of liberalism in French society in the 1930s is subject to quite another diagnosis.

12

From the Ancients to the Moderns: The Reasons for the Liberal Revival

Jean-Claude Casanova

I want to emphasize at the start that I am not discussing the problem of continuity between the liberalism of the ancients, or classical liberalism, and contemporary liberalism. The former I take to be defined by three elements: individual liberties, representative government, and capitalist market economy. By the latter I mean neither the liberalism adopted by politicians in the same way as one chooses an attractive tie, nor the liberal vogue whose decline or rebirth the newspapers lie in wait for in order to satisfy their readers' unquenchable thirst for novelty. Instead, I take contemporary liberalism to mean a combination of democracy, the welfare state, and a market economy with state intervention. This model of liberalism derives from the classical model but differs from it to the point of having been characterized under the twofold influence of democracy and social welfare ideas, either as a synthesis of liberalism and socialism or as a sort of reformed liberalism.

Our problem is not to analyze the characteristics of this type of government but to ask why, since about the mid-1970s, both in the United States and in Europe the wind has been blowing more strongly in favor of a purer, less diluted brand of liberalism. We hear talk of the revival and even the triumph of liberalism. It is a change that is all the more surprising because on the eve and on the morrow of World War II, and even in the 1950s, our period was believed to be witnessing the collapse or the rout of liberalism.[1]

THE DEFEAT OF LIBERALISM

The historical vulgate is well known. It holds that liberalism was born between the English and French revolutions. The Golden Age was attained at the end of the nineteenth century. The turning point was reached between 1870 and 1914. The crisis opened with World War I. The death certificate bears the date of World War II.

For Joseph Schumpeter, the diagnosis was straightforward. Liberalism was defeated during the interwar period because liberalism changed to the point of renouncing its own principles. Confidence in laissez-faire disappeared; personal taxation developed; socialist parties masterminded by middle-class intellectuals grew; several nations adopted protectionism; mutually hostile alignments of peasant farmers, bureaucrats, nationalists, and Catholics sprang up; the alliance between economic science and liberalism, which had dominated the nineteenth century, was broken; social Catholicism opted for corporatism; and finally, intellectuals adopted a hostile attitude to the market economy. Passing from its traditional form to its modern form, liberalism changed and lost its soul as it became tinged with socialism and nationalism.

But this change appears to me better described in a few lines in an article by Pierre Manent.[2] For him, social democracy was born of the dialectic between the two principles dominating liberalism: the principles of the market and of representative government, and of the gradual predominance of the latter over the former. Blue-collar and white-collar workers are at the same time citizens and voters. When they do not realize their aspirations from the workings of the economy, they try to achieve their economic objectives via the ballot box. To the detriment of the market, democracy allows them to do this. It matters little whether liberals are the adversaries or the political authors of this operation. As authors, liberals try to keep an electoral clientele by cutting the ground from under their opponents' feet. As adversaries, liberals are opposed to conservatives who want to turn them to the left, and to socialists who, as Engels's testament suggested, are more concerned with elections than with revolution. In both cases, the outcome is the same.

This prospect highlights two basic traits of modern liberalism: the rise of the democratic principle, which leads to the confusion of the democratic idea and the liberal idea, and the separation of the economy and politics.

THE DEMOCRATIC IDEA AND THE LIBERAL IDEA

If the features of democracy are defined as equality among citizens, the sharing of sovereignty, universal suffrage, and the competition of multiple parties to exercise political power, and if liberalism is defined to mean the existence of constitutional guarantees of personal liberties, we are forced to note that our societies are characterized by the fusion of democratic and liberal ideas[3]—a theme that is commonplace for Americans but less so for Europeans.

Traditional European liberalism admitted that a society could be liberal without being democratic. For such a society it was enough to lodge executive power in customary or hereditary authority and to reserve prerogative in a fraction of the population—the rich, the enlightened, or those with power—leaving the masses (including all women) outside the political city.

Even present-day liberalism necessarily mixes the two ideas to such an extent that they cannot be separated in everyday language. The fact is that two symmetrical and complementary relationships have engendered much confusion. First, it is said that over time the situation developed in which the exercise of individual rights led to their encompassing a fragment of sovereignty; the doctrine according to which a society can remain liberal without becoming democratic is only a temporizing doctrine: democracy is the ultimate consequence of liberties and individual rights. Second, it is held that society cannot be democratic if it is not liberal. Universal suffrage and multiple parties require the existence and preservation of individual liberties. In other words, liberalism is the requirement for a democracy. That is why those "popular democracies" in Eastern Europe were not true democracies.

From these relationships, present-day liberalism draws an interpretation of the past and a set of questions about the present. It rereads the history of the nineteenth century as that of the development of universal suffrage and sees in this change,[4] a continuous and uniform process of democratization. The histories of Britain, France, Germany, or Switzerland can be clarified in this light. The episodes and stages may differ from one country to another, but the framework remains the same everywhere.

As for the present, the chief issues concern countries deprived of liberty. Authoritarian regimes are likely to become more liberal, as has been proved recently in Spain, as well as in the major Latin American countries. Should we consider recent changes in the Soviet regime in this light? Are not communist or totalitarian governments, as opposed to authoritarian ones, also capable of liberalization? Will the liberalization prove to be long-lasting in all the countries of Eastern Europe? The answers to those questions remain uncertain, but they are all dominated by the same prospect: the world is made up of some liberalized regimes and of some regimes that, to varying degrees, are susceptible of liberalization.

From this historical reinterpretation and analysis of current affairs, modern-day liberalism draws an acute awareness of the possibilities of failure and of difficulties for the liberal idea. The utopian view, according to which the liberal and democratic process is linear, easy, universal, and irreversible, has lost some of its strength. But was this illusion really one of the features of traditional liberalism? In the eyes of the first liberals, did not the failure of the French Revolution introduce the same elements of doubt and uncertainty as those which, for today's liberals, are engendered by the persistence of authoritarian regimes and the power of totalitarian states? The fact remains that present-day liberalism is dominated by the idea that it is inseparable from democracy.

THE SEPARATION OF THE ECONOMY AND POLITICS

In traditional liberalism, economic freedom and political freedom were fused. Among individual rights, property and the rights of entrepreneurship held an essential place. Taxation was to be limited and proportional. The ruling political class was mixed quite naturally with the privileged class in the economic order.

In modern-day liberalism, things are less clear, if not in doctrine at least in practice. For certain liberals, political freedom stems from principles, and economic freedom from expediency. In this pattern, economic freedom is subordinate; it is one of the instruments for serving the social ends of wealth, efficiency, and justice. Depending on conflicts over priorities among social ends, but also on particular circumstances, economic liberalism can be reformed, amended, or abandoned without calling political liberalism into question.

For their part, socialists, at least those who are democrats, have always asserted that the two liberalisms were neither linked nor complementary and even that political liberty could be fulfilled only in socialism: that it would be better served through public than private enterprise, by an organized economy rather than by the market, and by the fiscal distribution of income instead of distribution among factors of production. One wing of socialism constructed a societal model that would combine the political institutions of liberalism with various degrees of collectivized property and central planning.

In the capitalist world, economic liberalism has been limited and sometimes destroyed by the interests it was meant to unshackle. Thus corporations, trade unions, farmers, and consumers have called economic freedom into question to claim state aid, to increase taxation, and to promote protectionism. All have used democracy to correct the market.

What was the liberal response to this twofold questioning, theoretical and practical? On the one hand, in the economic order, liberalism has moved from apology to criticism. On the other hand, it has rediscovered a political argument against too great a separation of economics and politics.

Returning to liberalism in the name of efficiency and collective interest has revived the old polemics against waste, vested interests, interventionism, corporatism, and mercantilism. Thus, protectionism may serve the interests of a politically powerful economic sector but is opposed to the general interest of the country and of the world as a whole.

In the political order, liberalism has reacted in two ways, the one extreme, the other moderate. Hayek tried to demonstrate that economics undermines politics and that even a partial renunciation of economic liberties unavoidably leads to the loss of political liberties. Thus, for him the "road to servitude" is marked with planned-economy or socialist measures. It is in the light of the totalitarian experience, considered as the logical outcome of this process, that the possible effects of the corruption of the liberal model must be measured.

The same criticism is formulated in less systematic and more qualified fashion (but the root of the argument is the same) by those who consider economic freedom as one of the conditions of political freedom, who regard the complete disappearance of economic liberalism as incompatible with a minimum of political freedom, and who think that the existence of private firms and the preservation of family patrimonies are necessary for decentralized decision making and political pluralism. In this light, the existence of commodities and labor markets is one of the conditions of pluralism and individual liberties.

Here again, modern liberalism goes back to its origins. In the seventeenth century, Locke defended private property to guarantee freedom of conscience. If, in the 1980s, the Poles preferred contractual labor relations to state control, it is because they wanted to guarantee the workers greater independence vis-à-vis the Party-State. However legitimate these criticisms may appear to us, however legitimate it is for the disciples of Montesquieu to condemn nationalizations in the name of a sociological interpretation of the separation of powers, or for the disciples of Adam Smith to demonstrate the inefficiency of socialist economies or of state interventions in capitalist economies, I do not believe that the pertinence of these analyses explains the revival of liberalism that we are witnessing today. Had there been only those estimable authors whom we all revere—Hayek, Milton Friedman, Jacques Rueff, and the society of Mont-Pélérin—it is pretty unlikely that a historical movement of such dimensions could have taken place.

THE LIBERAL-SOCIAL-NATIONAL MODEL

Rather than offering an intellectual explanation, I wish to propose a historical explanation of the return of liberalism. The liberal-social-national model that, after World War II, took the place of the traditional liberal model is today the object of thorough reexamination. This model is based on three elements: the market economy more or less tempered by the intervention of the state within the national framework, the welfare state (that is, spending on health, retirement pensions, education, and unemployment benefits), and political democracy. The reexamination takes different forms. Among them are denationalization of public firms and reduction of the state sector, deregulation, reduction of taxes, challenges to progressive taxation, the weakening of state controls over the market and reform of social institutions, and criticism of certain aspects of Keynesian policies. It is sufficient to observe the change in policies and ideas in the United States, Britain, continental Europe, and Japan since the mid-1970s, to realize that the phenomenon is both broad and deep. Liberalism is no longer regarded as retrograde ideology.

We do not intend to analyze these developments in detail or to argue about various terms chosen to characterize this change: neo-conservatism, neo-liberalism, return of the market. We do not intend to deny the differences either. The starting points and evolutions are not identical in the United States, Sweden, Britain, and France. But everywhere there clearly appears the contrast between the model dominant in the 1950s and 1960s and the one appearing in the 1980s: the return of the market and reduced state power. The modalities are different, but the direction of the change is the same. I am not saying that one model succeeds another. I am merely saying that the previous model is being reevaluated and weakened; it has become less attractive and is being profoundly reformed.

In the same way, socialist economies have lost prestige. As for poor countries, today developmental economists and international organizations advise them to adopt less interventionist and less protectionist policies than those recommended in the 1960s. Thus, India, Argentina, and South Korea nowadays practice more liberal policies than those practiced (under European influence) just after World War II. But let us leave aside the special problem of Eastern and poor countries, and limit our discussion to the Western democracies. How can we explain the new liberalism? I suggest four causes.

FOUR CAUSES OF THE RETURN OF LIBERALISM

The first cause for the return of liberalism is traditional. I have already mentioned it. It is quite simply the exercising of critical thought, amplified and reinforced in our societies, it must be added, by the prospect of the communist model. We have looked at freedom in the mirror of totalitarian systems, and the sight of their guided economy, planning, public property, and state monopoly has magnified criticism of our own institutions, bureaucracies, and social systems. The results have been to weaken, in the minds of intellectuals and voters in general, the social-national-liberal model and to strengthen the defense of political freedoms, to favor a systematic return to the market, and to foster suspicion of bureaucratic, state, corporate, and protectionist formulas. But that cause has not been the decisive factor.

The second cause was brought to light by Pierre Manent.[5] The liberal-social-national model made citizens dependent on government. Democratic society, by its very nature, fosters the criticism of all forms of dependency. And what happened to the dependent order and corporations under the ancien régime happens with regard to dependencies under systems of social protection, bureaucracies, unions, and the state. As in the eighteenth and nineteenth centuries, people are quite naturally led to the market economy because in modern society it represents the least power. In the same way that Turgot and Sieyès criticized corporations and monopolies, so we today criticize bureaucracy in the name of the market. In the spirit of our age, the market is reborn because it is a refuge and a more equitable arbitrator than the powers of established institutions and of a state perceived as being partisan, arbitrary, or despotic. Neutrality and economic laws confer on the market the virtues with which secularism and public interest invested the state in juridical utopias.

Third, the growing role of the international market over the past thirty years and internationalization of the economy have led to a weakening of the liberal-social-national model. Take, for example, the

Commissariat du plan in France, which lost all its political and economic
meaning when its founder, Jean Monnet, created the Common Market.
The commissariat survives, naturally, because there are always studies
to be carried out, commissions to be convened, and civil servants to be
paid. But it survives like some sort of compensatory myth. This example illustrates the effect of the international market on certain national and social elements of the liberal-social-national model. In
Western countries, leaders must adjust their political and economic
decisions to a constraining international whole whose principal element is a market economy. France cannot overturn its economy, or
modify its tax system or its system of redistribution, or follow a macro-
economic policy without taking into account the structural features
and present economic evolution of the group to which France belongs
(a group more liberal than France)—not to mention the constraints on
French firms and foreign businesses.

The fourth cause is political. To safeguard all liberties, Guizot preferred to entrust political freedom to a limited number of people. The
fear of the democratic principle was clear. In his eyes, universal suffrage could provoke demagoguery and tyranny. But some liberals saw
profoundly conservative principles in the democratic principle and
on this point shared the Bonapartists' analysis.

Events have proved the second school of thought right. Universal
suffrage throws up majorities that prefer the distribution of income
via the market to their distribution by political power. Since the
mid-1970s a fiscal reaction has been developing in Britain, the United
States, Sweden, West Germany, France, and other countries—a reaction that has led not only to a reduction of taxes levied on households
but also to a reduction in the progressiveness of income tax.[6] This
reaction is the consequence of a twofold movement: (1) the slow transformation of the income pyramid into a sort of diamond shape in
which the middle class constitutes the majority and (2) the increase in
taxation over recent years that has affected many households because
their incomes were rising and more often than not both partners in a
marriage were earning a wage. Perhaps we could prepare ourselves to
write a history of progressive income tax? In the first phase, from the
end of the nineteenth century to the 1960s, majorities had no trouble
increasing both fiscal progressiveness and fiscal pressure. A few years
ago, the second phase—a reaction—set in, and income taxes have been
holding steady or even diminishing. The political majorities appear to
fear that they might be victimized by progressiveness and thus find
themselves unwilling custodians of the fiscal status quo. As a result,
governments say they prefer revenues that stem from the market and

from the appreciation of products on an international market to revenues determined by fiscal levy and redistribution.

This phenomenon of conservative democracy, which was sought for by some nineteenth-century liberals but for which they were not always able to prepare, combined with the world market, gives empirical power to the intellectual phenomenon described by Pierre Manent.

A DETOUR VIA ELIE HALÉVY

Let us reconsider the analysis by Elie Halévy on the eve of World War II,[7] when he compared the traditional model of liberalism to what we are calling the liberal-social-national model. Halévy questioned himself about socialism as Tocqueville had questioned himself about democracy. For Tocqueville, democracy could lead to liberty or tyranny. For Halévy, socialism had two sides. Combined with the effect of wars in Europe, it could lead democracies either to the total state (Fascist, National-Socialist, or Communist) defined by the organization of the economy, the omnipotence of the state, and the single party; or to a sort of "social democracy" exemplified by Sweden and Britain, combining high taxation, developed social services, and democratic and pluralistic institutions. The meeting of liberalism, socialism, and nationalism, with the last two reinforced by the democratic principle, thus rendered the historical outcome uncertain for liberty, because state organization and nationalism might have carried the day to the detriment of liberal institutions.

If, fifty years later, we reread Halévy's studies, the historical question they invite is whether peace, prosperity, and international trade in the Western democracies will result in the maintenance of mixed governments, the most complete type of which is Sweden (and was Britain), or will force our societies into a greater dose of economic liberalism—given that we are not concerned here with fundamental oppositions but only with orientations that differ in degree.

What Schumpeter[8] had not foreseen when he announced the necessary transformation of capitalist economies into socialist democracies was the contrary (and perhaps provisional) effects of two developments: the growth of the international economy (whether we like it or not, the Keynesian vulgate is protectionist and even autarkical), and the explosion of individual enrichment (Keynes believed in stagnation and the end of technical progress; he also favored collective saving). These effects force the directed economies we call social-democratic, for simplicity's sake, to become more capitalistic. That is why people speak today of the return or revival of liberalism.

In the space of fifty years, liberalism has been presented first as defeated, now as victorious. And thus liberals will have gone from pessimism to optimism. But during this time we have not returned to traditional liberalism. Modern liberalism remains defined by the democratic idea and by the separation of the economy and politics. But certain phenomena have caused social-democratic elements of the modern-day model to be inflected in a more liberal direction, economically speaking, as if the molders of democratic and socialist sentiments (that is, the spirit of equality) were the free trade from which no country can escape without sacrificing its standard of living and the iron law of electoral majorities.

So, to make discussion easier, let us consider three illustrations of the dialectic movement I have just outlined: changes in public spending, denationalization of public firms, and the problem of power in the workplace.

PUBLIC SPENDING

In most European countries, public spending—which includes military spending, the costs of running of the state, and social welfare spending (health, education, retirement pensions, and unemployment benefits)—accounts for half of the gross national product (GNP). In the United States and in Japan, countries that have never had socialist governments, public spending accounts for only 30 percent of the GNP. A major feature of the post–World War II period is the growth of social spending under the influence of two factors, the generalization of insurance, which is liberal in origin, and its financing by various forms of taxation, which is democratic in origin. If we study the change in the amounts devoted to the financing of this expenditure, we can clearly see how the democratic idea has transformed the liberal economy.

In the mid-1970s, this process was interrupted, and most countries have undertaken to reduce or, more often, simply to maintain the level reached. Two brakes are at work here. One is domestic and political; it stems from taxation and is expressed through majorities who refuse to increase taxes or try to reduce them. The other is international and economic. Every Organization for Economic Corporation and Development report imputes to excessive public spending a part of inflationary pressure, insufficient savings, shrinking productivity, the persistence of unemployment, and the absence of business. Therefore, so as to rediscover its source of dynamism and not to be outdistanced, every Western country is led to embark—with considerable difficulty, moreover—on the policy of limiting public expenditure. Symmetrically, this policy is rendered different because public spending satisfies large sections of the electorate and because, in terms of state machinery and social spending, most countries have reached similar levels. Thus, the democratic game and the international environment put a brake on the pursuit of increased spending and favor the status quo. The fact is that the level reached is at the balance point of three forces: international competition, democratic pressure for reduced taxation, and democratic pressure for increased spending and redistribution. The pressure thus exerted can vary according to the distribution of income within the economy and in the world.

DENATIONALIZATION OF PUBLIC FIRMS

It is quite obvious that the wave of denationalization in Europe today is not due simply to charges of inefficiency and confusion of politics and economy that are leveled at public firms nationalized between 1920 and 1960. The denationalization also stems from the facts that the public sector is costly and denationalization profitable and that the public sector is better adapted to the forms of national state monopolies and is less well adapted to international competition, which demands independent multinationals.

THE POWER OF CREDITORS

The question of power in the workplace deserves more space. This power, as it was defined in traditional liberalism (expropriation of workers and exclusive appropriation by the holders of capital), was subjected to criticisms that, in the final analysis, are based on the democratic idea. Outside its original political framework, this idea influenced the various institutions of society. On this topic, Pierre Manent[9] has spoken of the calling into question, by extension of the democratic idea, "of the status of commandments in civil society." An old text written by John Stuart Mill perfectly expresses the present-day problem:

> The form of association, however, which if mankind continue to improve, must be expected in the end to predominate, is not that which can exist between a capitalist as chief, and working people without a voice in the management, but the association of the

laborers themselves on terms of equality, collectively owning the capital with which they carry on their operations, and working under managers elected and removable by themselves.[10]

The enterprise is defined as a democratic entity composed of individuals distinct by virtue of their functions but equal in rights. A threefold criticism of capitalist power is contained in the passage just quoted: first, there is criticism of the authority of management, that is, power is not legitimated by its origins and is exercised without consultation. Second, there is criticism of inequality within a company between those who hold the capital and the workers, between the hierarchy and those who carry out the orders. Last, there is criticism of expropriation, because the workers have no share in the profits. A threefold solution is suggested: elections and consultations to legitimate authority, power sharing to transform the firm into an association reinforcing equality and attenuating the consequences of hierarchy, and the sharing of capital to put an end to the expropriation of workers. Because Mill condemned appropriation by the state and favored the market and decentralization, his model remained compatible with some of the elements constituting liberalism.

To these arguments, several replies may be put forward. The first reply is traditional. It defends the pure capitalist model. Workers are protected by their contract. The capitalist assumes the risks. It is the assumption of risks and the combining function of the factors of production that legitimate the power of capital. The differentiation of economic roles and competition are guarantees of efficiency. A second reply is sociological. Mill's firm would not work well. It would be inefficient. Elections would not produce sufficient or stable power of arbitration. At best we would end up with an oligarchic corporatism and at worst with state control. A third response is historical. The type of firm that people would like to reform no longer exists. Today, ownership and management are two distinct things. Ownership now offers only a residual power in the event of crisis and a vague consecration of the real power of managers and technostructure. The evolution in forms of command has fulfilled Mill's prophecy. Fourth, there is a conciliatory response that accepts Mill's criticism but puts forward less radical solutions. We know this response well from the working community of Marshal Pétain, de Gaulle's association of capital and labor, various forms of participation in the workers' representation committees, the distribution of shares to workers, and so forth.

Recent developments bring to light a fifth reply, which the preceding ones could not foresee and which goes in a new liberal direction. We are witnessing a "delocalization" of interests. Let us suppose that the democratic ideal has triumphed in a firm. Would the workers be satisfied with it? If the steel workers had been told, "From now on, you will be the owners of your firms and you will elect your leaders," a fine pickle they would be in! They would learn from the newspapers and EEC reports that the steel industry in Europe must be reduced and will perhaps disappear altogether. Doubtless they would consider the owners' situation as being more enviable than the workers' situation. The owners have invested in different assets or, as we can just as well say, in different debts: in debts in the steel industry, that might lose their value, and in more viable assets. Why should present-day society not say to the workers, "Your rights are debts. Rather than keeping your debts in your firms (in this case, the steel industry), you should be indebted to the economy as a whole. That is the safest way of protecting your income, for a debt is merely a right to future resources. It is better to have several debtors than a single one. General debts are preferable to private ones because they are safer, because the risks are spread over several ventures, several companies, several industries, and several countries." In the same way as British pension funds do not invest their reserves in the (often declining) industries of their principals but have assets all over the world, today's salaried workers, defined as debtors, must do the same. In this light, the appropriation of their firm, that is, of an asset that is by nature unstable and perishable, would scarcely make any sense. But this does not mean that partial and voluntary appropriation should be discouraged.

It is as if, by breaking the individual's attachment to his firm through the generalization of debts, today's economy makes more difficult the links that Mill and his disciples who favored self-management wished to introduce. For why should a worker become the "citizen" of his own firm if his interests are not linked to the firm as such, defined as a provisional technical community, but instead are linked to a world economy to which one is indebted on a worldwide basis? If the salaried worker is considered a universal creditor (a concept that is more legitimate, because throughout his retirement he is a creditor and during his years of training he is a debtor), his power must grow on a scale with his debts and that power will necessarily be more diffuse than if he worked in a purely localized firm.

Two patterns of spreading and managing debts then become conceivable. In one, society (thus, the state) alone holds all the debts in the name of the workers and distributes the added value among them while they are employed, but also when they are unemployed, changing jobs, and retired. In the other pattern, plurality is maintained: the workers hold debts in their companies and in other firms and institutions.

Economic movement leads to a division of risk and hence to a greater spreading of debt. In the same way that the retirement pension will not depend on the fate of the firm, a greater share of income during the worker's working years will not depend on his employment, whether the worker holds other assets or whether the risks concerning his work are assumed by relationships other than the one linking him to his company.

The second model is obviously the more liberal of the two, and it is inevitably favored by the existence of electoral majorities wishing to preserve the free disposal of savings and inheritances and by the development of international financial markets. The first model is well adapted to a centralized society. The second entails the plurality of retirement systems, the spread of corporate capital, the private holding of savings in the form of financial debts, and so forth. But this model also forces us to consider the problem of power within the firm in a different light. Of course, it does not do away with the tension brought about by the consequences of private appropriation, of the functional hierarchy within the company, and of democratic aspirations, but it does weaken and reduce that tension. Democratization ceases to be a resolution of this conflict, for it would tether the worker to the firm just as feudalism tied the serf to the glebe.

This brings me back to my overall interpretation. The comeback staged by liberalism is not merely the result of a victory of light over darkness, of the laying low of the bureaucratic or socialist hydra. By a sort of ruse of history, it stems instead from a turnabout that has resulted in the weakening of nation-states by international trade and in the decision by social democracy to limit itself as its citizens become enriched. It is as if, having assimilated the benefits of systems of redistribution, of social security, and of national protection, modern societies wished to give themselves an extra margin of freedom to face the difficulties of a richer, more cosmopolitan, more competitive world.

What liberals must not do is to mistake this change or this phase for the birth of a new world or for the return to the world of yesteryear. Both in opposition and in government, both by criticism and by reform, their task remains to tame and civilize the spirit that they have brought to life, one that will not cease to grow in stature, namely, the spirit of democracy.

NOTES

1. To measure the intellectual state of liberalism in the 1930s, we have to go back to the *Colloque Walter Lippmann*, which was held in Paris in August 1938, on the initiative of

the International Centre for the Renewal of Liberalism; Walter Lippmann's *La Cité Libre* had just been published by the Librairie de Médicis (1938). Among others taking part were R. Aron, A. Detoeuf, F. A. Hayek, E. Mantoux, R. Marjolin, L. von Mises, M. Polanyi, W. Röpke, L. Rougier, J. Rueff, and M. van Zeeland. The papers presented were published by the Librairie de Médicis (Paris, 1938). During the congress, the delegates endeavored to answer the following questions: (1) What are the causes of the decline of liberalism? (2) Are these causes endogenous or exogenous? (3) Can liberalism fulfill its social tasks? (4) Is decline inevitable? (5) If decline is not inevitable, what remedies can be drawn from an analysis of the causes? See also Abba Lerner, "Economic Liberalism in the Postwar World," in *Postwar Economic Problems*, edited by S. E. Harris (New York: McGraw-Hill, 1943).

2. Pierre Manent, "Situation du libéralisme," *Commentaire*, No. 35, Autumn 1986.

3. On this matter, see Raymond Aron's two major articles "La définition libérale de la liberté" in *Archives Européennes de sociologie*, vol. II (1961) and vol. V (1964).

4. On the notion of liberalization, see Raymond Aron, "De la libéralisation," in *Penser le temps: Mélanges offerts à Jeanne Hersch* (Lausanne, L'Âge d'homme, 1964); and Ernest Geliner, "From Revolution to Liberalization," *Government and Opposition* (London, 1976), vol. II, 3.

5. Manent, "Situation du libéralisme."

6. On the evolution of personal taxation in Western countries, see the OECD report, *L'imposition du revenu des personnes physiques dans un contexte économique en évolution* (Paris, 1986).

7. Elie Halévy, *L'ère des tyrannies: Etudes sur le socialisme et la guerre* (Paris: Gallimard, 1938).

8. Joseph A. Schumpeter, *Capitalisme, socialisme et démocratie* (French translation) (Paris: Payot, 1951).

9. Manent, "Situation du libéralisme."

10. *Principles of Political Economy*, 3rd edition (London, 1852), Book IV, chapter vii, 6.

13

Free Persons and the Common Good

Michael Novak

In the last years of the twentieth century, the flame of the liberal idea has again leapt to life. The liberal idea is intensely practical. It envisages institutions to realize the three great liberations: (1) from tyranny and torture; (2) from poverty; and (3) from the censorship and oppression of conscience, information, ideas, and creativity. In most countries, the term *progressive* (often now used ironically) has been captured by Marxist and socialist parties. The party of liberty, which is committed to the three liberations just mentioned and which owes its political roots to French, British, and North American thinkers of the eighteenth and nineteenth centuries, has achieved, in fact, the most institutional progress. Despite this quiet record, the party of liberty has long been pictured by its foes on the left as "conservative" and by its foes on the right, the traditionalists, as "modernist" or even "decadent." No one in France will forget that in the late 1930s both the Nazis in Germany and the foes of the liberal society in France united in condemning "decadent" bourgeois liberalism.

Experience has been a harsh teacher. After the shedding of unimaginable amounts of human blood, after mature inspection of a planet strewn since 1945 with failed social experiments, the peoples of the world still cry out for and move toward liberty, more scarce on this planet than oil. They would move faster, did not walls and guards prevent them.

What are the secrets of societies of free persons? They lie in forgotten concepts of *order* and *system*. I mean to show here that it is an error to think of liberalism as primarily a theory about *individuals* or *individualism*. It is, above all, a social theory. Its aim is the common good. Its greatest work has been the building of *social institutions*. To show all this, however, I need to describe some recent intellectual developments.

1. THE RETURN TO THE LIBERAL TRADITION

In the United States, many persons who have begun, belatedly, to appreciate the wisdom of the liberals of a century or two ago have been termed (by their socialist critics) *neo-conservatives*.[1] Earlier in their lives, most "neo-conservatives" had been democratic socialists or social democrats. Confronting the many failed socialist experiments since World War II, they tried to believe, first, that socialist theory is true but that the world had not yet learned how to practice it successfully. Only reluctantly did they come to the second step, before which most hesitated: when socialist *practice* fails again and again, something must be wrong with socialist theory. Because some form of socialism is the lens through which most intellectuals think about the future, they felt for a time like men with cataracts. Thus, a neo-conservative, the wits say, is a progressive who has been mugged by reality. Most are either Jewish or Catholic—a point not without significance, because most of them have a strong social sense and an inherent respect for history, tradition, and experience.

In the United States then, a neo-conservative is a person brought up as a person of the left who grew dissatisfied with the ideas and the spirit of the left.[2] Typically, this dissatisfaction arose because the way of life of the left seemed to demand so many forms of false consciousness, not least a loathing of the American system. Most American neo-conservatives can recall in their family memory a real and urgent poverty. Yet, the United States liberated nearly all the offspring of poor immigrant families from poverty. Other nations to which inhabitants of our original lands of birth also migrated (as, for instance, those in Latin America) did not so liberate their immigrants. This difference is crucial to our self-identity; we cannot deny our own experience. American capitalism helped us and many millions of others from the poor working class, who within two or three generations, had acquired many goods once solely the prerogative of the rich.

In the aristocratic literary tradition and in the socialist tradition— the twin sources of most of our education[3]—it is always asserted that capitalism is "exploitative." But was that, even in 1830 or 1897 or 1931, a fair picture of events? If so, why did our families migrate in such great numbers precisely toward the centers of capitalist activity? They well knew the exploitation of traditionalist societies. They found capitalist forms comparatively liberating.

This is not to say that the three liberations to which democratic capitalist societies are committed (political, economic, and moral) have been accomplished. There is much yet to do. But it is important to compare the *realities* of the liberal society with the *actual* historical alternatives, and to compare the *ideals* of the liberal society with other active ideals.

In my judgment, the liberal society is superior in the realm of practice, and its ideals are morally more attractive. Those ideals are the ideals of the future, both because they work and because they are most consonant with human nature itself. Thomas Jefferson succinctly stated the ideal of the liberal society: "The God who gave us life, gave us liberty."[4] And Alexis de Tocqueville observed quite correctly that the heart of Christianity discerns in human liberty the dignity of the child of God. In trying to bring Catholic Christianity, belatedly, to the support of the ideal of the democratic republic, John Courtney Murray, S. J., wrote in *We Hold These Truths*:

> The American Bill of Rights is not a piece of eighteenth-century rationalist theory, it is far more the product of Christian history. Behind it one can see, not the philosophy of the Enlightenment but the older philosophy that had been the matrix of common law. The 'man' whose rights are guaranteed in the face of law and government is, whether he knows it or not, the Christian man, who had learned to know his own personal dignity in the school of Christian faith.[5]

He meant that ironically the liberal society, some of whose first historical protagonists were antireligious, owes its originating insights about the dignity of the human person and the nature of community to Jewish and Christian inspirations. Even those scholars who prefer to stress the sharp "break" between ancient and modern traditions might accept such belated support as a compliment. Pluralist in practice, the democratic republic is also susceptible of a pluralism in philosophical justifications. (But, some of these may be better than others, and some may in the long run be dangerous to its survival.)

2. THE REDISCOVERY OF THE SOCIAL DIMENSION

Perhaps the greatest lesson American neo-conservatives have learned is that a society of free persons is rooted in *ideas*—and that these ideas are easy to forget. That they themselves had neglected these ideas now sharpens their fascination with the founding fathers of the liberal idea—with Montaigne, Montesquieu, Bastiat, and Tocqueville; with Adam Smith, Edmund Burke, John Stuart Mill, and Lord Acton; with

Madison, Jefferson, Hamilton, Franklin, and Lincoln. The experience of two centuries has not diminished the foresight of such thinkers and builders. Their stature has grown, even as the harsh tests of experience have diminished the reputations of the thinkers who dominated later generations.

But there is one further lesson the neo-conservatives retain from their socialist past: the necessity of thinking universally, about the common good, and for the future. Those who have lately come to admire the liberations wrought by democracy in the political order, by capitalism in the economic order, and by pluralism in the moral and cultural order now hold that democratic capitalism—the proper name for the political economy of all three liberations—is the best hope for the poor of the world. As the practice of a social theory, democratic capitalism works.

Still, the tasks that democratic capitalism sets for itself are always unfinished, for its vision is radically transcendent. In our generation, the least developed and least understood side of democratic capitalist theory understood is its *social* vision. Adam Smith did not focus his inquiry on the wealth of individuals; he focused it on the wealth of nations. The political economy of democratic capitalism is primarily a *social* theory, intended to benefit the common good of all, especially the poor. Democratic capitalism represents a novel solution to the problem of the common good.

3. THE DECLINE—AND RESURRECTION—OF THE COMMON GOOD

The concept of the common good, F. A. Hayek says, is an atavistic concept that harks back to the primitive instincts of tribes of hunters, when collectivist instincts dominated.[6]

But unlike Hayek, I believe that the notion of the common good (and, by derivation, "social justice") has great importance for liberal thought. The great liberal thinkers of France, Britain, and the United States had in mind the good of "nations," "the general welfare," and the improvement of the human condition everywhere on Earth. Nonetheless, to talk about such matters in the frame of reference of all the nations of the world and in complex, differentiated modern societies required on their part a break from earlier and simpler notions of the common good. Besides, the foes of the liberal revolution used against them the claims of the common good as earlier understood. Thus the phrase itself dropped from sight, but the reality did not.

To understand the notion of the common good useful to our own future, it is important to grasp several underlying concepts. It is no longer possible to understand modern societies simply by personal inspection, by looking at them with one's eyes. Modern societies are constructs of ideas. An effort of abstraction (or at least of sustained reflection on concrete phenomena) is necessary. This is why the Statue of Liberty—that great gift of one liberal society to another—is pictured as a serene woman, not as a warrior, with the upraised torch of enlightenment against surrounding darkness in one hand and a tablet of the laws in the other. To defend liberty is primarily to defend certain ideas, learned through much sweat, bloodshed, and bitter disappointment but gentle and powerful in their sway.

A word of caution is necessary. In speaking of ideas about the common good, I am not speaking of clear and distinct ideas reached by mind alone. Human experience is often richer with ideas than the human intellect of any one generation can put into words. Experience is a great teacher, the most subtle and astute of all. In social thought, ideas apart from experience are nearly always mischievous, if not pernicious. The human race does not arrive at laws, traditions, customs, and habits apart from hard-won even if inarticulate wisdom. (The survival and prospering of the race until now suggest that such wisdom has staying power.) The liberal party is a progressive party that respects the wisdom of the past and is constantly revitalized by the study of experience. (One of its often unrecognized progenitors is Saint Thomas Aquinas, "the first Whig."[7])

The essence of the common good is to bring about in social life the benefits of human cooperation. A modern concept of such cooperation for the common good must be open to change, and open to the invention, enterprise, creativity, and free choices of multitudes of free persons. In a traditional rural society, each villager knew virtually every other through lifelong familiarity. In a modern society such as France or the United States, citizens can know only a tiny fraction of the millions of their fellow citizens.

Furthermore, the characteristic mobility of modern people means that most persons do not have lifelong familiarity even with most of their associates. So vast is the differentiation of modern trades, crafts, occupations, professions, technologies, and economic skills that no one person can have that learned experience in each that counts as true knowledge. A central characteristic of modern societies, then, as contrasted with traditional societies, is the ignorance of each citizen regarding many sectors of life in which other citizens live. To speak of the common good of a modern society, therefore, is to speak without concrete experience of the worlds of a vast majority of others. It is to speak without concrete knowledge, behind a veil of considerable ignorance.

4. BUT HOW CAN THERE BE A COMMON GOOD?

A further difficulty must be attended to. Traditional societies were not pluralistic, as modern societies are. The free persons of modern societies are expected to form their own judgments about the good, not only about their own personal and familial good but also about the common good. Whereas the common good of a premodern society is collective, universally subscribed to, and binding on all, the common good of a modern society must respect the pluralism of free persons. The common good of modern societies, then, cannot be defined in substantive terms. Or, rather, it can be so defined only in times of national emergency, under attack by alien forces. (This helps to explain why, in modern societies, powerful leaders who seek to unite the citizenry behind common purposes *must* take demagogic refuge in appeals to nationalism, xenophobia, and external aggression.) The issue runs even deeper. The common good of pluralistic modern societies must leave space for the personal definitions of the good cherished by free persons. In this context, is it even conceptually possible to think of a common good that does not do violence to the goods freely decided on by free persons?

5. A COMMON INTENTION NOT NECESSARY

The liberal solution to this dilemma has two parts. First, it is important to shake the concept of the common good free from the image of the concrete good expressed in a particular state of affairs. Collectivist societies can bend every individual will to collective purposes, defined by command and announced as the collective good. Societies of free persons cannot. What free societies can do, however, is to establish general rules designed to bring to all the benefits of human cooperation. When these general rules are framed in such a way as to proscribe certain particular behaviors, they leave free a large field of liberty for creativity and enterprise. Liberty should never be conceived apart from law. Liberty rests upon law. Rules, wisely constructed, empower liberty and by no means destroy it.

Second, it is also important to shake the tribal notion of the common good free from conscious intentions, aims, and purposes. In a

homogeneous, collective, monist society, it is possible to infuse individual wills with a common purpose, to direct all to common aims,
and to nourish in all a common intention. Not so in pluralistic societies of free persons. What makes a person free is a capacity to form
his or her own life purposes, immediate and ultimate aims, and personal motivations and intentions. It does not follow, however, that free
persons cannot cooperate with one another, cannot give loyalty to
common laws and rules, and cannot achieve dynamic societies that
manifestly improve the lot of all.

A sharp distinction must be drawn, therefore, between concepts of
the common good whose essence consists in common intentions, aims,
and purposes, and concepts of the common good whose essence consists in mutual cooperation apart from common intentions, aims, and
purposes. A footpath along a river or up a mountainside may have
been formed cooperatively by human beings over centuries, but quite
apart from the intentions of any one person, and in pursuit of aims as
various as the multiple motives of the multitudes of persons who have
used such a path. There are common goods apart from common intentions, aims, and purposes. Were it not so, societies of free persons
could not exist.

To cooperate, it is not necessary for atheists and theists to share
common views of the purposes of human life. When institutions and
rules are defined in appropriate ways, a full pluralism of intentions,
aims, and purposes may be defended. Meanwhile, free participation in
such institutions and rules may not only encourage vital cooperation,
dynamic advances, and the liberation of much personal creativity, but
also inspire significant love for the commonwealth that has achieved
such a design.[8]

A notion of the common good suitable for a society of free persons,
therefore, abandons the tribal project of commanding a particular
and concrete state of affairs and sets aside the tribal requirement that
common intentions, aims, and purposes should be made to infuse the
inner life of every person. Naturally, the human race has a profound
longing for such tribal solidarities, but such solidarities are incompatible with personal freedom. Personal freedom is such a valuable good
that it is more than worth the surrender of tribal solidarities.

Conversely, a society that protects personal freedoms reaps immense social benefits. Through liberating the creativity, enterprise,
and inventiveness of its citizens, the free society acquires an enormous
upward thrust in history. Such a society can hardly be static, even if it
wished to be. More than that, in the face of rapid change it has capacities for flexible adjustment and innovation. In long-repressed human

capacities for invention and discovery, free societies activate the primary cause of the wealth of nations. (Japan, a densely populated island with virtually no natural resources, has laid hold of these causes to a world-astonishing degree.)

In the relatively brief span of two hundred years, free societies have, in fact, demonstrated before the bar of history that their social design is eminently able to attain for all the benefits of the human cooperation of all, by a new definition of the constitutive features of the common good. The essential feature of the common good is "the benefits of cooperation." Rather than commanding cooperation, free societies have learned by experience how to elicit it. The underlying insight, rooted in experience, is that human beings are by nature cooperative animals (Aristotle said "political animals"). This does not mean that they are *always* cooperative, but rather that they *can* be, for their own sake *should* be so, and in well-designed systems are likely to be so *more* often. In short, it is not necessary to coerce them into cooperation. Human beings need one another. Their fates are interdependent.

The great modern liturgies of athletics, therefore, quite appropriately celebrate team playing, in soccer, cricket, American football, baseball, and basketball. Similarly, other institutions may be so designed as to make it in the personal interest of each person (as it demonstrably is) to seek cooperation and to be "other-regarding," whatever the state of each person's own motivations. That is to say, although human beings are naturally inclined toward cooperation, their natural instinct may be augmented by other rewards that will incline them toward cooperation, even if they are among those human beings moved best by considerations of selfishness.

This last point is important. The liberal party in history has been chastened by human experience and has learned to think quite realistically. To design a political economy for saints is a thankless task; there are too few of them. To design a political economy for human beings as they are is to design a political economy that has a chance to succeed, even if most of its members are sinners. Any political economy that will work must be designed for sinners. To check the worst instincts in humans and, simultaneously, to encourage the best (by incentives and rewards) is not the least of the arts of designing institutions and rules that will, in practice, promote the common good.[9]

6. THE COMMON GOOD AS A BENCHMARK

Thus far, we have uncovered two useful meanings of the classic concept of the common good. A third must now be added. Allusion has been made to the Jewish, Christian, and humanistic concept of sin (or fallibility). In Jewish, Christian, and humanistic thought, the concept of the common good has also supplied a *benchmark*, in whose light any achieved social order must be judged. The liberal party is a party of progress, and progress implies a measure. For Jewish and Christian thought, humans have been created in the image of the Creator. Humans are not only individual in the way that every cat or every dog is an individual but they are also persons, that is, creatures of two capacities they share with God: capacities for insight (inquiry) and choice (love). Because they are capable of insight and choice, they are by nature both free and responsible; that is, endowed by their Creator with certain inalienable rights—and inalienable responsibilities. They are always under judgment, by their own conscience, by the consciences of their fellows, and by God. Moreover, theologically, as Saint Thomas Aquinas put it, their common good consists in their enjoyment together of the Presence of God in eternity.[10] In more worldly terms, their common good consists in giving witness to the brotherhood of insight and choice, freedom and responsibility they enjoy on Earth. This vision sets a very high standard for the common good of any Earthly society.

Taken as a benchmark, then, the concept of the common good obliges the citizens of any particular society to lift up their eyes in order to see how well they are doing, by some standard that transcends present achievement. No progressive party can object to such a standard, providing only that it is applied with some regard for realism. Consider the economic order alone. (It is in regard to economic performance, in fact, that the concept of the common good is today most often advanced.) Is it really true that "the benefits of cooperation" are being extended to *all*? What is the condition of the poor and the disabled? What is being done for the elderly and for children? What about foreign laborers, migrants, and illegal immigrants? Is the level of employment what it ought to be? How about interest rates, foreign debt, and trade policy? What about competition from foreign goods, Third World debts, the openness of markets to Third World goods? Then there are the "externalities": Do damages to the environment outweigh improvements in the environment (such as irrigation, erosion control, forest management, the development of sources of clean water, and the like)? These represent only a small fraction of the claims of perfection on today's worldly economies. All such claims represent legitimate benchmarks. Altogether, they can be pressed as utopian claims demanding paradise on Earth. One by one, though, each such benchmark has its own validity. Critical intelligence always discovers the shortcomings of the present.

Therefore, societies of free persons properly dream of further progress. The concept of the common good, employed as a set of benchmarks, can be a spur to progress. In the second draft (1985) of their later pastoral letter on the U.S. economy, for example, the U.S. Catholic bishops invoked the "common good" twenty-three times.[11] Moreover, when all their demands on the economy are added up, the bishops desire low inflation, low unemployment, a healthy physical environment, lower spending on defense, higher spending for the poor, creativity and innovation, progressive taxation, a higher minimum wage, greater equality of incomes, gains in savings and productivity, some form of "planning" for cooperation, some declaration of "economic rights" to include income and medical care and old-age security, and so on. If wishes were horses, the bishops would ride as cavalry. Yet who can object that this long list of goods is not *desirable?* The bishops recognize explicitly that, in the real order, "choices" and "trade-offs" are the best that can be hoped. Their essential exhortation seems to be, do better. Every progressive society wishes to, but how?

7. THE ECONOMY: A NEW IDEA OF THE COMMON GOOD

The chief contribution of the liberal party in the late eighteenth and nineteenth centuries was to uncover the crucial importance of economics in "political economy." To such classic treatises on politics as those of Plato, Aristotle, Aquinas, and Machiavelli they added the art of economics to the moral responsibility that statesmen would have to bear.

The first liberals, people who gave themselves that name and were called so by their foes, envisaged for the human race, as we have seen, three liberations. (Appropriately, the typical flag of the liberals was a *tricouleur.*) All three liberations are components of the common good in a society of free persons. Yet, perhaps because against the traditionalists, Tories, and the ancien régime they stressed the emergence of the individual from the collectivities of the past, later generations have read liberal social theory as fundamentally a theory about the individual and individualism. In fact, the effect of the liberal vision was primarily *social.* They were trying to imagine a *society* of free persons and to sketch the framework of institutions, laws, and rules that would achieve "the benefits of cooperation" for all. Implicit in their vision is a historically original approach to the common good.

As I have already suggested, the path that liberals at last discerned toward the common good came to their attention (as did so many of their discoveries) counterintuitively. Instead of attempting to achieve the common good by direct frontal assault, as premodern societies did, they approached the common good indirectly, by establishing institutions, laws, and rules designed to enable free persons to employ their own inventiveness and creativity in cooperative ways. They tried to root the natural impulse toward the common good in the pre-conscious rather than the conscious life of free persons. It is worth trying to rethink how this task must have appeared to them.

In all nature, there is no model for the way in which a specifically human order of free persons ought to arrange itself to secure the common good. Neither a herd of cattle nor a colony of ants nor a beehive nor a bevy of geese, neither the stars in their orbits nor the forest in its primeval ways, suggests the social forms through which free persons might order themselves. And although in the history of human orders through the ages there were many fertile clues and false starts to study, there were no full-blown human models. Once the individual had emerged in history—a person neither a noble nor a serf by birth, fixed neither in status nor in potential, a person with his or her own proper name and inalienable responsibilities—the prob-lem of any good thought of as *common* became acute.

In the political order, the discoveries of the first liberals concerning representative democracy, constitutionalism, a limited government, checks and balances, free political parties, an independent judiciary, and other institutional devices have been much celebrated. Less cele-brated, but equally important, are the new "democratic" habits and virtues they put in the place (as Tocqueville noted) of "traditional" or "classic" tables of the virtues.[12] The free person in democratic societies requires moral skills beyond those of the citizens of the ancien regime: enterprise more than resignation, civic virtue more than familial piety, respect for law and lawmaking rather than submission to command, self-improvement and self-realization more than contentment with an assigned station, skills in practical compromise and loyal opposition rather than in unbending moral absolutism.[13]

Yet it is in the economic order that the most profound originality of the first liberals lay, a fact that may explain why the work of many of them has remained more nearly in the province of students in economics than in the province of the humanities, philosophy, and theology. To a remarkable degree, liberal insights are seldom the patri-mony of well educated persons today. First, a great many such persons now live and work in social organizations safely removed from the pressures and experiences of economic activities: in government, the universities, research institutes, and other large organizations whose daily experience is rather more that of the moral, cultural, or political order than specifically economic. F. A. Hayek writes quite truly, if I may measure his words by my own experience: "An ever increasing part of the population of the Western world grows up as members of large organizations and, thus, as strangers to those rules of the market which have made the great open society possible. To them the market economy is largely incomprehensible."[14]

Second, economic history is both sadly neglected in the educations of most of us and treated in public discourse in a highly ideological way. Before students even read Adam Smith, they have normally been taught to think him wrong about the "invisible hand," "self-interest," and "pure laissez-faire." Third, those parts of the world deeply influenced by the socialist or Marxist critiques of the market economy learn first the prosecution's case against capitalism and only later, if at all, do they examine market theory in an unprejudiced way.

Thus, two features of markets, in particular, are widely neglected.[15] First, the market is a social device, designed to serve the common good. It is not so much the individual qua individual that the market serves; it serves the needs of all. To think of markets primarily as advancing individual interests is an analytic error. For one thing, markets are typically no respecters of persons qua persons; in fact, it is more nearly correct to criticize markets for their "impersonality." Trading in material things, markets occupy a point in space and time. They are physical places. But they are primarily constituted by systems of rules, lawlike and impersonal, tacit and explicit, and drawing on centuries of practical experience. They are institutions of high intelligibility, even though many of the skills required for using markets well can be learned only through long years of experience. It is not easy for the untrained eye to recognize instantly, for example, the actual quality of goods. Neophytes in markets often err.

For another thing, although entry into markets is open and uncoerced and many entrants come only to stroll and to observe (learning all they can), people who enter markets in order to buy or to sell are drawn by the rules themselves into an "other-regardingness" that their practice of the virtues in other areas of their lives may or may not exemplify. I use this odd word advisedly. "Other-regardingness" does not imply that selfless concern for others implied by altruism. It implies, rather, a concern for others from which self-concern may not be entirely absent. For example, in order to sell, a salesman must be able to enter into the world of the buyer. The buyer's satisfaction is in the seller's interest, particularly because the lifeblood of sellers is enduring relationships across many years. More generally, the rules of market behavior include the rule of voluntary mutual contract. Both parties must be satisfied. The ideal outcome for market transactions cannot, therefore, be expressed as "win-lose"; it must be "win-win." At the end of the day, most parties must leave with a sense of satisfaction. Ideally, all should do so.

These two characteristics of markets—that they are rule-based (therefore suffused with practical intelligence) and that they enforce "other-regardingness" and a pattern of mutual satisfaction, through transactions freely arrived at—suggest a fresh path to the question posed by our inquiry. Markets are institutions designed simultaneously to advance the common good and to respect the dignity, autonomy, and interdependence of free persons. The objection that respect for free persons must lead to anarchy is disproved by the orderliness, cooperativeness, and even courtesy found, in fact, in markets. It is quite astonishing, really, to walk into "convenience stores" in Japan (or any other free place) and to find there products from France, Italy, Britain, China, South Korea, Brazil, Israel, Jordan, and almost every other place on earth. How did all this orderliness and cooperation, normally displayed in cheerful surroundings and often at attractive prices, come about? Make of it what you will, we tend to take contemporary miracles of cooperation for granted.

In the economic sphere, then, markets serve to illustrate that there can be—because there are—institutions and rules of conduct that exemplify free persons at work cooperatively and with much intelligence at the service of the common good. There is a form or order that is not ordered from above, by an International Orderer. On the contrary, this order emerges from the multiple acts of free intelligent actors, aimed at maximizing social intelligence in their own concrete circumstances. In the sense that it is un-ordered (from above), this order is perhaps to be thought of as spontaneous; still, it is to a high degree suffused with intelligence. As a model for human order of high internal intelligibility, freely arrived at, the market has a fascination for the human mind that is far from being exhausted. The workings of markets show that liberty and order, the free person and the common good, are not antinomies.

8. THE CHALLENGING TASK OF MORALS

But what about those larger issues of the "common good," issues of the moral and cultural order, not usually embraced today under the sphere of economic activities: a taste for excellence in all fields, a noble character, scholarship, the arts, research, teaching and education, the quest for the divine, worship, prayer, contemplation, and the rest? Here the accusations against the liberal society do not ordinarily take the form of protesting against the absence of liberty but, rather, of protesting against the corruptions of liberty. What is the preferred symbol of the liberal idea—the Statue of Liberty, a torch against darkness in one hand and a tablet in the other, or the porn shops near Times Square? To their foes, liberal societies trail off too easily into libertinism, relativism, decadence, violence, and nihilism.

To some extent, one can reply properly enough that the liberal society constitutes a free and open expression of what individuals choose to do (alas) with their liberty. But the charge against liberalism is actually more precise than that. The liberal society, in its youth, became accustomed to imagining itself in perpetual conflict with an older and unfree establishment. Liberals imagined themselves to be carrying torches of light against the traditions of the darker past. Now in adulthood, however, it is no longer becoming for liberals to shout on *all* questions "Greater liberty!" and "No restrictions!" For there are forms of thought, feeling, and action that are inimical to freedom. Authentic freedom is rooted in intellect and insight. Those practices that darken the mind dim in humans the root of their liberty.

Today, the struggle for liberty is not waged solely against the external powers of a repressive traditionalism. Those powers have long since atrophied. The struggle for liberty must now be waged within every single mind and heart. Human beings can destroy the image of God in themselves—their own agencies of insight and choice—through drugs, fanaticism, violence, and the aberrations of self-destructive passion. Liberals, focused upon hereditary enemies easily externalized, have paid too little attention to the darkness within every human heart, including the liberal heart.

One of the great weaknesses of the liberal spirit is that it has neglected the internal life of human beings: the struggle for character; the learning of moral and intellectual habits; the quest for God; and the battle against egoism, the flesh, and demons. The roots of this weakness probably lie in an unconscious reliance on the spiritual capital of past ages; on sound habits consciously passed from one generation to another; and on the body of ideas and images that support the range of moral skills indispensable to the daily practice of liberty.

9. RETHINKING A RHETORICAL STRATEGY

In opposing the traditionalists, it must be remembered, the early liberals were driven away from the language of religion by the use their foes made of it. Moreover, the traditionalists used the high-minded language of the classical virtues in an attempt to make the liberals seem vulgar and materialistic. Making a virtue of necessity, the first liberals boasted of their plain speech, common sense, and ethical modesty. They even preferred to minimize moral claims they might have made. They preferred a language of great ethical neutrality, words such as interest and *utility*, which are consistent both with the heroism of the saints and the villainy of the base. They deliberately flattened out their moral vision. Perhaps this was in the interest of protecting the broadest possible pluralism. But it was also no doubt a calculated rhetorical stratagem against the pompous moral claims of the past, and influenced by scientific method in its attempt to extrude subjective factors from inquiry.

In our own time, the situation is quite different. One of the most urgent items on the intellectual agenda is to forge an explicit moral language for the moral insights of liberalism. There is no longer any reason to disguise them behind an affected neutrality, and there are many reasons to announce them straightforwardly and honestly, both in their strength and in their limitations.

10. LIBERAL HABITS

The chief constituent part of the common good of a free society is the habits of soul developed by its citizens. As James Madison said, the rights of Americans are not defended by "parchment barriers" but by the habits and the institutions of our people. If these habits weaken, the decay of institutions cannot be far behind. The liberal idea works only when embodied in habits and institutions, and it can be sustained only through a vigorous moral life. The decay of the moral habits of our citizens would speedily entail the collapse of our political, economic, and cultural institutions.

In a sense, though, such a diagnosis is hopeful. The strengthening of the moral life of each of us lies not in our stars but in ourselves. Fidelity, loyalty, bravery, honesty, enterprise, creativity, kindness, compassion and other commonplace virtues still thrive in American families. They are not so highly visible, alas, in the media presentations of ourselves that our culture offers to the world—or even to our own families, in reinforcement.

11. SUMMARY

In sum, the concept of the common good is useful as a benchmark. It pushes us beyond its ancient meaning as a concrete state of affairs and turns us instead to an indispensable idea: the rules that make an open society possible. It pushes us beyond its ancient meaning as a set of common aims, intentions, and purposes and turns us instead to practices of cooperation. It reminds us, finally, to think beyond the political struggles that occupy the news and the economic outcomes of daily transactions. It encourages citizens to be alert to goods not now being attended to and to evils that would choke the tree of common blessings. In a free society every citizen depends on the virtues of every other. The market that allows each to pursue his or her own private dreams is a social institution. Hence, the dreams most consonant with it entail building up thriving and virtuous communities, whose depth and vigor will nourish and inspire yet another generation. When each citizen builds up the universe around him or her, the sum of such universes (material and of the spirit) measures exactly the common good attained by all together. To achieve the common good, there is always more for each of us to do.

NOTES

1. The origins of the term *neo-conservatism* are not clear, but so far as I can discover it was first applied to Daniel Patrick Moynihan, Nathan Glazer, and Daniel Bell in a discussion of their work by Michael Harrington, "The Welfare State and Its Neoconservative Critics," *Dissent* 20 (Fall 1973): 453–4. That issue contains a symposium of six articles, including Harrington's titled "Against the New Conservatism." The following year Lewis A. Coser and Irving Howe edited a collection of critical essays on *The New Conservatives* (New York: Quadrangle, 1974).
2. This and the following five paragraphs have been adapted from my essay "The Liberal Society as Liberation Theology," *Notre Dame Journal of Law, Ethics, and Public Policy* 2 (Fall 1985): 27–42.
3. See the observations of Joseph Epstein, "The Education of an Anti-Capitalist," *Commentary* (August 1983): 58–9: "Would anyone dispute that, apart from certain religious schools and certain colleges in the South and perhaps in Utah, the reigning ethos in American colleges and universities today is the anti-capitalist ethos. . . ? The better—or, to be more precise, the more prestigious—the school, the more the ideas of anti-capitalism tended to hold sway. From the schools to the culture at large: Joseph Schumpeter . . . had foreseen the process years before it had quite come about: 'Perhaps the most striking feature of the picture,' he wrote, 'is the extent to which the modern bourgeoisie, besides educating its own enemies, allows itself in turn to be educated by them. It absorbs the slogans of current radicalism and seems quite willing to undergo a process of conversion hostile to its very existence.' "
4. Thomas Jefferson, "A Summary View of the Rights of British America," in *Thomas Jefferson*, Library of America (New York: Literary Classics of the United States, 1984), 122.

5. John Courtney Murray, S. J., *We Hold These Truths: Catholic Reflections on the American Proposition* (New York: Sheed and Ward, 1960), 390.
6. See, e.g., F. A. Hayek, *Law, Legislation and Liberty*, vol. 2: *The Mirage of Social Justice* (Chicago: University of Chicago Press, 1976). For a useful compendium of other references in Hayek, see Eamonn Butler, *Hayek: His Contribution to the Political and Economic Thought of Our Time* (New York: Universe Books, 1983), especially "The Criticism of Social Justice," 86–105.
7. In *The Constitution of Liberty* (Chicago: Henry Regnery, 1960), Hayek acknowledges that the tradition of practical wisdom is common both to the Whigs and to Aquinas, observing that "in some respects Lord Acton was not being altogether paradoxical when he described Thomas Aquinas as the first Whig" (p. 457, n. 4).
8. Hector St. John Crevecoeur wrote in 1780: "The American ought therefore to love this country much better than that wherein either he or his forefathers were born. Here the rewards of his industry follow with equal steps the progress of his labor; his labor is founded on the basis of nature, *self-interest*; can it want a stronger allurement? Wives and children who before in vain demanded of him a morsel of bread, now, fat and frolicsome, gladly help their father to clear those fields whence exuberant crops are to arise to feed and to clothe them all without any part being claimed, either by a despotic prince, a rich abbot, or a mighty lord." J. Hector St. John Crevecoeur, *Letters from an American Farmer* (1782; reprint ed., New York: Fox, Duffield & Co., 1904), 55.
9. This point was made by Alexis de Tocqueville, *Democracy in America*, edited by J. P. Mayer, translated by George Lawrence (Garden City, New York: Doubleday, 1969), 526–7. "Self-interest properly understood is not at all a sublime doctrine, but it is clear and definite. It does not attempt to reach great aims, but it does, without too much trouble, achieve all it sets out to do. Being within the scope of everybody's understanding, everyone grasps it and has no trouble bearing it in mind. It is wonderfully agreeable to human weaknesses, and so easily wins great sway. It has no difficulty in keeping its power, for it turns private interest against itself and uses the same goad which excites them to direct passions.

    "The doctrine of self-interest properly understood does not inspire great sacrifices, but every day it prompts some small ones; by itself it cannot make a man virtuous, but its discipline shapes a lot of orderly, temperate, moderate, careful, and self-controlled citizens. If it does not lead the will directly to virtue, it establishes habits which unconsciously turn it that way.

    "If the doctrine of self-interest properly understood ever came to dominate all thought about morality, no doubt extraordinary virtues would be rarer. But I think that gross depravity would also be less common. Such teaching may stop some men from rising far above the common level of humanity, but many of those who fall below this standard grasp it and are restrained by it. Some individuals it lowers, but mankind it raises."
10. Lest this seem exaggerated, the reader should consult Jacques Maritain, *The Person and the Common Good*, translated by John J. Fitzgerald (New York: Charles Scribner's Sons, 1947). Because Thomas Aquinas is one of the architects of modern notions of the "common good" and "social justice," it is instructive to study his distinction between the "individual" and the "person," and his vision of the ways in which the "common good" exceeds the achievements and the claims of any "state." See also Thomas Gilby, *The Political Thought of Thomas Aquinas* (Chicago: University of Chicago Press, 1958), especially "Personal and Common Good," 237–50.
11. Nos. 75, 83, 87, 90, 101, 108, 109, 113, 115, 122, 234, 247, 251, 270, 284, 285, 294, 295, 306, 309, 310, 311, and 313 as printed in "Catholic Social Teaching and the U.S. Economy: The Second Draft," *Origins* (10 October 1985): 257–96.
12. The difference between the classical aristocratic virtues and the new democratic virtues is a pervasive theme in Tocqueville's *Democracy in America*. Relevant to our current subject, consult such passages as these: "I doubt whether men were better in times of aristocracy than at other times, but certainly they talked continually about

the beauties of virtue. Only in secret did they study its utility. . . . [By contrast,] the inhabitants of the United States almost always know how to combine their own advantage with that of their fellow citizens. . . . In the United States there is hardly any talk of the beauty of virtue. But they maintain that virtue is useful and prove it every day" (p. 525).

"It would not be fair to assume that American patriotism and the universal zeal for the common good have no solid basis. Though private interest, in the United States as elsewhere, is the driving force behind most of men's actions, it does not regulate them all. I have often seen Americans make really great sacrifices for the common good, and I have noticed a hundred cases in which, when help was needed, they hardly ever failed to give each other trusty support. The free institutions of the United States and the political rights enjoyed there provide a thousand continual reminders to every citizen that he lives in society. At every moment they bring his mind back to this idea, that it is the duty as well as the interest of men to be useful to their fellows. Having no particular reason to hate others, since he is neither their slave nor their master, the American's heart easily inclines to the public interest, afterward by choice. What had been calculation becomes instinct. By dint of working for the good of his fellow citizens, he in the end acquires the habit and taste for serving them" (pp. 512–13).

13. I have attempted to outline some of the virtues necessary for democratic virtue in a lecture given in Santiago, Chile, in 1983. See Peter L. Berger and Michael Novak, *Speaking to the Third World: Essays on Democracy and Development* (Washington, D.C.: American Enterprise Institute, 1985).

14. F. A. Hayek, *Law, Legislation and Liberty,* vol. 3: *The Political Order of a Free People* (Chicago: University of Chicago Press, 1979), 105.

15. One might consult, for example, Graham Walker's criticism of the ethical principles of F. A. Hayek, from a Christian point of view. Walker suggests that the moral foundations Hayek chooses are not adequate to the system whose workings Hayek brilliantly articulates; they will not take Hayek as far as he wants to go. See *The Ethics of F. A. Hayek* (Washington, D.C.: American Enterprise Institute, 1986).

Author's Note: This lecture became the seed of a longer book, *The Free Person and the Common Good* (Lanham, Md.: Madison Books, 1989).

14

Michael Novak on Liberalism

Pierre Manent

I can only express my general agreement with the main points of Michael Novak's remarkable essay but I wish to raise two issues on which he may give the impression of erring on the side of optimism: when he supposes a preestablished harmony first, between liberalism and human nature, and second, between liberalism and the "Judeo-Christian tradition."

On the first point, it is doubtless true that, generally speaking, whatever "culture" they belong to, people prefer liberty to its opposite if they have the choice. But this general truth must not blind us to the fact that circumstances fairly often provoke a natural hostility toward liberalism and liberal regimes. That is particularly true of bodies politic whose national or ethnic pride has been or still is humbled by past colonization (formal or informal) or by the present successes of liberal countries. In such places, the love of liberty has a powerful rival in patriotic resentment. Admittedly, this resentment is not very enlightened, and it is easy to show that free political and economic institutions could do more for the development of the countries in question than authoritarian or totalitarian governments. But it is in fact extremely difficult to dissociate two political ideas—here, free regimes and national humiliation—once they have been associated by a natural, powerful political passion. In other words, the attitude of many of the political elites of the Third World to liberal regimes seems to be perfectly summed up by a sentence from Flaubert's *Salammbô*: "The sight of Carthage irked the barbarians; at one and the same time, they would fain have annihilated it and dwelt in it."

Naturally, these remarks apply especially to the countries of the Third World, but, with modifications, they may also on occasion apply to certain Western countries. British and American observers have long called attention to the illiberal features of French institutions and political temperament. In doing this they are often right. But to a large extent this situation stems from the fact that France experienced or imagined it experienced its greatest political and military successes and attracted the gaze of Europe—in a word, encountered "greatness"—under two illiberal regimes, namely those of Louis XIV and Napoleon. Thus French national awareness does not identify with a free regime. In Britain, on the contrary, and in quite a different form in the United States, the increasing power of the nation coincided with the development of liberal institutions.

Thus the rational calculation that concludes in favor of liberty and liberal institutions often finds itself stifled or distorted by political passions that it would be useless to deplore, passions that must be considered when political decisions are made. Admittedly, it is easy to show that blacks in South Africa, as individuals, would gain nothing by being governed by the African National Congress rather than by the Afrikaners, but the fact remains that the desire to be governed by one's fellows often prevails over the desire to be free individually, as Raymond Aron pointed out to Friedrich Hayek.

I believe that Michael Novak could accept these remarks without difficulty. My second point is more important and more delicate. Novak maintains that liberal institutions and ideas are rooted in Judeo-Christian and humanist traditions. Let us leave aside the "humanist" tradition, whose definition is too uncertain. Let us even leave aside the problem posed by the idea of a Judeo-Christian tradition, an idea that would be intolerable for orthodox Jews, and, truth to tell, for many Jews, whether orthodox or not. Let us limit ourselves to the Christian tradition and to the place of liberalism in it, or to the attitude of liberalism toward it.

First, it is quite obvious that we must distinguish between two periods. During the first, covering the two hundred years preceding the French Revolution, liberalism directly or indirectly fought Christianity in all its forms. Even if the Catholic church was the main target, Christianity as a whole was seen as intolerant of and hard on human nature: it fostered sloth, hypocrisy and so forth. After the French Revolution, the picture changed. Liberals drew closer to Christianity, willingly recognizing its "value." But I believe that Michael Novak is wrong in presenting Tocqueville as "a Catholic thinker." Admittedly, he was Catholic insofar as he had been baptized and brought up in the Catholic religion, but he did not have faith—or at least, he did not have faith during all his life as a thinker—no matter how his last moments are interpreted. He simply considered that in a society that wished to govern itself, in a democratic society, it was indispensable that religion should remain as a fixed point, to give consistency and firmness to the individual souls of the citizens. In short, it is difficult not to conclude that Tocqueville considered Christianity first as a civic religion, as a religion useful and even indispensable for democratic society and not as a true religion in the traditional Christian sense.

Here I shall not try to establish whether the essence of the relationship between liberalism and Christian tradition is best revealed in the era of conflict or in the phase of reconciliation. I should merely want to indicate what *separates* the two traditions, a fundamental separation compatible with "conflict" as well as with "rapprochement."

Despite the authority of Lord Acton, it is not possible to describe Thomas Aquinas as a liberal. Saint Thomas was not a liberal. Nor was he antiliberal, which goes without saying. He described, analyzed, and pronounced what appeared to him to be the objective order of things and the nature of man, founded on an objective hierarchy of what was good. Now, it was such a "dogmatic" presupposition that was rejected by those authors who developed the liberal viewpoint. The starting point of the idea and of the liberal undertaking was skepticism: the idea of what was good is an uncertain one and that is why men fight. As Hobbes and Locke took pleasure in proclaiming, there is no *summum bonum.* One may well inquire into the subjective feelings of those authors who pronounced the presuppositions of the liberal point of view. It is certain that, by radically criticizing the idea of good, the idea of conscience, and the idea of an objective morality, they undermined a vital presupposition of Christian doctrine. That is why, when Michael Novak deplores the fact that liberalism neglected the soul, his criticism is doubtless a fair one, but it takes aim at what was the very project of the founders of liberalism who *set aside* the soul, not because they could be considered as men without souls, but because all ideas of the soul and its well-being were for them a motive for or cause of war, and they first of all wanted peace. That is why as virtuous an author as Locke can explain that murder and incest, like all moral notions, are cultural artifacts and have their roots not in the nature of things but in the productive capacity of human understanding.

As a result, if I willingly agree with Michael Novak that the liberal order in fact rests to a considerable extent on moral content, inherited from Christian tradition, I should add that this Christian support, these Christian roots if you like, cannot be easily admitted and recognized publicly, that is, institutionally. The logic to which liberalism tends is to dismiss this moral content and replace that "objective" morality, held as valid by the different Christian churches, by a formal morality of "reciprocity" or "respect" by all of the "individuality" of all. To choose a crucial illustration, it is impossible for a society claiming to be in the Christian tradition to admit that the right to abortion be written into law, and it is impossible for a liberal society to refuse its members this right.

Instead of hoping for a reconciliation between the two traditions, perhaps we could limit ourselves to asking those who are more Christian than liberal not to make themselves unbearable to liberal opinion, and those who are more liberal than Christian not to render liberal society unbearable for religious people.

ABOUT THE AUTHORS

Maurice Agulhon is professor of history at the Collège de France. A specialist on contemporary France, Professor Agulhon is the author of *Marianne au combat, Marianne au pouvoir,* and *1848 ou l'apprentissage de la République.*

François Bourricaud is professor of sociology at the Université de Paris IV. Former technical counselor in the cabinet of Alain Peyrefitte (minister of national education), Professor Bourricaud has written *Dictionnaire critique de la sociologie, Le bricolage idéologique,* and *L'individualisme institutionnel.*

Jean-Claude Casanova is professor of law and economics at the Institute for Political Studies in Paris and weekly contributor to *L'Express.* His previous positions have included counselor for education to Prime Minister Raymond Barre, director of studies and research at the National Foundation of Political Science, and co-founder with Raymond Aron of the journal *Commentaire.*

Eric Foner is professor of history at Columbia University. Professor Foner's publications include *Politics and Ideology in the Age of the Civil War* and *Free Soil, Free Labor, Free Men: The Ideology of the Republican Party before the Civil War.*

Walter D. Gray is associate professor of history at Loyola University in Chicago. His publications include *The Opposition of the Notables during the Second Empire* and numerous articles on modern French history.

Michael H. Haltzel is director of West European studies at The Woodrow Wilson Center. Formerly deputy director of the Aspen Institute Berlin, he is the author of *Der Abbau der deutschen ständischen Selbstverwaltung in den Ostseeprovinzen Russlands 1855–1905.*

Donald R. Kelley is James Westfall Thompson Professor of History at Rutgers University. He is also executive editor of *The Journal of the History of Ideas* and author of *History, Law, and the Human Sciences, Historians and the Law in Postrevolutionary France,* and *The Human Measure: Social Thought in the Western Legal Tradition.*

George Armstrong Kelly was visiting professor in the Humanities Center and in the Department of Political Science at Johns Hopkins University. A scholar of philosophy and political thought, Professor Kelly wrote *Idealism, Politics and History: Sources of Hegelian Thought, Lost Soldiers: The French Army and Empire in Crisis, 1947–1962,* and *Religious Consciousness in America.*

Joseph Klaits is professor of history at Oakland University. His publications include *Servants of Satan: The Age of the Witch Hunts, Printed Propaganda under Louis XIV: Absolute Monarchy and Public Opinion,* and *Animals and Man in Historical Perspective.*

Jean-Claude Lamberti was professor of sociology at the Université de Paris V. A scholar of Alexis de Tocqueville, Professor Lamberti's works include *La Notion d'Individualisme selon Tocqueville* and *Tocqueville et les deux Democraties.*

William E. Leuchtenburg is William Rand Kenan, Jr., Professor of History at the University of North Carolina at Chapel Hill. He has written many books on twentieth-century American history, including *Franklin D. Roosevelt and the New Deal, 1932–1940, The Great Age of Change, A Troubled Feast,* and *War and Social Change in Twentieth-Century America.*

Pierre Manent is maître des conférences at the Collège de France. He is the author of many works on intellectual history, including his most recent book entitled *Histoire intellectuelle du libéralisme.*

Michael Novak is resident scholar in religion and public policy at the American Enterprise Institute, Washington, D.C. Former U.S. ambassador to the Experts' Meeting on Human Contacts of the Conference on Security and Cooperation in Europe (CSCE), Ambassador Novak is the author of numerous publications including *American Philosophy and the Future, The Spirit of Democratic Capitalism, Moral Clarity in the Nuclear Age,* and *Human Rights and the New Realism.*

René Remond is president of the National Foundation of Political Science, Paris. Formerly president of the Université de Paris X and director of the *Revue Historique,* he is the author of many historical works on religious and political issues including *Forces religieuses et attitudes politiques dans la France contemporaine* and *Introduction à l'histoire de notre temps.*

Jean Rivero is professor emeritus of history at the Université de Paris II. He is the author of *Manuel de droit du travail, Précis de droit administratif,* and *Les libertés publiques.*

James T. Schleifer is professor of history and director of the Gill Library at the College of New Rochelle. A specialist on Alexis de Tocqueville, Dr. Schleifer has published *Alexis de Tocqueville Describes the American Character: Two Previously Unpublished Portraits,* and numerous other works on European-American intellectual and cultural relations.

INDEX